The
Acadians
of
Nova Scotia

Past and Present

Sally Ross
Alphonse Deveau

NIMBUS
PUBLISHING

Nimbus Publishing Limited
P.O. Box 9301, Station A
Halifax, N.S. B3K 5N5
(902)-455-4286

Design: Kathy Kaulbach, Halifax
Printed and bound in Canada by Printcrafters Inc.

Cover illustration: Alex Colville, *The French Cross.* 1988. Acrylic polymer emulsion on panel. 56.5 x 80 cm. Garth H. Drabinsky Collection, Toronto.

Nimbus Publishing Limited acknowledges the financial support of the Government of Canada through the Canadian Studies Directorate of the Department of the Secretary of State of Canada.

Canadian Cataloguing in Publication Data

Ross, Sally.

The Acadians of Nova Scotia past and present

Includes bibliographical references.
ISBN 1-55109-012-0

1. Acadians—Nova Scotia. 2. Canadians, French-speaking—Nova Scotia.
* I. Deveau, J. Alphonse, 1917- II. Title.

FC2350.5.R67 1992   971.6'004114   C92-098564-5
F1040.A2R67 1992

CONTENTS

La culture est l'âme d'une communauté. La langue transmet cette culture de génération en génération.

— Denise Samson (1951–1991)

FOREWORD

It is one of the ironies of Acadian history that most Acadians now live outside Nova Scotia. This situation is, of course, no accident. It arises from the forced migrations that followed the *Grand Dérangement*—the expulsion of the Acadians—in the eighteenth century. The irony is that, by comparison with the large numbers in New Brunswick, francophones in Nova Scotia form a much smaller minority in the very province that includes the lands first settled—one excludes the short and disastrous sojourn on Ile Sainte-Croix—by the founders of Acadie. Among the results has been a tendency among writers to assume that the real Acadian experience of the last two hundred years has been lived in New Brunswick, and a related disposition among analysts of contemporary affairs to see the increasingly successful re-empowerment of New Brunswick Acadians in political and economic life as eclipsing in importance the efforts that have been made in Nova Scotia.

To any statement as sweeping as the one I have just made there must, of course, be some qualifications. The New Brunswick Acadian experience *is* extremely important, as nobody would seriously deny. Furthermore, it would be foolish to assert that the distinctiveness of *acadianité* in Nova Scotia has lacked able and eloquent expositors. The work of current scholars at the Université Sainte-Anne and the Université de Moncton offers impressive examples, and especially evident is the long and distinguished tradition of folklore analysis that stretches from Anselme Chiasson's classic treatment of *Chéticamp: histoire et traditions acadiennes*

(1961) to Ronald Labelle's recent work on *La vie acadienne à Chezzetcook, Nouvelle-Ecosse* (1991).

Nevertheless, the reality remains that the history of Nova Scotia Acadians is not as well known as it ought to be. This is especially true regarding historical treatments in the English language. General histories of Nova Scotia tend to allow Acadians to drop out of sight after 1755, just as the Micmac have been frequently—and just as regrettably—ignored from an even earlier period. Regarding the Acadians, and giving attention too to the significance of the Acadian-Micmac relationship, this book makes a major contribution towards restoring the balance. Alphonse Deveau and Sally Ross are to be congratulated on many aspects of their fine work. They have skilfully synthesized the history of the Acadians prior to the *Grand Dérangement*, drawing on the most appropriate and up-to-date sources. Their treatment of the Acadian return, and of the subsequent rebuilding of Acadian life in seven areas of Nova Scotia, adds greatly to our knowledge of these communities. It pays tribute to Acadian cultural resilience, while illustrating the rich diversity of the Acadian experience in the province. The final chapter sets out the choices that have faced Nova Scotia Acadians in the present century, many of which still present difficult challenges. The authors do not shy away from the complex and sensitive questions surrounding the issue of linguistic assimilation but they make these dilemmas understandable by setting them carefully in the appropriate historical and cultural context.

Finally, but very significantly, this history of Nova Scotia's Acadians is written in a clear and vigorous style that highlights the value of what the book has to say to us. This is a work that can only increase understanding—among Nova Scotians and others—of a crucially important element of the history of the province and the history of the Acadian people.

John G. Reid
Saint Mary's University

PREFACE

At first glance, the painting on the cover of this book might appear quite innocent. However, in his inimitable and masterful fashion, Alex Colville invites the inquisitive mind to look again and to ask questions. The young girl is riding across the marshlands of Grand Pré, one of the most historically significant landscapes in Nova Scotia. She is obviously intrigued by the large wrought-iron cross which she has just passed. If she follows her curiosity, she will discover that this cross marks the location where more than two thousand Acadians from the Grand Pré region were embarked on to boats to be rowed over to transport ships lying at anchor in Minas Basin. The French Cross or the Deportation Cross was erected by Acadians in 1924 to commemorate the tragedy of the Expulsion that began in 1755. This disastrous event, which lasted for almost ten years, shattered and dispersed the entire French-speaking population of the Atlantic region.

In recent decades, many books have been written about the Acadians, but this is the first work devoted exclusively to the Acadians of Nova Scotia. The first three chapters of our study relate to the collective past shared by the ancestors of all the Acadians scattered throughout the world. In order to provide a fresh perspective on that part of Acadian history which has been chronicled and analyzed by so many historians, we have returned to the original texts of Jacques Cartier, Samuel de Champlain, Marc Lescarbot, Father Pierre Biard, Father Laurent Molins, Nicolas Denys and Sieur de Dièreville. We have also attempted to

incorporate the results of recent historical and archeological research which has facilitated a cultural approach.

The Deportation constitutes a pivotal point in the history of
the Acadian people. As a result of the decision to ship ten thousand
individuals out of the Atlantic region, the cohesive fabric of the
Acadian people was fractured into many pieces that were to evolve
in different ways. One of the principal goals of our work is to
examine the Acadian communities that developed in Nova Scotia
after 1764, in other words to show regional differences within the
confines of one province. The Acadians were able to resettle in
seven main areas in the territory covered by present-day Nova
Scotia. In tracing the evolution of these regions during the first
century after the Deportation, we have attempted to focus on
elements that in some way explain the distinctive features that can
be observed today.

Although our seven regional portraits contain new material,
we have benefited from the research of scholars such as Father
Clarence d'Entremont and Father Anselme Chiasson who have
published extensively on their native regions. Father d'Entremont's
monumental study entitled *Histoire du Cap-Sable de l'An Mil au
Traité de Paris (1763)* has been a constant source of inspiration,
along with his work on Nicolas Denys. Father Chiasson's numerous publications form the basis of any examination of Chéticamp.
Within the context of the post-Deportation period at a regional
level in Nova Scotia, we have also drawn on the work of other
researchers including Neil Boucher, Joan Bourque Campbell,
Ronald Labelle, Barbara LeBlanc, Laura Sadowsky, Karin Flikeid,
Betty Dugas-LeBlanc, Régis Brun, Ephrem Boudreau, Paul
Touesnard, Gabriel LeBlanc, Father Charles Aucoin and Stephen
White. The majority of the sources and reference materials we
have used are written in French. If a translation of the original text
exists we have quoted it, otherwise we have provided our own. All
translations are followed by (TR).

The final section of our book is devoted to the choices and
challenges that Acadians in Nova Scotia have faced in the twentieth
century, especially since the late 1960s. In a period when technology has tended to homogenize differences and break down the
isolation of the past, preservation of distinctive cultural features is

extremely difficult. The pressures of the mainstream culture are overwhelming. The survival of the French language amongst the Acadians of Nova Scotia constitutes the central issue of our last chapter. People of French origin form about ten percent of the population of this province, however less than half of them are francophones. Since the beginning of the twentieth century, thousands of Acadians have been absorbed into the English-speaking majority. As a small linguistic minority scattered in communities at opposite ends of the province, the French-speaking Acadians in Nova Scotia today face challenges of heroic proportions.

We would like to express our gratitude to the Canadian Studies Directorate of the Secretary of State for their financial support. The writing of this book has been a long process. We would like to thank John Reid, Director of Atlantic Canada Studies at Saint Mary's University, for his very helpful suggestions and for agreeing to write the foreword to this book. We are grateful for all the editorial work, especially that of Elizabeth Eve who, with Dorothy Blythe, managing editor of Nimbus Publishing, helped bring this book to publication. We would also like to express our gratitude to Brenda Dunn and Wayne Kerr, Canadian Parks Service, Scott Robson of the Nova Scotia Museum, Margaret Campbell of the Public Archives of Nova Scotia, Joëlle Désy of the Fédération acadienne de la Nouvelle-Ecosse, Neil Boucher of the Centre acadien at the Université Sainte-Anne, Daniel Aucoin of the Société Saint-Pierre, and Frank and Jim Balcom at Atlantic Direct. We hope that our discoveries and our short-comings will inspire others to pursue the research.

Sally Ross and Alphonse Deveau   January 1992

Postscript
As this book goes into its second edition, we are both pleased and honoured to add that we received two prestigious literary prizes for our work: *The City of Dartmouth Book Award* and *The Evelyn Richardson Memorial Literary Award.*

November 1993

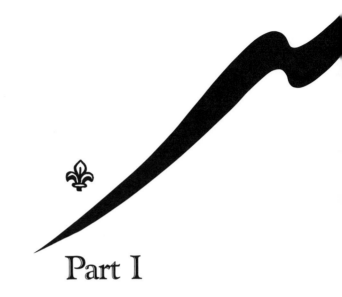

Part I

CHAPTER 1

The Foundation of Acadie

The ancestors of the Micmac and Maliseet peoples had been established in the territory now known as the Maritime Provinces for at least ten thousand years before the first European explorers and fishermen crossed the Atlantic Ocean. The first written description of the native people of Canada is provided by Jacques Cartier. In July 1534, the famous French explorer traded with a group of Micmac living on the south shore of the Gulf of St. Lawrence, near the Bay of Chaleur.[1] This was not the first cultural exchange between the Old and the New Worlds. On the contrary; by the time Jacques Cartier arrived on their shores, the native people had already met many European fishermen and discovered the value of iron and copper utensils. This explains the enthusiasm and excitement which Jacques Cartier describes:

The next day some of these Indians came in nine canoes to the point at the mouth of the cove where we lay anchored with our ships... As soon as they saw us they began to run away, making signs to us that they had come to barter with us; and held up some furs of small value, with which they clothe themselves. We likewise made signs to them that we wished them no harm, and sent two men on shore, to offer them some knives and other iron goods, and a red cap to give to their chief. Seeing this, they sent on shore part of their people with some of their furs; and the two parties traded together. The savages showed a marvellously great pleasure in possessing and obtaining these iron wares and other commodities, dancing and going through many ceremonies, and throwing salt water over their heads with their hands. They bartered all they had to such an extent that all went back naked without anything on them; and they made signs to us that they would return on the morrow with more furs.[2] (TR)

From a European point of view the Atlantic Ocean represented an unknown frontier, a potential source of food and riches. The push to explore this frontier was motivated by both economics and scientific curiosity. The success of any expedition was closely linked not only to the relative power of the seafaring nation but also to improvements in shipbuilding and navigation techniques. Around the year 1000, the Vikings had attempted to found colonies on this side of the Atlantic. However, several centuries elapsed before sailing vessels from Europe navigated the cold waters of the North Atlantic.

By the late 1400s and early 1500s, Portuguese, French and Basque fishermen were frequenting the rich fishing banks located off the south coast of the islands of Newfoundland and Cape Breton. They also sailed up the St. Lawrence River, along the shores of Labrador and Newfoundland, and down the coast to Cape Sable, the southernmost tip of present-day Nova Scotia.[3] These fishermen came to harvest the immense supplies of cod for the markets of Europe. Codfish was an invaluable commodity, especially in Catholic countries where there were more than 150 fast days in the year; in other words when it was forbidden to eat meat. But cod was also a very preservable food item: it could either be salted or sun-dried and then stored for several months.

Throughout the first half of the sixteenth century, the fishing fleets in the New World belonged mainly to France.[4] In the early days of the fishery there were numerous ports from which the fishermen set sail, the most important of which were Rouen and Dieppe in Normandy, St. Malo in Brittany (whose inhabitants gave their name to Cape Breton) and La Rochelle, the Protestant stronghold and capital of the old province of Aunis. The home port of the Basque fishermen was Saint-Jean-de-Luz, the gateway to the Spanish markets. The Basques, who had pioneered whaling, sailed the North Atlantic in search of both cod and whale oil.[5] By the mid-1500s, fishing fleets from all these ports were returning home with tons of green, or salt, cod and tons of cod which had been dried on wooden racks, or "flakes," placed

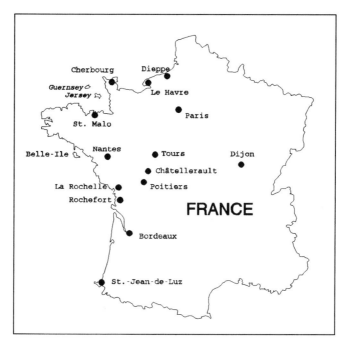

Map of France. (Courtesy: Atlantic Direct)

along gravel beaches. With the expansion of this so-called dry fishery, the more frequent encounters between the native people and Europeans brought about the first stages of the fur trade.

The fishermen did not settle on the west side of the Atlantic; their primary aim was to dry their cod and return to their home ports with the catches. They chose sheltered inlets with gravel beaches and a good supply of wood for their flakes. As the names on the earliest maps of Cape Breton show, each nationality tended to use specific harbours: English Harbour (Havre aux Anglais which was renamed Louisbourg in 1713), Spanish Bay (Baie des Espagnols which became Sydney in 1784), and St. Annes Harbour (Havre Sainte-Anne, named after the patron saint of fishermen).[6]

The story of the colonization of the Atlantic region is closely related not only to the development of the cod fishery but also, of course, to the great voyages of discovery. Inspired by Marco Polo's expeditions to the Far East, European monarchs and merchants hoped that one day a navigator in their employ would find the western route to China. Sponsored by King Henry VII of England,

Giovanni Caboto (John Cabot) crossed the Atlantic in 1497 and appears to have explored the northwestern Atlantic region. The Portuguese nobleman, Gaspar Corte Real, visited the North Atlantic in 1501 and apparently landed on the shores of Newfoundland. Thomas Aubert, a navigator from Dieppe, explored the coast of Labrador and supposedly took six Beothuks from Newfoundland back to France in 1509.[7] With the support of King François I of France, Giovanni Verrazzano crossed the Atlantic in 1524 and explored the coastline from Cape Breton to Florida. Ten years later, the king gave Jacques Cartier, the navigator from St. Malo, the support necessary to "travel, discover and conquer for France and to find the northern passage to China."[8] (TR)

The extraordinary voyages of Jacques Cartier in 1534 and 1535-1536 mark the beginning of French claims to New France or Canada. It was only after Jacques Cartier's expeditions that the island of Cape Breton and the south coast of the Gulf of St. Lawrence became distinguishable features on the map.[9] Not only did Jacques Cartier write detailed descriptions of the territory he explored, he proved that it was possible to survive the Canadian winter and therefore to establish a permanent colony. He provided convincing proof of the vast resources of fur, lumber, and fish and he contributed the first written observations of the indigenous cultures, although he succeeded in alienating the St. Lawrence Iroquois. Despite his efforts, Jacques Cartier could not provide the king of France with immediate profits. His voyages and those of his successor, Roberval, were extremely costly. However, from 1562 to 1598, France was torn apart by the Wars of Religion, shattering the dream of settlement in the New World. It was not until the end of the century, when peace was restored, that the king, Henri IV, could turn to colonial expansion.

Although political events put a halt to voyages of discovery, the fishing fleets continued to cross the Atlantic year in and year out. Every spring, hundreds of sailing vessels left the European ports and returned in the fall laden with dry and green cod. Unlike the explorers, the fishermen left no maps or written accounts of their expeditions. Perhaps they preferred not to divulge the whereabouts of their favourite fishing grounds or the most sheltered coves and inlets.

By 1581, the French merchants of Rouen, Dieppe, and St. Malo began sponsoring expeditions designed exclusively to bring back furs from the St. Lawrence River. Five ships left St. Malo in 1584 and returned so laden with pelts that it was decided to double the number of vessels the following year.[10] If exploratory voyages did not ensure quick profits, the fur trade certainly did. Rather than having to build forts to protect "their" supply routes and trading posts, merchants soon demanded monopolies of the fur trade over vast territories. At no point, however, did the fur trade in the Atlantic region ever reach the proportions that it did along the great inland waterways, such as the Saguenay, the Ottawa, and the Assiniboine rivers. Various factors, including the climate and the shorter river systems, prevented the growth of vast populations of aquatic mammals like the beaver.[11]

In accordance with his ambition to colonize the New World and thus ensure permanent control of both the territory and the resources, Henri IV began to distribute concessions, or huge tracts of land, in exchange for certain guarantees. Although he was assassinated in 1610 before he could reap the benefits, it was his support that resulted in the founding of Port Royal in 1605 and of Quebec in 1608.[12] He granted concessions to numerous individuals who attempted, with varying degrees of proficiency, to found a colony. The least successful of these men was the Marquis de la Roche who abandoned 50 convicts and a few head of cattle on Sable Island in 1598 with the intention of founding a colony in a more favourable location. Eleven survivors were rescued from the island five years later.

The first successful attempt to establish a French settlement in the New World took place in 1604. Henri IV granted Pierre Dugua de Mons, a native of the province of Saintonge in western France, a monopoly for the lands situated between the 40th and the 46th parallels. De Mons was granted fishing and fur trading rights on the condition that he settle and cultivate the land, prospect for mines, and bring about the conversion of the native peoples. The tract of land that de Mons received was immense. It excluded the St. Lawrence River but it included "the entire eastern seaboard from present-day New Jersey to Cape Breton."[13] The territory or colony was referred to as La Cadie or l'Acadie. The boundaries of this colony shifted and changed many times throughout history. In general terms, however, the Acadie of the seventeenth century refers to the territory covered, in today's terms, by Nova Scotia, New Brunswick, Prince Edward Island and part of the State of Maine.

Verrazzano was the first explorer to use the name "Arcadie" to designate a land mass in the New World. Mapmakers who followed Verrazzano moved "Arcadie" northward on their maps until it covered the territory corresponding roughly to present-day Maine and the Maritimes. "Arcadie" or "Arcadia" referred to a famous and beautiful region in ancient Greece. The "r" appears to have been dropped as contacts with the Micmac increased, and gradually the territory became known as *la Cadie* and then *l'Acadie*—resembling Micmac place names like Shubenacadie, Tracadie or Passamaquoddy.[14]

De Mons set sail for Acadie from the French port of Le Havre in March 1604. There were 79 men on board two vessels. Most of these men were simply vagabonds recruited for the occasion. However, two of the noblemen on board—Jean de Biencourt (Sieur de Poutrincourt) and Samuel de Champlain—were to play an important role in the development of Acadie. Since Catholicism had not yet been firmly established as the official religion of France, the expedition included a mixture of Catholics and Protestants. There were also two priests and one minister present.

Thanks to Champlain's diary it is possible to follow the precise itinerary of de Mons' vessels once they reached the coast of Acadie. Although Champlain did not have a specific role on this expedition, he was an accomplished navigator and cartographer. In the previous year he had travelled with Pont Gravé, commander of one of de Mons's vessels, up the St. Lawrence River. Champlain's diaries and maps provide extensive information pertaining to various expeditions and to the geography of Nova Scotia. In fact, many of the place names along the Atlantic coast and the Bay of Fundy were designated by Champlain. Of all the men on this first expedition, Samuel de Champlain appears to be the only one who settled permanently in the New World. He founded Quebec in 1608 and died there on Christmas Day, 1635.

According to Champlain, the two vessels arrived at Sable Island at the beginning of May 1604. They continued their journey along the coast, stopping at various points along the way, including LaHave, Port Rossignol (Liverpool), Port Mouton and Cape Sable. They also explored the Bay of Fundy and St. Marys Bay. They decided to spend the winter on a tiny island at the mouth of the St. Croix River. Champlain provides a description of the island indicating that the site was chosen because it was considered to be safe from a military point of view. The following passage shows that the desire of the French to establish good relations with the native people was not without ulterior motives. Champlain makes it quite clear that his main goal was to obtain furs and new converts to Christianity.

The island is covered with firs, birches, maples and oaks. It is naturally very well situated, with but one place where it is low, for about forty paces, and that is easy to fortify. The shores of the mainland are distant on both sides some nine hundred to a thousand paces, so that vessels could only pass along the river at the mercy of the cannon on the island. This place we considered the best we had seen, both on account of its situation, the fine country, and for the intercourse we were expecting with the Indians of these coasts and of the interior, since we should be in their midst. In course of time we hoped to pacify them, and to put an end to the wars which they wage against one another, in order that in the future we might derive service from them, and convert them to the Christian faith.[15] (TR)

As it turned out, the island was a disastrous choice. The supply of firewood and wildlife was limited. Almost half of the men died of scurvy or starvation. Consequently, it was decided to dismantle the habitation on St. Croix Island and resettle on the opposite side of the Bay of Fundy. Champlain and de Mons chose a sheltered location on the north shore of the Rivière Dauphin, later renamed the Annapolis River. Champlain named the settlement Port Royal. He describes the site and the reconstruction of the buildings:

Continuing two leagues on the same course, we entered one of the finest harbours I had seen on all these coasts, where a couple of thousand vessels could lie in safety. The entrance is eight hundred paces wide, which I named Port Royal. Into it fall three rivers, one of which...is called Equille...

From the mouth of the river to the point we reached are many meadows, but these are flooded at high tide, there being numbers of little creeks leading here and there, up which shallops and boats may pass at high tide...

Having searched well in all directions, we found no place more suitable and better situated than a somewhat elevated spot, about which are some marshes and good springs...

Having seen that the site for the settlement was a good one, we began to clear the ground, which was full of trees, and to erect the houses as quickly as possible. Everybody was busy at this work.[16] (TR)

The Habitation constructed in Port Royal in 1605 under the supervision of Champlain served as a comfortable shelter for a small group of men for two years. During their travels throughout the region, de Mons and Champlain learned a great deal from the native people that helped them survive in the New World. The following passage, for example, describes some of the indigenous vegetables of North America and the organic farming methods of the Abenaki people living along the Kennebec River in present-day Maine:

The following day the Sieur de Mons went on shore to view their fields upon the bank of the river, and I went with him. We saw their grain, which is Indian corn. This they grow in gardens, sowing three or four grains in one spot, after which, with the shells of the aforesaid signoc [horseshoe crab], they heap about it a quantity of earth. Then three feet away they sow as much again; and so on in order. Amongst this corn they plant in each hillock three or four Brazilian beans [Bushbeans], which come up of different colours. When fully grown these plants twine around the aforementioned corn, which grows to a height of five to six feet; and they keep the ground very free from weeds. We saw there many squashes, pumpkins and tobacco, which they likewise cultivate. As for the beans, they were beginning to burst into flower, as were likewise the pumpkins and squashes. They plant their corn in May, and harvest it in September.[17] (TR)

With the exception of several labourers whose names are not known, Champlain was the only person in the de Mons expedition who actually spent the winters of 1605 and 1606 in Port Royal. Poutrincourt went back to France for supplies and did not return to Port Royal until the spring of 1606. With him came another group of skilled workmen along with several aristocrats. The latter included Poutrincourt's son, Charles de Biencourt; a cousin from Paris, Louis Hébert, an apothecary and horticulturalist who would live in Acadie for several years before moving to Quebec; a cousin from Champagne, Claude de Saint-Etienne de La Tour and his fourteen-year-old son, Charles de Saint-Etienne de La Tour, who was to play an important role in Acadie; and Marc Lescarbot, a lawyer-poet from Paris who wrote a major work entitled *Histoire de la Nouvelle France*.

Marc Lescarbot stayed for one year in the colony and was particularly interested in the customs of the native people. On the voyage to Port Royal, Poutrincourt's vessel laid anchor in the harbour of the well-established fishing station of Campseau (Canso). He and the other men on board were greeted by a group of fishermen from St. Malo and a group of Micmac. Lescarbot writes:

Meanwhile the two long-boats came up, one manned with savages, who had a moose painted on their sail, the other by Frenchmen from St. Malo who were fishing off Canso harbour; the savages showed the greater diligence, for they arrived first. They were the first I had ever seen, and I admired their fine shape and well-formed faces. One of them made his excuses that on account of the inclemency of the weather he had not brought his beautiful beaver robe. He wore only a piece of coarse red frieze, with Matachiaz [decorations] around his neck and wrists, above his elbows, and at his waist.[18] (TR)

All the men at Port Royal were forced to return to France in 1607 when it was learned that de Mons's monopoly in Acadie had been revoked. Lescarbot describes their return journey to France. They stopped at various points along the coast including Port Mouton where they traded furs with the Micmac. They also stopped in Canso. On this visit, Lescarbot met a Basque sailor who had been fishing off Canso every year since 1565. The following passage provides eloquent proof of the continuity of the dry cod fishery and of contacts with the Micmac.

Finally, we arrived within four leagues of Canso, at a harbour where a fine old sailor from St. Jean-de-Luz, named Captain Savalet, was fishing. He received us with every possible courtesy and, inasmuch as this harbour, which though small is excellent, has no name, I have given it on my map the name of Savalet. This worthy man told us that that voyage was his forty-second to this parts, and one must remember that these Newfoundlanders [fishermen who frequent the banks] *make but one trip a year. He was wondrous content with his fishing and told us that he caught daily a good fifty crowns' worth of cod, and that his voyage was worth to him ten thousand francs. He had sixteen men in his employ, and his vessel was of eighty tons' burden, and able to carry one hundred thousand dry fish. He was at the time troubled by the savages encamped there, who too boldly and impudently went on board his ship, and carried off what they listed.*[19] (TR)

The Frenchmen were forced to return to France thus abandoning the settlement of Port Royal which had only been inhabited for three winters. What were the accomplishments of this short-lived establishment? First of all, the experience instilled in several of the men a firm determination to return to the New World. Poutrincourt, for example, was able to find the financial backing to start another colony in Port Royal. Claude de La Tour, the young Charles de La Tour, the young Charles de Biencourt, Champlain and Hébert all came back to settle in either Acadie or Canada. Obviously, this first settlement had been a crucial learning experience. A considerable amount of practical knowledge was accumulated in the space of four years—precise observations related to the geography, climate, growing conditions, plants, animals, etc.

The most important accomplishment of Port Royal, however, was the relationship established with the Micmac. Needless to say, it was very much in the interests of the French to cultivate friendly relations with the native people. They were the suppliers of furs, in other words, the commercial life-line of the colony. Their extensive and profound knowledge of the country and their numbers put them in a very advantageous position.[20] Both Champlain and Lescarbot indicate that Chief Membertou and the other *Souriquois*, or Micmac tribesmen, and their families who lived in the vicinity of Port Royal were received regularly in the Habitation. Charles de Biencourt and Charles de La Tour both learned the Micmac language.[21] The bond between the Micmac and the French was to be strengthened in the future. The Micmac eventually adopted the Catholic religion although the process of conversion was neither instant nor subservient.[22] The British, who were soon to enter the territory claimed by France, were never able to match the alliance between the French and the Micmac.

Poutrincourt returned to Port Royal in 1610 with Claude and Charles de La Tour, Louis Hébert, Abbé Jessé Fléché, a Catholic priest, and about twenty colonists. The Habitation was intact and they were welcomed by Chief Membertou and his band. The primary goals of the colony were to carry out fur trading and to convert the native people to Catholicism. This double mission proved complicated because of the religious struggles in France. The commercial backers were Protestant merchants from Dieppe who disliked Jesuit priests whom they associated with the Counter-Reformation, an organized movement within the Catholic Church opposing Protestantism. The religious backer was Madame de Guercheville who had connections with the French court and with the Jesuits who had already established successful missions in South America. Father Pierre Biard, a Jesuit priest, left France from Dieppe and arrived in Port Royal in the late spring of 1611. Like Champlain and Lescarbot, Father Biard wrote an extremely detailed account of his stay in the colony. In his *Relations* or reports to his superior in Paris, he describes the tension in Dieppe that ultimately resulted in the withdrawal of the Protestant merchants supporting Poutrincourt.

[There] *was great excitement among those of the Reformed Religion. For sieur Robin, who (as we have said) took entire charge of the shipping, had given a commission to two merchants of the Pretended Faith* [Calvanist], *called du Chesne and du Jardin, to attend to the repairing and loading of the ship, under promise to remunerate them for their time and expense, and to form a partnership with them to divide the profits which be derived from the trade in skins, and from the cod fisheries. Now the Merchants... began to delay more than ever. For they were very obstinate, swearing with their loudest oaths, that if the Jesuits had to enter the ship, they would simply put nothing in it; that they would not refuse all other Priests or Ecclesiastics, and would even support them, but as to the Jesuits, they would not abide them...*

The Court was informed of this, and the Queen ordered sieur de Cigoigne, Governor of Dieppe, to signify to the superintendents of the Consistory, that she desired what her deceased Lord and husband had planned in his lifetime, namely, that the Jesuits should go to the countries of New France; and therefore, if they opposed this voyage, they were opposing her purpose and good pleasure.[23] (TR)

Although the colonists in Port Royal planted crops and had a grist mill, they could not survive without supplies from France, implying successful fur trading and solid financial resources. The future of Port Royal did not look promising. However, it was not the disputes in France that brought the final blow, but an attack from Jamestown, Virginia, commanded by Samuel Argall in 1613. He had been sent by the English to destroy the French settlement of Saint-Sauveur on the coast of present-day Maine. After destroying this mission post, Argall learned of the presence of Frenchmen at Port Royal. He and his troops sailed to the settlement where they looted and burned the Habitation. The inhabitants were spared as they were off working in the fields and woods. This attack destroyed Poutrincourt's dreams forever but it was not the end of Acadie. This raid by the British signalled the start of a struggle for the American continent which would last for the next 150 years.

A number of the men from the Habitation, including Charles de Biencourt, Claude and Charles de La Tour, decided not to return to France. Little is known of their activities except that they continued fur trading and therefore maintained close contact with France and the Micmac. They supplied David Lomeron (acting on behalf of two Protestant merchants from La Rochelle) with fish and pelts from 1614 to 1623. Lomeron met them in Port Royal for several years and then in Cape Sable where they were established by 1617.

The shift of headquarters from Port Royal to the southern tip of the peninsula may have been dictated by Lomeron and his partners in France. Cape Sable was a well-known fishing station that had been frequented by Basque and Portuguese fishermen. Being closer to the shipping routes, it was more accessible for supply ships. There was also a Micmac settlement in Cape Sable which meant a supply of furs and possible protection against the attacks of English or Dutch traders—equally anxious to establish themselves in a strategic location.

The habitation post in Cape Sable was called Fort Lomeron and was located near present-day Chebogue Point, just south of Yarmouth.[24] The actual name and location of the fort changed at various times over the years but it was in the Cape Sable region which, in general terms, corresponded to the southern corner of Nova Scotia from Cape Fourchu to present-day Shelburne.

Poutrincourt's son, Charles de Biencourt died in 1623, leaving his thirty-year-old cousin, Charles de La Tour, in charge of a "resolute band of Frenchmen."[25] This group of men lived in close alliance with the Micmac. At some point Charles de la Tour married a Micmac woman, probably a chief's daughter (historians rarely record the names of Micmac women). The union, later blessed by a Récollet missionary, gave rise to three daughters, all of whom were baptized—obvious evidence of the Christian and evangelical dimension of the colony. One of the daughters eventually entered the convent of Val-de-Grâce in Paris, thus becoming the first Acadian nun.[26] Other men in the group also married Micmac women, further strengthening the political alliances of this tiny colony. The first known child of French blood born in Acadie was the son of Louis Lasnier and a Micmac woman, André Lasnier, born in Cape Sable in 1620.

By the time Biencourt died, the foundations of a settlement in Cape Sable were established. Situated on the Atlantic seaboard, it was economically linked to the nearby fishing banks and the growing markets of the Massachusetts Bay colony.

In 1627, Charles de La Tour sent two letters to France from Fort Lomeron, one addressed to King Louis XIII and the other to his First Minister, Cardinal Richelieu. The content of the letters is the same. Basically, Charles de La Tour asks for support from France in the form of an official commission that would give him the right to protect and defend the coast of Acadie. He explains that because of the destruction of Port Royal by the English, he and the other Frenchmen have been living and dressing like *les peuples du pays* (the people of this land). Perhaps because he is closer to the Micmac, Charles de La Tour does not use the word *sauvages* (savages) that one finds in virtually all French writings of the time, including Champlain's and Lescarbot's.[27] The commission from France did not arrive until several years later. Despite the lack of official support, Charles de La Tour continued his trading activities in Cape Sable and later returned to France, bringing back a number of families who settled in this corner of the peninsula.

The proximity of Acadie to the shipping routes, to the fishing banks and to the British colonies along the Atlantic seaboard made it a very coveted territory. The first British attempt to establish colonies in Acadie took place a number of years after Argall destroyed Champlain's Habitation in Port Royal. In 1621 James I, King of Scotland, granted the territory covered, in today's terms, by the Maritime Provinces and the Gaspé, to a Scotsman, Sir William Alexander, who renamed the country "New Scotland" and gave it a coat of arms. In 1629 he founded Fort Charles, a short-lived colony located on the south shore of the Rivière Dauphin. Sir William Alexander arrived with 70 colonists most of whom were repatriated in 1632.

War broke out between France and England in 1627, the same year that Cardinal Richelieu, the chief minister of Louis XIII, founded the Company of One Hundred Associates, designed specifically to establish French settlements in North America. One of the founding members of this company was Isaac de Razilly, a distant cousin of Cardinal Richelieu and an experienced commander in the French navy. Until peace was restored in March 1632, plans for colonial expansion were curtailed. One of the stipulations of the peace treaty was that Scotland give Acadie back to France.

In September 1632 Isaac de Razilly arrived in Acadie with three sailing vessels, 300 hand-picked men, three Capuchin Fathers and a few women and children.[28] Two of these men were to play crucial roles in the future of Acadie: Charles de Menou d'Aulnay, a cousin of Razilly, and Nicolas Denys who, like Razilly, was a native of Tours.

Motivated by military and commercial considerations, Razilly decided to found his settlement at the mouth of the LaHave River, a site which Champlain had already visited with de Mons in 1604.[29] Fort Sainte-Marie-de-Grâce was constructed to give protection to the new colony of LaHave. It was no doubt a safer location than Port Royal since the English had captured the French fort of Pentagouet across the Bay of Fundy from Port Royal. As well as being located on an important inland waterway, LaHave was situated between two fishing posts, Cape Sable and Canso.

In compliance with the aims of the Company of One Hundred Associates, Razilly was determined to make his colony a permanent commercial success. In a letter to Marc Lescarbot, Razilly gives a glowing description of LaHave in 1634. He paints a picture of happiness and abundance—a "paradise on earth." He complained, however, that his financial reserves were being depleted and that the fur trade was anything but profitable. According to the description of his letter, Razilly blamed the beavers (source of the most valuable pelts) for not being particularly cooperative.[30]

It is certainly not the beavers who helped [in the endeavour], *since there were none to speak of and it cost him twice as much as he received to win the friendship of the savages.* (TR)

During the summer of 1634 Razilly also addressed a letter to Cardinal Richelieu.[31] Once again, he sings the praises of life in "this blessed land," and stresses the moral fibre of his colony where goodwill and friendship reign thanks to the spiritual guidance of the Capuchin Fathers. In the following lines, however, Razilly makes it quite clear that the establishment of a colony is a costly, if not ruinous, adventure:

My friends and I have already advanced 50,000 écus for the establishment of this work without having obtained the slightest profit, except for the buildings and fortifications armed with a battery of 25 cannons in good shape and able to defend the cross and the lilies. Until the very last drop of my blood, I shall continue to devote myself to this effort while waiting for the help that it pleases the King to give us through your Eminence... (TR)

Nicolas Denys came as Razilly's second lieutenant. He is described as "the most attractive but the least fortunate" of Acadian leaders.[32] He established a fishing post at Port Rossignol (Liverpool) from which he also exported squared timber. He describes the construction of his dwelling and the preparation of the lumber.

I had a dozen men with me, some labourers, others makers of planks or staves for barrels, others carpenters, and others for hunting. I was provided with all kinds of provisions, and we made good cheer, for the game never failed us. On the upper part of my little river, passing four or five hundred paces into the woods, I went to large ponds full of game, where I did my hunting, leaving the main river to the Commander. In these places all the woods were nothing but Oaks, and this was what I sought. There I set my makers of planks and carpenters at work, and for two years I had a lot of planking and of beams for building all squared, as well as rafters. Monsieur de Razilly who wished only to make known the goodness of the country in order to attract people there, was charmed that I could load all the timber upon the vessels which brought him his provisions, as otherwise they would have been obliged to return empty to France.[33] (TR)

Nicolas Denys was granted a large monopoly which stretched from Cape Breton to Miscou Island. He established other fishing posts at Canso, Saint-Pierre (St. Peters, Cape Breton) and Nepisiquit on the Bay of Chaleur. After suffering setbacks due to his creditor, Emmanuel LeBorgne, and to Charles d'Aulnay, Nicolas Denys returned to France around 1669.[34] Having spent more than 30 years in the New World, he then wrote and published a work entitled *Description géographique et historique des costes de l' Amérique septentrionale (Acadie)* which, along with Champlain's, Lescarbot's and Father Biard's writings, constitutes an invaluable description of Acadie in the seventeenth century. Nicolas Denys travelled extensively along the coastline of Nova Scotia and Cape Breton and provided accurate information pertaining not only to the geography but also the natural resources of the entire region. He remained close friends with Charles de La Tour. One of his sons married a Micmac woman and his daughter, Marie, married a nobleman from Trois-Rivières, Michel LeNeuf de la Vallière, who later became governor of Acadie.

Charles de Menou d'Aulnay came to Acadie as Razilly's first lieutenant. When the latter died prematurely in LaHave in the summer of 1636, d'Aulnay inherited his cousin's title as Governor of Acadie.[35] He remained in charge of the colony until he drowned in the Rivière Dauphin in 1650. Throughout this period he consolidated, at the expense of Charles de La Tour and Nicolas Denys, his military and economic control over the entire territory from Cape Breton to the Bay of Chaleur.

In 1636, on d'Aulnay's initiative, most, but not all, of the colonists at LaHave were moved to Port Royal. His decision may have been related to the fur trade and the distribution of monopolies, but it does not appear to have been made for agricultural reasons since Razilly's letters indicate that the land in LaHave was fertile and productive. The reinstatement of Port Royal as the principal settlement of Acadie marks the birth of the Acadian heartland. The new settlement was not rebuilt on the site of Champlain's Habitation, but further upriver.

Charles de La Tour lived in Cape Sable until 1636 when he was forced to shift his fur-trading operations to the mouth of the Saint John River. This move was partly related to the supply of pelts and partly due to the fact that officials in France had a very vague notion of the geography of Acadie which resulted in poorly defined or overlapping land grants. At some point, La Tour's first wife died and he contracted to marry a French woman, Françoise Marie Jacquelin, in 1639. She became known as Madame de La Tour and arrived with two servants at Fort La Tour, at the mouth of the St. John River, sometime in 1640. Five years later, the fort was destroyed by Charles d'Aulnay while La Tour was away trading in Boston. He returned to find himself without headquarters and a widower once again. He left Acadie for the safety of Quebec but in 1650 he learned that his rival, Charles de Menou d'Aulnay, seigneur of Port Royal, had drowned. La Tour went to France to be reinstated as governor, and on his return to Acadie he took up residence in the then well-established settlement of Port Royal and married d'Aulnay's widow, Jeanne (née Motin) in 1653. They had three daughters and two sons, all of whom settled and married in Acadie. La Tour died in 1663, having spent almost 60 years in the New World.[36]

When Charles de La Tour returned from France in 1651, he brought back several families who were prepared to settle in Acadie. The most well-known in this group were Madeleine (née Hélie) and Philippe Mius d'Entremont. They arrived in 1651 and by 1653 were settled in Cape Sable where Philippe d'Entremont had been granted the barony of Pombomcoup (Pubnico). Several other families established themselves in Cape Sable with the d'Entremonts, at least one of which came from La Rochelle.[37] Given the very limited number of eligible bachelors, it is not surprising that two of Charles de La Tour's daughters married two of d'Entremont's sons! D'Entremont's third son, Philippe II, married into the Micmac nation. D'Entremont's eldest daughter, Marguerite, married Pierre Melanson who founded Grand Pré in 1682.

It is not known exactly how many of the first permanent settlers in Acadie were brought out as a result of the recruiting efforts of Razilly, d'Aulnay or La Tour.[38] This information would facilitate research on the precise geographic origin of the founding families. However, most of the settlers arrived during the years that d'Aulnay was seigneur of Port Royal—from 1636 to 1650. Immigration to Acadie was extremely limited both in time and numbers: only about 50 families came from France to settle in Acadie and very few colonists arrived after 1670. The number of people who immigrated to Acadie was negligible in comparison to the nearby Massachusetts Bay colony where there were 11,000 inhabitants by 1645.[39] Around the time of d'Aulnay's death in Port Royal and La Tour's marriage to the widow, Jeanne d'Aulnay (née Motin), there were about 450 permanent settlers from France and more than 3,500 Micmac living in Acadie.

Prior to the first census of Port Royal in 1671, one of the few documents that provides information on the names and origin of a certain number of permanent settlers is the passenger list of the *Saint Jehan* which sailed from La Rochelle on April 1, 1636. There were approximately 90 passengers on board this vessel, including 12 women and about 12 children. Only three of the names on the passenger list appear in the census of Port Royal in 1671: Pierre Martin (with his wife whose name is not given), Guillaume Trahan (with unnamed wife) and Louis Blanchard. Given the fact that France was attempting to populate a colony, the number of women or couples on board the *Saint Jehan* seems very low. There were seven women identified simply as "wife of" and five women who are named: La Veuve (widow) Perigault; Anne Motin; her younger sister, Jehanne Motin; a cousin, Jacqueline de Glaisnée; and Jehanne Billard, an attendant. The *Saint Jehan* is often compared to the *Mayflower* which arrived in Plymouth, Massachusetts in 1620. However, there were more true colonists, as opposed to labourers, on board the *Mayflower* and there were 19 married women and 32 children.[40] As the 1671 census of Port Royal proves, almost all of the passengers of the *Saint Jehan* eventually made their way back to France. Although the *Saint Jehan* constitutes an important key to the colonization of Acadie, it did not play a role comparable to that of the *Mayflower*.

One of the women on board the *Saint Jehan* was the aforementioned Jehanne or Jeanne Motin whose family originated from Dijon in eastern France. Jeanne's older sister, Anne, was married to Sieur de Breuil, Isaac de Razilly's lieutenant at Fort St. François in Canso.[41] Shortly after Jeanne Motin arrived in Port Royal in 1636, she became the wife of Charles de Menou d'Aulnay and after his accidental death in 1650, she married Charles de La Tour. The children of this second marriage form the first generation of Acadians born in Port Royal, cradle of the heartland.

Ironically, Charles de La Tour spent his last years in the place that he had first come to settle with Poutrincourt in 1610. During his lifetime in Acadie, La Tour had experienced devastating attacks by the English, the Scottish, the Dutch and by his rival, Charles d'Aulnay. Like Nicolas Denys, Charles de La Tour had founded trading posts. He had visited Boston and witnessed the extraordinary growth of the Massachusetts colony, only two days' sailing from Cape Sable. By the time La Tour returned to Port Royal in 1651, it had been inhabited and farmed continuously by the French for 15 years. The dykeland farming was well established and was to characterize the Acadian way of life in Nova Scotia until 1755. Port Royal and the other communities which gradually developed along the Bay of Fundy would constitute the Acadian heartland. From the mid-1600s to the beginning of the 1700s, only a few families—like the d'Entremont, the Amirault, the Pitre and the Mius—lived in settlements outside this agricultural society.[42]

NOTES

1. The name Micmac does not appear in written documents until 1676. Champlain uses Souriquois and Father Chrestien Le Clercq uses Gaspésiens. See Andrew Hill Clark, *Acadia: The Geography of Early Nova Scotia to 1760*, University of Wisconsin Press, 1968, p. 58.

2. *The Voyages of Jacques Cartier*, translated by H.P. Biggar, Publications of the Public Archives of Canada, 1924, pp. 52-53.

3. Father Clarence-J. d'Entremont, *Nicolas Denys: sa vie et son oeuvre*, L'Imprimerie Lescarbot Ltée, 1982, p. 303.

4. Harold A. Innis, *The Cod Fisheries: The History of an International Economy*, Toronto, University of Toronto, 1954, pp. 43-49.

5. The Basque country now straddles the border between France and Spain. Until the early 1800s, the Basques negotiated as a separate nation. The Basque language is unrelated to any other tongue in Europe.

6. J.S. McLennan, *Louisbourg: from its foundation to its fall (1713- 1758)*, Bryant Press Ltd, Toronto, 4th edition, 1978, pp. 8-9.

7. Yves Jacob, *Jacques Cartier: De Saint-Malo au Saint-Laurent*, Editions Maritimes et d'Outre-Mer, 1984, p. 40.

8. Ibid., p. 61.

9. Henry Harisse, *Découverte et évolution cartographique de Terre-Neuve et des pays circonvoisins, 1497-1501-1769*, Amsterdam, N. Israel, 1968, p. 125.

10. Yves Jacob, op. cit., p. 217.

11. Harold A. Innis, *The Fur Trade in Canada*, Toronto, University of Toronto Press, (1st ed. 1930), 1977 ed., pp. 9-10.

12. M.A. MacDonald, *Robert Le Blant: Seminal Researcher and Historian of Early New France*, The New Brunswick Museum, 1986, p. 28

13. John G. Reid, *Six Crucial Decades*, Halifax, Nimbus Publishing, 1987, p. 6. France and England were limited to northern latitudes, while Spain and Portugal were limited to southern latitudes. France lies

between the 43th and the 50th parallels. Nova Scotia is situated between the 43rd and 47th parallels.

14. Andrew Hill Clark, op. cit., p. 71.
15. *The Works of Samuel de Champlain,* translated by H.P. Biggar, Champlain Society, Toronto, 1922-1936, Vol. I, p. 271.
16. *The Works of Samuel de Champlain,* translated by H.P. Biggar, Champlain Society, Toronto, 1922-1936, Vol. I, pp. 258-259; pp. 368-369.
17. *The Works of Samuel de Champlain,* translated by H.P. Biggar, Champlain Society, Toronto, 1922-1936, Vol. I, pp. 327-328.
18. *The History of New France* by Marc Lescarbot, translated by W.L. Grant, The Champlain Society, Toronto, 1907-1914, vol. VII, p. 309.
19. *The History of New France* by Marc Lescarbot, translated by W.L. Grant, The Champlain Society, Toronto, 1907-1914, vol. VII, p. 362.
20. John Reid, op. cit., pp. 17-21.
21. M.A. MacDonald, *Fortune and La Tour,* Methuen, 1983, pp. 5-6.
22. See: Cornelius J. Jaenen, *Friends and Foe: Aspects of French-Amerindian Cultural Contact in the Sixteenth and Seventeenth Centuries,* McClelland and Stewart Ltd., 1976. See also: H.F. McGee, *The Native Peoples of Atlantic Canada,* McClelland and Stewart Ltd., 1974.
23. *The Jesuit Relations and Allied Documents* (Father Biard's Relation, 1616), translated and edited by Ruebeun Gold Thwaites, Pageant Book Co., New York, 1959, Vol. 3, p.173.
24. Father Clarence d'Entremont, *Nicolas Denys: sa vie et son oeuvre,* pp. 293-296.
25. M.A. MacDonald, *Fortune and La Tour,* op. cit., p. 18.
26. Father Clarence d'Entremont, *Histoire du Cap-Sable de l'An mil au Traité de Paris (1763),* Hebert Publications, 1981, Vol. II, pp. 408-9.
27. M.A. MacDonald, *Fortune and La Tour,* op. cit., p.18. Text of letter in Alphonse Deveau, *Notre héritage acadien,* L'Imprimerie de l'Université Sainte-Anne, 1979, pp. 55-56.
28. A. H. Clark, op. cit., p. 94 ; Michel Roy, *L'Acadie des origines à nos jours,* Québec-Amérique, 1981, p. 41.
29 A. H. Clark, op. cit., p. 95; Joan Dawson, *The Map Maker's Eye,* Nimbus Publishing Ltd. and the Nova Scotia Museum, 1988, pp. 14-15, p. 72.
30. Authors' translation from Razilly's letter to Lescarbot dated August 16, 1634. The only existing text is a third person account of the letter: France, Bibliothèque nationale, Fonds français, vol. 13423, folios 348-350. Photocopy of original provided by Joan Dawson.
31. Authors' translation from Razilly's letter to Cardinal Richelieu dated July 25, 1634, France, Archives du ministère des Affaires étrangères, Mémoires et Documents, vol. 4, folio 130-130v. Photocopy of original provided by Joan Dawson.
32. A. H. Clark, op. cit., p. 93.

33. *Description and Natural History of the Coasts of North America (Acadia)* by Nicolas Denys, translated and edited by William F. Ganong, Toronto, The Champlain Society, 1908, pp. 149-150.

34. Father Clarence d'Entremont, *Nicolas Denys*, op. cit., pp. 41-52. Emmanuel LeBorgne's son. Alexandre LeBorgne de Belle Isle, inherited his father's title in Port Royal. It is on this estate that the archeological digs referred to in Chapter 2 took place.

35. Until Father d'Entremont's recent research, it was thought that Razilly died in 1635. In fact, he died on July 2, 1636. See: *La Société historique acadienne: les cahiers*, 19, 1988, pp. 139-42.

36. M.A. MacDonald, op. cit., pp. 177-9.

37. Father Clarence d'Entremont, "Histoire de Pubnico" in *Les régions acadiennes de la Nouvelle-Ecosse, Histoire et Anecdotes*, Centre Acadien, Université de Sainte-Anne, 1982, pp. 47-48. The family in question: Antoine Hervieux and Marguerite Pesseley from La Rochelle.

38. For the colonization efforts of Poutrincourt, Razilly, d'Aulnay, de La Tour see d'Entremont, *Histoire du Cap Sable*, op. cit. Vol. 2, Chapter 15, pp. 641-670.

39. M.A. MacDonald, op. cit., p. 91.

40. Kate Caffrey, *The Mayflower*, Andre Deutch Ltd., London, 1975, pp. 335-41.

41. Joan Dawson, *Isaac de Razilly, 1587-1635: Founder of LaHave*, Lunenburg County Historical Society, LaHave, 1982, p.5.

42. For the development of the Micmac branch of the d'Entremont family which became known as the Mius, see d'Entremont, *Histoire du Cap Sable*, op. cit., Vol. 3, Chapter 20, pp. 963-1018.

CHAPTER 2

The Heartland: 1636–1755

By the middle of the seventeenth century there were about 50 families living in or near the settlement of Port Royal. This tiny cluster of families, some of whom had been established on the fertile lands along the Rivière Dauphin (Annapolis River) since 1636, and others who had arrived in subsequent decades, constitutes the foundation of the Acadian people.

Until recently, historical accounts of Acadie have concentrated on the military and political struggles between France and England, rather than the social fabric of the Acadians as a people. This is partly due to the fact that Acadie occupied a strategic geographical position and served as a pawn in international politics. From a maritime point of view, Acadie was the key not only to the trade routes and the fishery of the North Atlantic, but also to the Gulf of St. Lawrence and the fur trade. This key was tossed back and forth between the two superpowers for more than a century. In fact, Acadie changed hands nine times between 1604 and 1710. This political instability obviously had an effect on the flow of French settlers. For example, Acadie fell to the English in 1654. As a result, no new immigrants were able to establish themselves in Port Royal until after the Treaty of Breda in 1667 when the colony was given back, once again, to France. Over the next few decades, only about one hundred immigrants arrived in Acadie. Port Royal suffered a disastrous attack in 1710 which, once again, placed the colony in jeopardy. In 1713, the Treaty of Utrecht transferred ownership of mainland Acadie, or Nova Scotia, to the British. Ile Royale (Cape

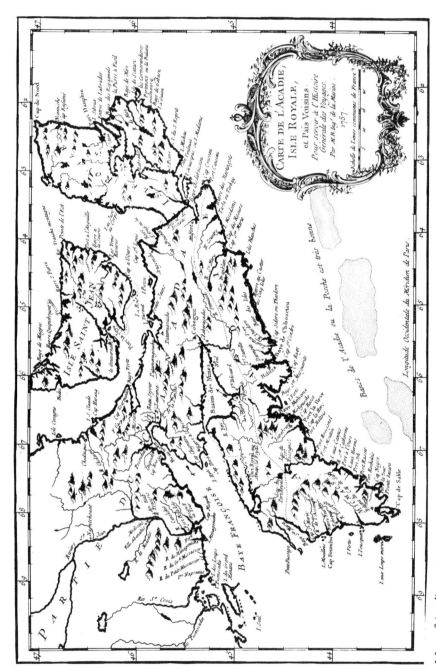

Map of Acadie

Fortress Louisbourg (Courtesy: Canadian Parks Service)

Breton) and Ile Saint-Jean (Prince Edward Island) remained French. The treaty was unclear as to which country owned the tiny islands off Canso and the territory north of the Missaguash River forming present-day New Brunswick.

One of the most immediate consequences of the fall of Acadie and the Treaty of Utrecht was the establishment of a French colony on Ile Royale. Louisbourg became the capital of the colony which also included Ile Saint-Jean. In 1719 work began on the enormous fortress which was designed to protect France's fishing and commercial interests in the New World. Until its final destruction in 1758, Louisbourg constituted one of the busiest ports on the Atlantic coast and an important trade link between France and the sugar plantations of the French West Indies.

In 1713, mainland Nova Scotia became a British colony, although the Acadians had no particular reason to think that France would not regain control of their homeland as it had done on numerous occasions in the past. Until the founding of Halifax in 1749, the British made no effort whatsoever to colonize Nova Scotia and restricted their presence to a fishing post at Canso and a small garrison in Port Royal, renamed Annapolis Royal. Despite the fact that the Acadians were now officially under the control of the British, they were able to continue living, at least for a few more decades, in relative safety and prosperity. Their presence along the periphery of the territory did not threaten the hunting grounds or fur-trading activities of the Micmac whose numbers had declined to about 1,500.[1]

Over the years, Port Royal had grown considerably and had produced generations of young men and women who gradually moved away to found new communities. By the end of the 1740s, Acadian settlements dotted the marshlands along the Baie française (Bay of Fundy). The Acadians were thus well-established over a vast territory and had developed a life-style that, in many ways, was quite unlike other cultures in the New World.

Little is known about daily life in Port Royal during the first 40 years of the permanent settlement. In order to paint a picture of the settlers established on the shores of the bay, one must draw on several sources, including modern statistical analyses and recent archeological discoveries. From 1636 to the end of the century, few of the French officials and missionaries who visited Acadie left descriptions that give any idea of family or community life. There are no diaries that compare with those of Lescarbot and Champlain who recounted the century's opening years. Although Nicolas Denys arrived with Razilly in 1632 and travelled in Acadie for almost forty years, his activities were centered far away from the marshlands of Port Royal in his outposts at Saint-Pierre, Ile Royale (St. Peters, Cape Breton) and Nepisiquit, near present-day Bathurst, New Brunswick. Consequently, his writings provide no clues to life in the part of Acadie that formed the heartland.

The first document that gives a clear picture of the people in Port Royal is a census taken in 1671 by a French missionary by the name of Father Laurent Molins who was a member of the Cordelier Order, a branch of the Franciscans. The census covers Port Royal, the most populated area, and all the small outlying settlements like Cape Sable and LaHave where the settlers and the Micmac lived in close contact. Father Molins gives the name and age of all the men, women and children along with the occupation of the heads of households, the amount of land they had cultivated and the number of sheep and cows they possessed. According to Father Molins, there were 66 families, including three widows and their children, living in Port Royal in 1671. One century later, direct descendants of some of these families were still living in the Annapolis Valley. They were granted land on St. Marys Bay and founded the first settlements in the township of Clare. The surnames of these pioneer families whose ancestors appear in the census of 1671 are Gaudet, Babin, Terriau, Trahan, Thibaudeau, Doucet, LeBlanc, Comeau, Dugas, Melanson, Robichaud and LaNoue.[2]

Father Molins begins his enumeration with the family of Jacob or Jacques Bourgeois, a doctor and the only professional man in the settlement of Port Royal. He was 50 years old at the time and his wife, Jeanne Trahan, was 10 years younger. They had 3 sons and 7 daughters. Jacques Bourgeois had 33 head of cattle and 24 sheep, which was more than any of the other families. In addition to being a doctor, Bourgeois had served as lieutenant in Port Royal in 1654 when it was attacked by the English. When Father Molins conducted his survey, the administrative seat of Acadie was located in Pentagouet. Consequently, there were no French officials living in Port Royal so that, as a doctor and former lieutenant, Jacques Bourgeois and his family were at the top of the social scale.

Most of the heads of families are identified by the old term of *laboureurs* or ploughmen but the census also lists several specialized tradesmen. For example, there were 4 coopers including Pierre Commeaux [sic] who was 75 years old and married to Rose Bayol. They had 9 children between the ages of 6 and 21. The other skilled workers living in Port Royal in 1671 were: Pierre Melanson, a tailor; Mathieu Martin, a weaver; Pierre Doucet, a mason; Thomas Cormié [sic], a carpenter; Laurent Granger, a sailor; Guillaume Trahan and Jehan Pitre, blacksmiths; and Pierre Sire and Abraham Dugast [sic], gunsmiths.

Of the women enumerated in Port Royal, some were undoubtedly Micmac, including a 27-year-old by the name of Anne Ouestnorouest, married to Pierre Martin the younger, a 40-year-old farmer. They had 4 children between 2 ½ and 10 years old. One of the elderly women listed by Father Molins is called Marie Sale. As the women in the census are usually identified by their maiden names, and as marriages between Micmac men and Acadian women were rare, in all likelihood Marie Sale was a Micmac widow whose husband had been an Acadian. Intermarriage and conversion to Catholicism tended to strengthen the cultural and commercial ties between the Micmac and the Acadian settlers.

The Acadian population was enumerated on ten occasions between 1671 and 1714. The original parish register of Saint-Jean-Baptiste in Port Royal has survived and is in the Public Archives of Nova Scotia. It covers the period 1702-1755, in other words, the last decade of the French regime before the Treaty of Utrecht and 40 years of British rule. These records, along with the ten enumerations and other reports compiled by French officials who visited the colony at the end of the seventeenth century, portray a healthy and growing population that was well-adapted, both physically and socially, to the local environment.

The health of a population can be measured in several ways, but longevity is normally considered to be a good indicator. Although he was later appalled by the effects of wine and brandy distributed by fishermen and fur traders, Nicolas Denys was struck by the number of elderly people and the lack of diseases among the Micmac. Referring to the early days of travels, he notes, for instance,

They lived long lives. I have seen Indians of a hundred and twenty to a hundred and forty years of age who went to hunt Moose...

They had knowledge of herbs, of which they made use and straightway grew well. They were not subject to the gout, gravel, fevers, or rheumatism. Their general remedy was to make themselves sweat, something which they did every month and even oftener.[3] (TR)

Like the Micmac, the Acadians lived in a clean and uncrowded environment with a plentiful supply of food and water. There is every reason to believe that they had access to Micmac knowledge of the curative value of certain plants.

Father Molins enumerated a number of individuals over 60 years of age and one man, Jehan Gaudet, who was 93. To illustrate a typically healthy Acadian family, one might take the example of Charles Melanson and Marie Dugas who were married in Port Royal in 1664. Within seven years of their marriage, the young couple owned 20 *arpents* of cultivated land in the Port Royal area on the site known today as the Melanson Settlement.[4] Charles and

Marie had 9 daughters and 5 sons. Several of the children married and settled near their parents. Their daughter Cécile married Abraham Boudrot, a successful ship captain and merchant who participated in the trade between Port Royal and Boston. Charles Melanson died at the turn of the century at the age of about 57 but Marie Dugas lived for many more years and was about 90 years old when she died in 1737.

The recent analyses of the parish registers of Port Royal show that Acadians respected the religious customs of the time and that they lived within the rigid framework of their farming activities.[5] Marriages never took place during Lent or Advent—the holiest periods in the Christian calendar. Most couples married between late October and February, in other words during the cold months outside spring planting time and the harvest season. The first child was usually born nine months or more after the wedding. Various records also indicate that between 1671 and 1730 the average household in Port Royal had about seven children. Generally, women married at a younger age (between 15 and 21) and had more children than their contemporaries in France. Men always married, even if they had to wait a number of years before they could find an eligible bride. Genealogical research shows that Mathieu Martin appears to be one of the rare bachelors in Acadie. His parents arrived as passengers on board the famous *Saint Jehan*. Mathieu was born in Port Royal in 1636 and is believed to be the first child born in Acadie of French parents. He was 35 years old at the time of Father Molins's census. In 1689, he moved away from Port Royal to carry out fur-trading and was granted land in Cobequid (Truro).[6]

The most important first-hand description of life in the settlements along the Rivière Dauphin (Annapolis River) was written by Sieur de Dièreville, a Frenchman from Normandy, who arrived in Port Royal in 1699 and lived among the Acadians for one year. By this time, the first generation of children, like Mathieu Martin, had grown up and many of them had married and moved away to the newly founded settlements of Beaubassin (1672) and Grand Pré (1682). When Sieur de Dièreville landed on the shores of the Rivière Dauphin, there were about five hundred settlers living along the river in the general vicinity of Port Royal.[7] He provides the following explanation for his readers in France:

Let me say, to begin with, that there are only three Settlements to divide so vast a Territory, and that the People of these places have the same occupations. Port Royal is the first… The second is Minas [Grand Pré], and Beaubassin is the third. I have never been to these two places, and shall therefore give no Description of them. I only know that Minas provides more Wheat than all the rest of the Country, because its Marshes, which are quite extensive, have been drained; and that the People of Port Royal have established their children there on concessions they have purchased, in order that the land may be settled and rendered fertile; in this they are very successful. In regard to Beaubassin, so called because of its situation, it is the least populous Settlement, and also the least productive.

The Climate of all this region is like that of France, and it lies in almost the same latitude; the Summer is warm, but the Winter is colder; it snows almost continuously at this season, and the winds are so cold that they freeze one's face…[8] (TR)

Dièreville describes the countryside around Port Royal as being "faultlessly beautiful" although many of the houses were in poor condition because of the numerous raids and attacks Port Royal had suffered over the years. The parish priest did not live in luxury and the church was obviously much more rudimentary than anything Dièreville was used to in France:

I asked for the Church which I had been unable to identify, because it differed in no way from the other buildings; and I should have been more inclined to take it for a Barn than for the Temple of the True God; while I was on my way there to give thanks to Him for his mercy in having brought me here in safety, I saw Monsieur le Curé coming to meet me; we paid one another reciprocal compliments, after which he conducted me to the Church, and honoured me by the offer of Holy-Water. I said my prayer, and then Monsieur le Curé took me to his room, which was ill-furnished, and contrary to the rules concerning Presbyteries, at one end of the Church and adjoining it.[9] (TR)

Having overcome his initial disappointment with regard to material comfort in the colony, Dièreville goes on to paint a picture of productive farms which he could see as he travelled up the Rivière Dauphin. He was impressed by the efficient dyking methods that enabled the settlers to produce a sizeable wheat crop.

He also discovered that the most popular vegetables were cabbages, turnips, peas, beans, onions and corn because they kept well. Like the many varieties of apples which Dièreville observed, the turnips and cabbages could be stored in the cellars for the winter. Other vegetables like peas and beans were dried and kept in the attic. The wheat was obviously made into flour since Dièreville saw both flour and lumber mills.

Contrary to other observers, both French and English, Dièreville does not criticize the Acadians for dyking the marshes rather than clearing the forests on higher ground.[10] He comments on their efficiency and their hard work:

It costs a great deal to prepare the lands which they wish to cultivate. To grow Wheat, the Marshes which are inundated by the Sea at high Tide, must be drained; these are called Lowlands, and they are quite good, but what labour is needed to make them fit for cultivation! The ebb and flow of the Sea cannot easily be stopped, but the Acadians succeed in doing so by means of great Dykes, called Aboteaux [sic].[11] (TR)

This lowland farming, which entailed the reclamation of salt marshes by means of co-operative dyking, became the single most distinctive characteristic of Acadian culture. It is difficult to know exactly how or when the complex and labour-intensive technology of dykes developed in Acadie. The first dykes were probably constructed between 1640 and 1650. It is possible that some of the settlers from France were familiar with dyking techniques used for the reclamation of marshes in southwest Poitou, since a project was initiated by Henri IV as early as 1599 in order to create new farmland. This project along with others in the old French provinces of Poitou, Aunis and Saintonge were carried out under the direction of Dutch engineers. Throughout the seventeenth and eighteenth centuries, salt, an indispensable commodity in the fishery, was obtained by dyking the marshes around Brouage, just south of the famous seaport of La Rochelle. Although their knowledge of lowlands would be useful, even the most experienced saltmakers would not have been able to collect salt from the marshes along the fog-bound coast of Nova Scotia.[12]

It is not known whether any colonists who arrived between 1636 and 1650 were recruited specifically for their experience in

The construction of dykes and aboiteaux was based entirely on co-operative labour. (Painting by Azor Vienneau. Courtesy: Nova Scotia Museum)

lowland farming or dyke-building, although a number of them originated from La Rochelle and other lowland areas in southwestern France. It is interesting to note, however, that the well-known Acadian name, Saulnier, which originally referred to a person involved in the extraction of sea salt from marshlands, does not appear in the nominal census of either 1671 or 1686. It would appear then that the development of dyking techniques was the result of a combination of skills and of factors dictated by the very distinctive features of the landscape along the Bay of Fundy.

Obviously the first settlers in Port Royal would have been aware of the extraordinary fertility of the immense salt marshes that surrounded them. The height of the wild grasses alone would have been a clear sign of a very productive soil. But until the movement of water through the flat wet marshlands was controlled, the fertility would remain untapped. Not only would the ground be too damp for cultivation, but the salt content would prevent the growth of essential crops like wheat and barley.

No other group which colonized North America developed settlements based on the reclamation of salt marshes. No other group perfected the techniques of dyke-building. No other group preferred to settle on lowlands rather than clear the forests on higher ground. The term *aboiteau*, which designates the wooden clapper valve that controlled the flow of salt water on the marshes, has no equivalent word in English or modern French. Like the word *igloo*, the word *aboiteau* is inextricably linked to a specific cultural context. As witnessed by Dièreville's description, by the end of the seventeenth century, the Acadians were very proficient builders of dykes and aboiteaux. He explains the complex construction and stresses the absolute necessity for team work.

The ebb and flow of the sea cannot easily be stopped, but the Acadians succeed in doing so...and it is done is this way; five or six rows of large logs are driven whole into the ground at points where the Tide enters the Marsh, and between each row, other logs are laid, one on top of the other, and all the spaces between them are so carefully filled with well-pounded clay, that the water can no longer get through. In the centre of this construction, a Sluice [the aboiteau] is contrived in such a manner that the water on the Marshes flows out of its own accord, while that of the Sea is prevented from coming in.

An undertaking of this nature, which can only be carried on at certain Seasons when the Tides do not ride so high, costs a great deal, and takes many days, but the abundant crop that is harvested in the second year, after the soil has been washed by Rain water compensates, for all the expense.

As these Lands are owned by several Men, the work upon them is done in common; if they belonged to an Individual, he would have to pay the others, or give the Men who had worked for him an equal number of days devoted to some other employment; that is the manner in which it is customary for them to adjust such matters among themselves.[13] (TR)

The Acadians thus developed co-operative farming methods that relied on the rich clay soil which is naturally fertilized by sediments deposited by the tides. The Bay of Fundy and its numerous basins and inlets have the highest tidal ranges in the world—up to 15 metres in Minas Basin where the Acadians settled in the 1680s. The great rushes of water or tidal bores that flow over the mud flats transport tiny soil particles that constantly enrich the marshes.[14]

Within a few decades the Acadians learned how to exploit the natural fertility of the marshes that they first discovered at Port Royal and that they gradually came to prefer to any other type of farmland. Before the end of the French regime in 1710, the Acadians had built dykes and aboiteaux in all the great marshland regions bordering on the Bay of Fundy.

As in all pioneer settlements, the family formed the basic social unit in Acadie. The cohesiveness of the Acadian family was particularly important not only because of the isolation and vulnerability of the colony, but also because the marshland farming depended entirely on co-operative labour. As Dièreville and other visitors observed, the building and maintenance of dykes could not take place without the co-operation of a number of neighbouring households. This usually meant the members of an extended family. Although Charles Melanson and Marie Dugas, for example, had twice as many children as the average couple in the heartland, the settlement pattern followed by their offspring was typical of most families from the 1680s to the mid-1700s. Eight of the 14 Melanson children married in Port Royal and settled near their parents, thus ensuring the presence of a young labour-force to work the fields and maintain the dykes. The remaining children either moved away or established themselves elsewhere in the Port Royal area.

Maps made by the British surveyor George Mitchell in 1733 show the family settlements that gradually developed along the Annapolis River. Mitchell indicates the actual location of the various families who formed closely-knit units or villages. Typical surnames in the Port Royal area were Melanson, Bourg, Doucet, Robichaud, Dugas, LeBlanc, Thibodeau, Girroir, Bastarache, and Bourgeois. Because of the limited number of available surnames, the Acadians were often forced to use nicknames to distinguish between the different branches of a family. For example, Pierre Commeau had two sons named Pierre, one was known as *l'Esturgeon* (the sturgeon) and the other as *Loupmarin* (the seal). The Esturgeon (Commeau) settlement can be found on Mitchell's map, near the mouth of the Annapolis River.

Until very recently little was known about the buildings and houses that made up these family settlements. Dièreville, for instance, does not provide details either about specific families or their homes. However, several major archeological excavations carried out between 1983 and 1985 have shed new light on the material culture of the Acadians who lived along the Annapolis River in the 1730s. The digs took place at Belleisle and at the so-called Melanson Settlement, located 15 and 2 kilometres, respectively, to the east of the Port Royal National Historic Site.[15]

The results of these archeological digs—particularly at the Belleisle site—show that the family dwellings built by the Acadians in the late 1600s and early 1700s were much more sophisticated than written documents from the period suggest. The Acadians in the heartland were not living in log cabins or in stockade-type constructions normally associated with trading posts and frontier life. Acadian families were not living in homes that looked in any way like Champlain's Habitation which has become well known thanks to the 1939 reconstruction at the Port Royal National Historic Site. Their houses were made from solid wood posts, beams and boards. Bunches of charred marsh grasses were uncovered during the excavations which indicate that the roofs of these frame houses were thatched. Judging from other materials unearthed, the Acadians appear to have lined the walls of their homes with clay that they whitewashed to provide clean bright walls. They also used both stone and clay to construct a large hearth inside the house, with an exterior bake oven, a feature that appears to be quite distinctive and has not been found elsewhere in North America.

Perhaps the most striking discovery made at the Belleisle and the Melanson archeological sites was the wide range of ceramics and other artifacts that provide concrete proof of the extensive contacts the Acadians had with Louisbourg, France, England and the Anglo-American colonies. Although their farms provided them with the basic agricultural products, the Acadians were not self-sufficient. In other words, they relied on outside markets for many items ranging from firearms to molasses. They traded raw materials—furs, wheat, barley and cattle—in exchange for goods they could not (or did not) produce or manufacture themselves.

Written documents dating back to the 1680s and 1690s indicate that trade between the English in Boston and the Acadians in Port Royal was commonplace—despite the fact that it was officially illegal until the Treaty of Utrecht in 1713. As was noted earlier, Charles de La Tour, for example, visited Boston on several occasions for commercial reasons. The following translation of an invoice signed by Abraham Boudrot of Port Royal (a son-in-law of Charles and Marie Melanson[16]) is an obvious illustration of the commercial ties between Acadie and the Massachusetts Bay colony. The items listed indicate that Acadian women did not sew entirely with homespun cloth and that they used spices like cloves and nutmeg from the British West Indies in their cooking.

Invoice of the merchandise that I, André Faneuil and brother, have given to Mr. Boudrot to sell for us at Port Royal plus our profit as follows:

For:

26½ yards of gingham @ 3s 3d — £4 4s 10d
7½ yards of red cloth @ 11s 6d — £4 6s 3d
5½ yards of blue cloth @ 11s 6d — £3 3s 1d
155½ yards of silk lace @ 2 — £1 5s 11d
16 yards silk ribbon @ 8 — £10
30 yards blue ribbon @ 4 — £3
92 pieces of serge — £1 17s 10d

1 piece of blue cloth No. 18,
  30 yards @ 15 per yard — £1 17s 10d
1 piece of ditto No. 10,
  27 yards @ 15 — £1 13s
1 piece of red cloth @ 4s per
  yard, 38 yards — £7 12s
3 t of nutmeg @ 17d per pound — £2 11s
2 t of cloves @ 17d per pound — £14 1s
12 pairs of mens' stockings — £2 1s
1 parcel of wampons [beads] — 9s 6d

I, the undersigned concede having received from Mr. André Faneuil
the above mentioned things that I promise to sell for him at Port Royal
plus his profit and as soon as they are sold to send the returns to Boston
to him or to his order. Done at Boston, April 26, 1691. (TR)

  Abraham Boudrot[17]

Another clue as to the importance of these trade links is
provided by Mathieu Des Goutins, a French civil officer or clerk
who sent regular dispatches to his superiors in Paris at the Ministry
of the Marine. In the following translation of one of his reports,
Des Goutins makes no secret of the fact that the Acadians relied on
the English, not the French, for salt and essential tools and utensils
like harrows, ploughs, scythes, axes and knives.

We would be very happy, Sir, if at present our enemies [the English]
would bring us the necessary items in exchange for beaver pelts which
we have in abundance. Without the goods they brought us the last time,
we would not even have had soup. The ground would not have been
cultivated. [With no scythes] *we would have had to pull up grass by*
the roots in order to make hay. [With no knives] *we would have had*
to bite off our bread with our teeth. We would have no pots, no ovens,
no scythes, no knives, no iron, no axes, no kettles for the Indians and
no salt for the inhabitants. (TR)

  Mathieu Des Goutins, December 23, 1707[18]

Although a number of written documents give historians a
glimpse of trading activities, the archeological digs carried out in
the 1980s have provided a clearer picture of the types of objects the

Acadians obtained from their French and British trading partners.

No artifacts made of wood, leather, or cloth have survived but metal objects and fragments of stoneware, earthenware, and glass provide the primary clues to the commercial activities of the Acadians living along the Annapolis River in the 1730s. It is evident from the discoveries at both the Belleisle and the Melanson sites that the Acadians relied entirely on outside sources for all their bowls, plates, jugs, bottles, cups, and mugs. Specialists have been able to identify the origin and approximate dates of almost all the fragments of these tableware items. The types of ceramics unearthed show that the Acadians in the heartland led a comfortable life but that they could not afford elegant or costly porcelains and glass. It would appear that they obtained most of their cooking and eating vessels from England and the Anglo-American colonies. However, they also used French tableware which, of course, implies trade links with Louisbourg or France. Numerous pieces of green earthenware were found. This glaze is typical of bowls and plates produced in the old French province of Saintonge, located near La Rochelle. As was noted previously, La Rochelle was the home port of many of the fishing vessels and passenger ships that came to Acadie during the seventeenth and eighteenth centuries.

Since smoking tobacco was a very popular pastime, it is not surprising that many fragments of clay pipes were found at all the archeological sites. Because of the evolution of manufacturing techniques, archeologists are able to determine with considerable accuracy the date and country of origin of these pipes. The majority of the white clay pipes found at Belleisle, for example, were made in England in the 1730s. The archeologists also discovered red clay pipes at the Grand Pré, Belleisle and Melanson sites. The origin of these pipes is not known although they may have been made locally.

With a few exceptions like coins and gunlocks, archeologists have not been able to identify the source for metal artifacts such as buckles, straight pins, needles, awls, bale seals, mouth harps, and door locks. The following invoice dated January 12, 1696-97 is another example of the wide variety of goods the Acadians received from Boston during the French regime. It is interesting to note that, unlike many pioneers, the Acadians did not make their own soap—perhaps because it was such an easy commodity to obtain.

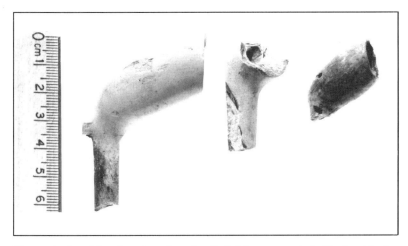

The majority of the clay pipes found at Belleisle were made in England in the 1730s. (Courtesy: Nova Scotia Museum)

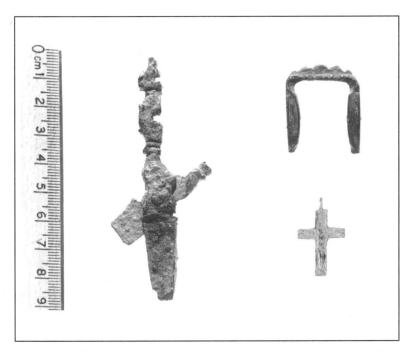

Archeological digs have provided concrete proof of the contacts the Acadians had with Louisbourg, France, England and the Anglo-American colonies. (Courtesy: Nova Scotia Museum)

The molasses mentioned in the invoice was a by-product of the sugar plantations in the West Indies and a very popular item in Acadian cooking. Dièreville obviously tasted it for the first time in his life during his stay in Port Royal and describes it as a "kind of raisin-coloured sugar syrup" used in the making of spruce beer. Fragments of a number of the items listed in the invoice (marked with an asterisk) were uncovered at both the Belleisle and the Melanson sites. The Charles de La Tour mentioned in the invoice was born in Cape Sable around 1665 and is one of the sons of the first Charles de La Tour.

These are to certifie all whom it doth Concern that Charles D Latour master of the shallop Jacob burthen ffifteen Tuns or thereabouts, no Guns mounted, navigated with three men, plantation built, did on the thirteenth day of September 1695 clear the said Vessel for Cape Sable having here loaden and taken on board by virtue of an order of the Honble the Lieut. Governor and Council dated the fifth of September aforesaid:

Two pieces of white cotton
One piece of Penistone
Two pieces of Lining
ffour pounds of thred
Three dozen combs
*Two dozen ffish hooks **
Six lines
*Six dozen halfe knives **
Three dozen Tobacco Tongs
One hundred pound Tobacco
Sixteen pieces Tape and Gassooms
*Six dozen pewter Buttons **
One pound Vermillion
Two dozen halfe stockins
*One dozen Brass and Copper Kettles * [fragments of brass and copper]*
*Six dishes **
*Six plates **
Six hoes
*Two dozen Sizzors **

Six pounds pepper
One hundred Eighty Gall. Rum
One barrel of Molasses
One piece of Red Searge
One Gross Pipes *
ffour Barrels ffyal Wine * [fragments of glass]
Six pair Shoes
fforty pounds soap
Six dozen Axes *

and here became bound with Surety as the abovesaid order of Councill directs. Given under my hand at the naval office at Boston the twelfth day of January 1696/7

William Welsteed [19]

Scientific analysis carried out at the National Museum of Natural Sciences of all the bones discovered at the Belleisle site has provided valuable information with regard to the Acadians' eating habits and trading practices. Almost all the bones unearthed belong to domestic animals—cows, pigs, sheep and poultry. The remains from wild species such as passenger pigeon, goose and hare, constitute a very small percentage of all the bones uncovered. This fact enables archeologists to confirm that the Acadians were not hunters and gatherers. On the contrary, they depended to a large extent on the animals they raised for their food. Perhaps Acadians living in frontier settlements like Tatamagouche and LaHave would have relied more on wild birds and animals than the inhabitants of the Port Royal region.

Judging from the types of bones discovered at Belleisle, the Acadians traded the choicest cuts of meat and kept the less valuable ones for home consumption. The age of the cows and sheep when they were slaughtered indicates that the sheep were being kept for their wool and that the cows were slaughtered when they were no longer productive. Given the value of fresh meat in the eighteenth century, it is very probable that the Acadians sold many of the younger animals live. Written documents refer to cattle from Minas Basin being driven across the Isthmus of Chignecto to harbours on the Northumberland Strait for shipment to Louisbourg.

The most important of these ports was Baie Verte (near present-day Cape Tormentine, New Brunswick), although smaller Acadian outposts like Tatamagouche played a significant role in trade with Ile Royale. A few vessels made the long voyage out of the Bay of Fundy and around the south coast up to Louisbourg.[20] As it is known that the Acadians on Ile Saint-Jean exported calves to Louisbourg where fresh veal was considered to be a great delicacy among the French officials, one can assume that the Acadian farmers living in the heartland exported their livestock to the French fortress and to the even closer markets of Boston.[21]

Due to their fragile nature, very few fish bones were discovered at Belleisle. Obviously the Acadians ate fish, not only because it was plentiful, but also because, as Catholics, they would have observed all the days of abstinence and fasting in the liturgical calendar. In other words, when the consumption of meat was forbidden, fish was an accepted substitute. In his description of life in Port Royal in 1699, Dièreville states that he tasted a wide variety of fish caught locally. He mentions, in particular, smelts, flounder, gaspereaux, shad, bass, eels, trout, and salmon. He also describes fishing weirs that were built at the mouth of brooks and rivers. Obviously the Acadians learned this technique of fishing from the Micmac and they used, and still use, the Micmac word *nijagan* when referring to these weirs. The nijagan described by Dièreville differs only slightly from the ones the Acadians in southwest Nova Scotia build today.[22] The following passage illustrates how much the inhabitants must have relished the taste of fresh fish after months of salt cod, especially if the fish started running in time for Lent.

During the seasons when the Fish are running, for one does not have them all the time, quantities are caught in Fish-weirs [nijagan], *and from them the Settlers derive a great aid to existence. This is how a Fish-weir is made: stakes are driven, side by side, at the mouth of Streams and Rivers into which the Sea rises; the Fish pass over it at high Tide on their way to fatten on the ooze of the Marshes; when the Sea has run quite far out and the Fish begin to lack water, they follow the ebb, or reflux, and being no longer able to pass over the stakes, because the water is too low, they are arrested, and can be taken.*

The first Fish to be caught, comes in the Springtime, and is a

Modern fishing weir or nijagan made from brush and netting. Port Royal.
(Courtesy: Canadian Parks Service)

*variety of Smelt, not quite so good as that of France, although it will
pass as a substitute, and one is glad enough to have it to eat. That which
follows is the Flounder, and the Rivers are completely filled with it; it
is no better than elsewhere, but it is at least fresh, and if it could be
caught during Lent when there is nothing but salt Fish to eat, one
would be only too thankful to get it. I know how much I suffered from
having salt or dried Cod at every meal, which had, moreover, to be
eaten with oil, because of the lack of butter. Although butter is made
in the Country it is not good, and each Settler keeps only a very small
supply, preferring to use the milk.*[23] (TR)

No bones from the most valued fur-bearing animals (the
beaver, otter, muskrat and marten) were found around the houses
excavated at Belleisle. Although fur pelts constituted a significant
item in their commercial exchanges, the Acadians do not appear to
have been trappers themselves. One can conclude that they obtained all their pelts directly from the Micmac. This might not have
been the case for Acadians living in distant outposts like La Have,
Cape Sable or Tatamagouche. In the same way that the Acadians
relied on imported goods for their survival, the Micmac also
became dependent on items obtained through the fur trade.

Writing in 1611, Father Biard describes a well-established trading pattern that Nicolas Denys observed several decades later and that was still prevalent in the eighteenth century:[24]

They [the Micmac] *assemble in the Summer to trade with us, principally at the great river. To this place come also several tribes from afar off. They barter their skins of beaver, otter, deer, marten, seal, etc., for bread, peas, beans, prunes, tobacco, etc.; kettles* [iron cooking pots], *hatchets, iron arrow-points, awls, puncheons* [casks], *cloaks, blankets, and all other such commodities...*[25] (TR)

Archeological research in the Acadian heartland has provided visible proof of a well-established culture with unique characteristics and yet dependent on trade with the Micmac, the British and the French. Although the Acadians formed a distinct culture and a closely-knit society, they were not isolated from either regional or international influences.

To a certain extent the imperatives of these trade links explain the positioning of Acadian settlements along the Bay of Fundy. The creation of important marshland settlements outside the Port Royal area began in 1672 with the founding of Beaubassin (near present-day Amherst) by Jacques Bourgeois, the doctor enumerated in Father Molins' census, and by Michel Le Neuf de la Vallière (Nicolas Denys' son-in-law). A number of young couples left Port Royal with Bourgeois and his family to establish themselves in Beaubassin which was located much closer to the trade routes leading to Quebec.

The most intensive period of emigration from Port Royal took place in the 1680s and 1690s. The settlement of Grand Pré was founded in 1682 by Pierre Melanson and his young wife, Marguerite Mius d'Entremont. The settlements in the Minas Basin region grew very quickly since they were populated by young, fertile couples. The migration from Port Royal to other marshland regions along the Bay of Fundy gradually slowed down when Acadie fell to the British in 1710. The following figures show how the population centre gradually shifted away from Port Royal. By the 1720s the majority of Acadians were living in the settlements around Minas Basin (Grand Pré).[26]

YEAR	PORT ROYAL	GRAND PRE (Minas Basin region)	BEAUBASSIN (near the border of present-day New Brunswick)
1701	456	487	188
1707	570	677	326
1714	900	1,031	345
1730	900	2,500	1,010
1737	1,406	3,736	1,816
1748-50	1,750	5,000	2,800

The foundation of new settlements represents the natural expansion of a growing population. It is not surprising that it was the young couples of Port Royal, as opposed to the middle-aged or elderly, who moved away to forge new frontiers. But why did they move so far away from their birthplace since there was no shortage of marshland along the Annapolis River? Why did so many young people leave Port Royal during the peaceful years of the 1680s and 1690s? Although France was given back the colony in 1670, the administrative headquarters were located in various places including Pentagouet (on the coast of present-day Maine) and Beaubassin. Only in 1684 did the governor take up residence in Port Royal. Until then, the Acadians living along the Annapolis River had existed without any direct administrative control. By moving to Grand Pré and other locations further up the Bay of Fundy, young Acadians could distance themselves from the watchful eye of the governor and carry out unrestricted trade with their oldest and closest trading partners in the British colony of Massachusetts. Numerous observers commented on the independent spirit of the Acadians. Irritated by this tendency, Jacques-François de Brouillan, governor of Acadie between 1701 and 1704, referred to the Acadians in the Minas Basin region as semi-republicans.[27]

The Acadians' desire to avoid interference from the authorities was based on practical considerations. When Acadie belonged to France, trade with the Anglo-American colonies was officially

illegal although essential for survival. When mainland Nova Scotia
became a British colony in 1713, trade between the Acadians and
the French in Louisbourg was an illegal but common practice.
Given these political realities, it was in the interest of the Acadians
to settle in places like Grand Pré that were conveniently located
with regard to the fur trade and shipping routes and that were safe
from any official interference—French or English. In the light of
these considerations, Port Royal was a less favourable location.
Being the headquarters of the French garrison it suffered several
attacks before the final seige of 1710. It was renamed Annapolis
Royal by the British and remained the capital of Nova Scotia until
the founding of Halifax in 1749. Throughout this period the
Acadians continued to farm their lands along the Annapolis River,
and as there were no other European settlers in Nova Scotia, they
constituted the main source of food supplies for the British troops
stationed at Fort Anne.

By the beginning of the eighteenth century, the majority of
Acadians lived outside the Port Royal region. Being far removed
from civil authorities or administrative structures, the role of the
Church and in particular, the priest, became increasingly important. In 1676, Father Petit, pastor of Port Royal, was named the
first Vicar-general of Acadie by Bishop Saint-Vallier of Quebec.
Like all the French priests and missionaries who lived among the
Acadians, Father Petit served not only as a spiritual guide but also
as an educator and a mediator in civil disputes. He provides this
glowing picture of his parishioners:[28]

*One sees no drunkenness, nor loose living and hears no swearing or
blasphemy. Even though they are spread out four or five leagues along
the shores of the river, they come to church in large numbers every
Sunday and on Holy Days.* (TR)

Modest chapels and churches gradually appeared as the Acadians
established new communities along the Bay of Fundy. By 1710 there
were four churches in the Minas Basin region alone: Saint Charles
des Mines at Grand Pré; Saint Joseph at Canard; Notre Dame
l'Assomption and La Sainte Famille at Pisiquid (Windsor). Cobequid
(Truro) formed a parish with the mission of Tatamagouche, each
place having its own chapel. There were also chapels at Tintamarre

(Tantramar) and one or more at Cape Sable where the missionaries serving the Micmac also ministered to the settlers.

At various times when the French controlled Acadie, religious orders attended to the education of the youth. Capuchin Brothers, for example, provided religious instruction to the Acadian and the Micmac children of Port Royal during the early days when d'Aulnay was governor (1636-1650). Sister Chausson of the Congregation of the Holy Cross opened a school at Port Royal in 1701. After the British conquest in 1710, priests sent from Quebec were allowed to continue ministering to the spiritual needs of the Acadians but religious orders from France were no longer permitted in the colony.[29] The collapse of the French regime also meant that the Acadians were deprived of the presence of officers and administrators. As a result, the most educated person in Acadian settlements was the priest. Fewer and fewer children were able to receive any schooling. As the parish register of Port Royal indicates, illiteracy became increasingly common among the younger generations.[30] The situation appears to have been even worse in the Grand Pré area since only a few Acadian men were able to sign their name in 1714.[31]

A number of years after the British established themselves in Annapolis Royal they set up a system of representatives in order to maintain contact with the Acadians. At first, several Acadian men were appointed by the British to represent the major settlements. Later, the Acadians elected their own deputies: 6 from the Port Royal region led by Prudent Robichaud; 8 from the Cobequid (Truro) region led by Charles Robichaud; 12 from the Grand Pré region led by Alexandre Bourg; and 2 from the Beaubassin region.[32] These men were undoubtedly the most respected and influential members of their respective communities. In most cases they would have belonged to the older generation and would have received at least some formal education during the French regime. These deputies became the spokesmen and negotiators for their compatriots in a period of growing hostilities between England and France.

By 1710 the population of the Anglo-American colonies was more than 20 times that of New France. Despite these numbers, France did not initiate any programs that promoted large scale immigration. Rather than bringing out new immigrants, the French authorities attempted to encourage Acadians to move to Ile Royale and Ile Saint-Jean. A small scale migration of about one hundred Acadians to Ile Saint-Jean began in the 1720s. Since most of these people originated from the settlements around Beaubassin, they merely crossed the Northumberland Strait.[33] Even fewer Acadians appear to have been tempted to migrate to the more distant Ile Royale during the 1720s. According to the 1724 census, the inhabitants of Louisbourg came from various parts of France, probably via the former French fishing outpost in Placentia, Newfoundland. There were no Acadian men living in Louisbourg at this time although there may have been a few Acadian brides. There were, however, about 30 Acadian families living in Nicolas Denys' former settlement at St. Peters and a number of families in Petit-de-Grat on Isle Madame.[34]

The political climate in Nova Scotia changed dramatically after the founding of Halifax in 1749. The shift in British colonial policy can be measured in many ways, one of which being the sudden migration of hundreds and hundreds of Acadians to Ile Saint-Jean and Ile Royale. Due to this influx of settlers, between 1749 and 1752, the population of Ile Saint-Jean tripled and more than 500 Acadians moved to Louisbourg.[35]

Despite the fact that Acadie had been tossed back and forth between France and England, the Acadians had been able to live almost undisturbed for many generations. Now, after a century of relative stability, the Acadians were about to begin the life of an unwanted people. For thousands of men, women and children this meant deportation followed by years of wandering.

The Acadians had colonized a strategic territory overlooking all the great shipping routes of the North Atlantic and situated on the outer edge of both New France and New England. Caught in the war between France and England and victims of absolute political and religious intolerance, the Acadians were no longer able to thrive on British soil. On July 28, 1755, the Chief Justice of Nova Scotia, Jonathan Belcher, addressed Governor Lawrence and the Council in Halifax. At the end of a long submission on the conduct of the Acadians, Chief Justice Belcher stated that he was "obliged...to advise that all the French inhabitants may be removed from the Province."[36]

NOTES

1. Leslie F. S. Upton, *Micmacs and Colonists: Indian-White Relations in the Maritimes, 1713-1867*, University of British Columbia Press, 1979, pp. 25-26.
2. See: Recensement de Port Royal 1671, RG. 1 Vol. 1, copies available at the Centre Acadien de l'Université de Sainte-Anne; see also: *Les régions acadiennes de la Nouvelle-Ecosse: histoire et anecdotes*, Publication du Centre acadien, Université Sainte-Anne, March 1982, pp. 24-25.
3. *Description and Natural History of the Coasts of North America (Acadia)* by Nicolas Denys, translated and edited by William F. Ganong, Toronto, Champlain Society, 1908, pp. 399-400; pp. 415-416; pp. 446-451.
4. Research Bulletin No. 250, "The Melanson Settlement: An Acadian Farming Community (ca. 1664-1755)" by Andrée Crépeau and Brenda Dunn, Environment Canada, Parks, September 1986, pp. 2-3.
5. Gisa Hynes, "Some Aspects of the Demography of Port Royal, 1650-1755," in *Acadiensis*, vol. 3 No. 1, 1973. See also: "Settlement and Population Growth in Acadia" by Muriel K. Roy in *The Acadians of the Maritimes*, Moncton: Centre d'études acadiennes, 1985.
6. Bona Arsenault, *Histoire et Généalogie des Acadiens* Editions Leméac, Montréal, 1978, p. 674.
7. See: "Settlement and Population Growth in Acadia" by Muriel K. Roy in *The Acadians of the Maritimes*, Moncton: Centre d'études acadiennes, 1985.
8. *Relation of the Voyage to Port Royal in Acadia or New France* by Sieur de Dièreville, translated by Mrs. Clarence Webster [sic] and edited by John Clarence Webster, Toronto, The Champlain Society, 1933, pp. 89-90.
9. Ibid., p. 83.
10. A. H. Clark, op. cit., p. 231.

11. *Relation of the Voyage to Port Royal in Acadia or New France*, op. cit., p. 94. Dièreville uses the word "Aboteaux" as a synonym of dyke when in fact it is a valve in the dyke.

12. *Henri IV et la reconstruction du royaume*, Editions de la Réunion des Musées Nationaux, Archives nationales, Paris 1989, pp. 287-288 "la politique d'assèchement des marais du Poitou, confiée à l'ingénieur hollandais Humphrey Bradley..." and "le 8 avril 1599, Edit sur l'assèchement des marais" p. 430. See also Andrew Hill Clark, op. cit., note on page 107. See also: Yves Cormier, *Les Aboiteaux en Acadie*, Université de Moncton, Chaire d'études acadiennes, 1990, pp. 23-28.

13. *Relation of the Voyage to Port Royal in Acadia or New France*, op. cit., pp. 94-95.

14. See: "Geography and the Acadians" by Samuel Arsenault in *The Acadians of the Maritimes*, op. cit., p.98.

15. All references to the 1983 Belleisle digs are taken from: *Belleisle 1983: Excavations at a Pre-Expulsion Acadian Site* by David J. Christianson, July 1984, Curatorial Report Number 48, Nova Scotia Museum. All references to Melanson digs are taken from: Research Bulletin No. 250, "The Melanson Settlement: An Acadian Farming Community (ca. 1664-1755)" by Andrée Crépeau and Brenda Dunn, Environment Canada, Parks, September 1986. For information on earlier research, see: *An Archeological Survey of reported Acadian Habitation Sites in the Annapolis Valley and Minas Basin Areas 1971* by Brian Preston, Curatorial Report Number 20, Nova Scotia Museum. For information re 1972 dig, see: *Excavations at Site BeDi-2 Belleisle Annapolis County 1972* by Brian Preston, Curatorial Report Number 21, Nova Scotia Museum. Mitchell's map was first published in *Acadiensis*, Vol. III, 1909, p. 294.

16. Research Bulletin No. 250, "The Melanson Settlement: An Acadian Farming Community (ca. 1664-1755)" by Andrée Crépeau and Brenda Dunn, Environment Canada, Parks, September 1986, pp. 3-4.

17. Massachusetts Archives XXXVII, 93.

18. Quoted in *Une colonie féodale en Amérique: l'Acadie* by Edme Rameau de Saint-Père (Paris: Librairie Plon, 1889, p. 342). For information on Des Goutins see A.H. Clark, op. cit. p. 147.

19. Jean Daigle, "Les relations commerciales de l'Acadie avec le Massachusetts: le cas de Charles-Amador de Sainte-Etienne de La Tour, 1695-1697" in *Revue de l'Université de Moncton*, vol. 9, Oct. 1976, pp. 54-61. See also: "Preliminary Report on Source Material on Acadians Before 1755" prepared by Alphonse J. Deveau. Manuscript on File at the Nova Scotia Museum.

20. J. S. McLennan, *Louisbourg from its Foundation to its Fall*, Halifax, The Book Room Limited (first published in 1918), fourth edition 1979, p.77. See also: A.H. Clark, op. cit., pp.250-253.

21. Georges Arsenault, *The Island Acadians 1720-1980*, translated by Sally Ross, Ragweed Press, Charlottetown, 1989, p. 44.

22. Père Clarence-J. d'Entremont, *Nicolas Denys, Sa Vie et Son Oeuvre*, Yarmouth: L'Imprimerie Lescarbot Ltée., 1982, p. 451.

23. *Relation of the Voyage to Port Royal in Acadia or New France* by Sieur de Dièreville, op. cit., pp. 113-114.

24. Numerous missionaries and Nicolas Denys lamented the devastations among the native peoples caused by the use of alcohol as a "currency" in the fur trade. See: Father Chrestien Le Clercq, *New Relations of Gaspesia*, translated and edited by W.F. Ganong, The Champlain Society, 1910, pp. 100-108.

25. *The Jesuit Relations and Allied Documents* (Father Biard's Relation), translated and edited by Ruebeun Gold Thwaites, Pageant Book Co., New York, 1959, Vol. 3, p. 69.

26. Adapted from Muriel K. Roy, "Settlement and Population Growth in Acadia," in *The Acadians of the Maritimes*, op. cit., p. 138.

27. Emile Lauvrière, *La tragédie d'un peuple*, Paris 1924, Vol. 1, p. 185.

28. Quoted in *Le drame acadien depuis 1604* by Antoine Bernard, Montréal: Les Clercs de Saint Viateur, 1936, p. 165.

29. Gisa Hynes, "Some Aspects of the Demography of Port Royal, 1650-1755," in *Acadiensis*, vol. 3 No. 1, 1973, p. 8.

30. Gisa Hynes, op. cit., p. 7. According to Hynes' calculations about 20% of women and 60% of men in Port Royal could sign their marriage certificates in 1700. These figures dropped to 0% in the 1740s.

31. Lieutenant-Governor Paul Mascarene gives a list of inhabitants of Les Mines (Grand Pré) who ask for passage to Ile Royale. Virtually all the men mark a cross or an "x" beside their name. In his letter dated September 17, 1714 Mascarene writes: "La plupart des habitants ne sachant pas signer firent leur marque ordinaire." C.O. 217/1, f.227, P.A.N.S.

32. Jean Daigle, *The Acadians of the Maritimes*, op. cit., p. 36.

33. Georges Arsenault, *The Island Acadians 1720-1980*, translated by Sally Ross, Ragweed Press, Charlottetown, 1989, p. 25.

34. A.H. Clark, op. cit., p. 296. See also: Bernard Pothier, "Les Acadiens à l'Ile-Royale," *La société historique acadienne: les cahiers*, 23e cahier, Vol. III, No. 3, 1969, pp. 97-111.

35. Georges Arsenault, op. cit., p. 32; A.H. Clark, op. cit., p. 278.

36. John Reid, *Six Crucial Decades*, Nimbus Publishing, 1987, p.43.

CHAPTER 3

The Deportation: 1755–1763

The decision to "remove" the Acadians, announced by Chief Justice Belcher in July 1755, was the result of a series of events and circumstances that had evolved over a number of years. The Deportation is unquestionably the most traumatic event in the history of Nova Scotia. Had different men held positions of power in the British colonies of Nova Scotia and Massachusetts, the decision to deport might not have been made. The decision *was* made, however, and must be placed within the military, political and religious context of the eighteenth century.

The founding of Halifax in 1749 marked a turning point in the development of the colony of Nova Scotia. On the one hand, it established a solid British presence on the Atlantic coast mid-way between Boston and the French fortress at Louisbourg. On the other hand, it constituted the first step in an aggressive policy to colonize Nova Scotia with Protestant settlers who would eventually outnumber the French-speaking and Catholic Acadians. Within a few years, hundreds of families were settled at strategic locations along the Atlantic coast. These Protestants, loyal to the British Crown, were not only recruited in England, but also in Switzerland, Germany and in the tiny principality of Montbéliard in eastern France. They were Lutherans, not Huguenots, and were both German-speaking and French-speaking. These so-called *Foreign Protestants* founded the town of Lunenburg in 1753, not far from the Micmac and Acadian outpost at LaHave.[1]

Within the context of the rivalry between France and Great

Britain, Nova Scotia was a vulnerable colony for a number of reasons. Although Louisbourg had been captured in 1745, it was returned to France by the Treaty of Aix-la-Chapelle in 1748— much to the distress of Massachusetts and the other British colonies along the eastern seaboard who considered this fortress-town and trading port a serious threat.

The French presence at Louisbourg was not the only unsettling factor in the region. By 1750 there were at least 10,000 Acadians living in peninsular Nova Scotia. In comparative terms, this was not a large population but it was unusual to have a British colony populated with Catholic settlers of French descent. Ever since the Treaty of Utrecht in 1713, the loyalty of the Acadians to the British Crown had been a source of contention for most colonial or military officials in Nova Scotia.

Another stumbling-block with regard to the implementation of a large-scale settlement policy was the alliance of the Micmac with the Acadians and with the French on Ile Royale and elsewhere in the region. On their part, the Micmac had no desire to see any further intrusion on their hunting grounds and had already manifested their hostility on numerous occasions by raiding or harassing British posts or ships at various locations including Cape Sable, Canso, and Annapolis.[2]

With the arrival of large numbers of settlers, Britain began to solidify her position along strategic communication routes. In 1750 Fort Edward was built in Pisiquid (Windsor) at the confluence of the Avon and St. Croix rivers. This site was chosen not only because it overlooked a large Acadian settlement but also because it guarded access into the Bay of Fundy via inland waterways.

The next step in the British strategy was to establish a presence on the Chignecto marshlands where French troops and militia had been active since 1748. This was an extremely sensitive zone since, as noted earlier, the Treaty of Utrecht had left the western boundary of Nova Scotia ambiguous and undefined. France considered that it owned the territory north of the Missaguash River which cuts across the marshes on the Isthmus of Chignecto. The Acadians had been established in the settlement of Beaubassin on these marshlands for almost a century. Consequently, the decision of the British to build a fort on the east bank of the river (near present-day Amherst) was a provocative military move. Fort Lawrence was constructed in 1750 near the settlement of Beaubassin, which the Acadians had been encouraged to vacate not long before the arrival of British troops.[3]

The following year, France countered the British incursion onto these marshes by constructing Fort Beauséjour on the opposite bank of the Missaguash River and Fort Gaspereau at the important trading site of Baie Verte. Although military confrontations did not take place immediately, the establishment of these various forts certainly contributed to an atmosphere of increased tension which could not go unnoticed by either the Acadians or the Micmac. Trade routes were disrupted and political allegiances were pushed to the limit. The sudden migration of hundreds of Acadians to Ile Saint-Jean and Ile Royale in the early 1750s is an obvious indication that the political climate had changed drastically. Many of these up-rooted Acadians originated from the contentious region of the Chignecto marshlands where the two superpowers now faced each other, as if poised for war.

To a certain degree, both the Acadians and the Micmac were destabilizing elements on the checkerboard of international politics. As one French official stated: the Micmac "are of little account as our allies but could become quite important as enemies."[4] Obviously it was very much in the interest of France to preserve the goodwill of the Micmac. The fact that by the 1740s there were four French missionaries serving the native population throughout the region helped strengthen ties. In principle, the role of these missionaries was strictly spiritual. In practice, however, religion and national loyalties were impossible to separate. Two of these missionaries, Abbé Jean-Louis Le Loutre and Abbé Pierre Maillard, became deeply involved in political strategies which played the Micmac off against the British—Le Loutre at Shubenacadie and at Beaubassin and Maillard on Ile Royale at Port Toulouse (St. Peters) and at Louisbourg.[5]

Since the loyalty of the Acadians constituted the single most preoccupying political question in Nova Scotia from 1713 to 1755, it is essential to examine the issue as it unfolded. According to the Treaty of Utrecht, the Acadians could stay on their lands in Nova Scotia provided they swore an oath of allegiance to the monarch of

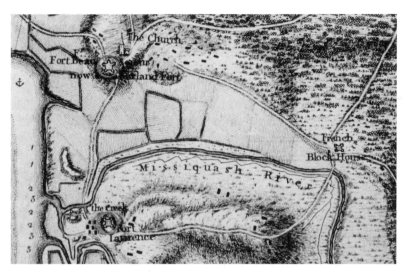

Fort Beauséjour and Fort Lawrence. The two superpowers now faced each other, as if poised for war. (Courtesy: Canadian Parks Service)

Great Britain. They were permitted "to enjoy the free exercise of their religion" as far as the laws of Great Britain allowed.[6] Basically this meant that they could practise their religion but that they could not vote, hold public office or join the army. This "freedom" was further complicated by the fact that the priests who served in the Acadian parishes were supplied by France and were directed by the Bishop of Quebec—in other words, they were outside the British sphere of influence. This was not the first time that the Acadians had found themselves under British rule, but it was the first time that they had been asked to define their political allegiance. They did not want to pledge loyalty to Britain if that meant fighting against the French or the Micmac in the event of war. Given the number of times that Acadie had changed hands in the past, war between France and England was not an abstract notion for the Acadians. They were prepared to sign an oath of allegiance, but only under certain conditions. By the end of the 1720s, the British authorities had convinced the majority of Acadians to sign an oath by promising them that they would not have to take up arms. In some cases this promise was written in the margin of the French translation of the oath and in other cases it was merely expressed verbally.[7] As noted previously, the degree of illiteracy was very high among the Acadians so verbal assurances had considerable weight.

In December 1729, Governor Philipps administered the oath of allegiance to Acadian men over 15 years of age in all the settlements along the Annapolis River. The following spring he travelled to the settlements around Grand Pré, Pisiquid (Windsor), Cobequid (Truro) and Beaubassin. The men pledged their loyalty by adding their name to the document which Philipps took from

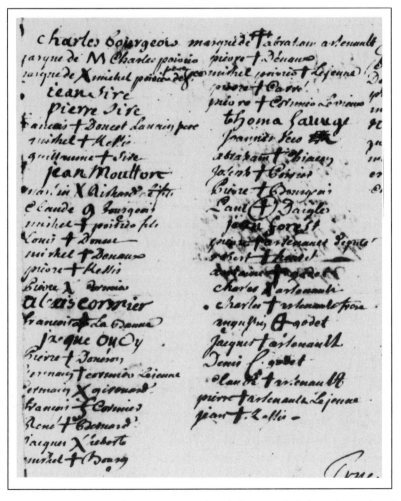

Acadian men signed their name or placed their mark below the oath of allegiance. Chignecto 1727. (Microfilm: Public Archives of Nova Scotia)

one district to another. If they could not write, they made their mark (usually in the form of a cross, rather than an X) and then the appropriate name was written beside the mark. Although Philipps did not inform his superiors in Britain, he promised the Acadians that they would not have to bear arms against France or the Micmac. The following text in French appears at the top of the document which Philipps presented in the various communities. Except for the "nous" (we) instead of "je" (I), this was the wording of the oath of allegiance which the Acadians took on several occasions.[8]

Nous Promettons et Jurons sincèrement en foi de Chrétien que nous serons entièrement Fidelle et Nous Soumettrons Véritablement à Sa Majesté George Le Second, Roy de la Grande Bretagne, que nous reconnoissons pour Le Souverain Seigneur de La Nouvelle Ecosse et L'Accadie. Ainsi Dieu nous soit en Aide.

The English text of the oath reads: "I sincerely promise and swear in the faith of a Christian that I will be entirely faithful and will truly obey His Majesty King George the Second, whom I recognize as the sovereign lord of Nova Scotia and of Acadie. So help me God."[9] It is interesting to note that the French name *Nouvelle Ecosse* was already in use by the early 1700s.

Since the political position of the Acadians was well known amongst British officials, they were generally referred to as the *Neutrals* or the *neutral French*.[10] A petition, signed in October 1744 by ten representative Acadians living in the Grand Pré area, addressed to the French commander at Louisbourg gives a clear indication of their desire to walk the line of neutrality and co-exist with both the French and the English. The petition is also significant because it illustrates the alliance between the French troops and the Micmac and it provides written proof that the Acadians in the heartland were supplying Louisbourg with both meat and grain.

We the undersigned humbly representing the inhabitants of Mines [Grand Pré], near Canard, Piziquid, and the surrounding rivers, beg that you will be pleased to consider that while there would be no difficulty by virtue of the strong force which you command, in supplying yourself with the quantity of grain and meat that you and M. Du Vivier have ordered, it would be quite impossible for us to furnish the quantity you demand, or even a smaller, since the harvest has not been so good as we hoped it would be, without placing ourselves in great peril.

We hope, gentlemen, that you will not plunge both ourselves and our families into a state of total loss; and that this consideration will cause you to withdraw your savages [Micmac] *and troops from our districts.*

We live under a mild and tranquil government, and we have all good reason to be faithful to it. We hope, therefore, that you will have the goodness not to separate us from it; and that you will grant us the favour not to plunge us into utter misery. This we hope from your goodness, assuring you that we are with much respect, gentlemen, Your very humble and obedient servants—acting for the communities above mentioned.[11] (TR)

As hostilities between the imperial powers grew, British authorities, especially Governor William Shirley of Massachusetts and Lieutenant-Governor Charles Lawrence of Nova Scotia, became increasingly suspicious of the Acadians' neutrality.[12] In the spring of 1755, for example, the Acadians in the Grand Pré area were denied the use of their boats and canoes and they were forced to hand over their guns and ammunition. These severe measures were obviously designed to prevent the Acadians from leaving their settlements and from participating in any armed conflicts.

In fact, the first major conflict took place on the Isthmus of Chignecto at the beginning of June 1755, not long after the restrictions were placed on the inhabitants of Grand Pré. Convinced that the French would use Fort Beauséjour as a springboard to attack Nova Scotia, Lieutenant-Governor Lawrence decided to take an aggressive stand in this sensitive border region. He was supported by Governor Shirley of Massachusetts who sent 2,000 volunteer troops to join up with Lieutenant-Colonel Robert Monckton's 300 British regulars. They attacked Fort Beauséjour on June 4 and the French troops were forced to surrender two weeks later. As a signed petition proves, several hundred Acadians had been compelled by the French commander to take up arms in defense of the fort. In other words, they had been forced to abandon their neutrality.

Following the capture of Fort Beauséjour and Fort Gaspereau, the large number of New England troops now in Nova Scotia were ordered to seize arms and ammunition from the Acadians. Later all

Acadians in Nova Scotia were ordered to surrender their firearms or be considered as rebels. Delegates from various Acadian settlements were sent to Halifax to request the return of their firearms. When they arrived, these delegates were informed that they must sign an unconditional oath of allegiance — in other words, an oath without any conditions whatsoever pertaining to bearing arms against the French or the Micmac. When they refused to sign, the delegates were imprisoned on George's Island in Halifax harbour.

In July 1755, Governor Charles Lawrence ordered the Acadians to send another group of delegates to appear before the Council in Halifax in order to settle the question of the unconditional oath of fidelity to the British Monarch. Despite the fact that Fort Beauséjour had been captured in June, that 2,000 New England soldiers were now stationed in Nova Scotia, and that Admiral Boscawen's fleet was present in the port of Halifax, the Acadians did not change their position. Like other representatives before them, they refused to sign an oath that would automatically mean that the Acadian population could not remain neutral. This second group of delegates was also detained on George's Island.

On July 28, 1755, when Lieutenant-Governor Lawrence assembled his council, which included for this meeting Admiral Boscawen and Chief Justice Belcher, the decision was made to proceed with the removal of the "French inhabitants" from the colony of Nova Scotia.[13]

Although Grand Pré has become the symbol of the expulsion of the Acadians, the deportation actually began on August 11, 1755, at Fort Beauséjour (renamed Fort Cumberland). The inhabitants in the area were rounded up and imprisoned in the fort prior to being shipped to the British colonies along the eastern seaboard.

One month later the deportation of the Acadians began at Grand Pré, the most populated of all the Acadian settlements. The male inhabitants were ordered by Colonel John Winslow, commander of the New England regiment stationed in the area, to assemble in the church Saint Charles des Mines on September 5 at three o'clock in the afternoon. The men of Pisiquid were ordered by Captain Alexander Murray to present themselves at Fort Edward. In both places, the assembled Acadians were informed that their lands, their houses, and their livestock would be confiscated and that they and their families would be transported out of the province.

THE DEPORTATION ORDER READ AT GRAND PRE BY COLONEL JOHN WINSLOW

Gentlemen,

I have received from his Excellency Governor Lawrence. The King's Commission which I have in my hand and by whose orders you are convened together to Manifest to you his Majesty's final resolution to the French inhabitants of this his Province of Nova Scotia who for almost half a century have had more indulgence granted them, than any of his subjects in any part of his Dominions. What use you have made of them you yourself best know.

The part of duty I am now upon is what though necessary is very disagreeable to my natural make and temper as I know it must be grevious to you who are of the same specia.

But it is not my business to annimedvert, but to obey such orders as I receive and therefore without hesitation shall deliver you his Majesty's orders and instructions viz.

That your lands and tenements, cattle of all kinds and livestock of all sorts are forfitted to the Crown with all other your effects saving your money and household goods and you yourselves to be removed from this his province.

Thus it is preemptorily his Majesty's orders that the whole French inhabitants of these districts, be removed, and I am through his Majesty's goodness directed to allow you liberty to carry of your money and household goods as many as you can without discommoding the vessels you go in. I shall do everything in my power that all those goods be secured to you and that you are not molested in carrying them and also that whole families shall go in the same vessel and make this remove which I am sensible must give you a great deal of trouble as easy as his Majesty's service will admit and hope that in what every part of the world you may fall you may be faithful subjects, a peaceable and happy people.

I must also inform you that it is his Majesty's pleasure that you remain in security under the inspection and Direction of the troops that I have the Honour to command.[14]

More people were deported from Grand Pré than from any

other location because not only was it the most populated of all the Acadian settlements, it was also the most important Acadian agricultural and commercial centre.[15] The population, encompassed by the parish of Saint Charles, was spread out between the present-day towns of Horton Landing and Wolfville. Although the settlement of Canard was often included as part of the Grand Pré area, it actually constituted a separate parish on the Minas Basin. The inhabitants of Canard were rounded up and loaded on to boats with the inhabitants of Grand Pré. A total of about 2,200 Acadians were thus removed from the greater Grand Pré area between October and December of 1755. Within a short time, all their homes and barns were destroyed by fire. Following orders to burn and lay waste, British troops travelled from village to village, torching every building in sight.

Today, a large wrought-iron cross marks the location where the men, women, and children of Grand Pré and Canard were embarked on to boats to be rowed over to transport ships lying at anchor in Minas Basin. Like the church now standing in the Grand Pré National Historic Site, the French Cross, or the Deportation Cross, was a monument sponsored and erected by Acadians to commemorate the horror and tragedy of the expulsion as it began to unfold at Fort Beauséjour, at Grand Pré, at Port Royal and at Pisiquid in the autumn and early winter of 1755. The cornerstone of the memorial church in Grand Pré was blessed on August 16, 1922 during a Mass said by Bishop Edouard LeBlanc, the first Acadian bishop in the Maritimes. The Deportation Cross was unveiled at a special ceremony held on August 19, 1924 attended by Acadians from the Maritimes and by a large delegation from Quebec led by the well-known journalist, Henri Bourassa.

It is estimated that there were about 6,000 Acadians deported from mainland Nova Scotia in 1755. Although many perished on board the transport ships, the survivors were distributed in allotments to the Anglo-American colonies from Massachusetts to South Carolina: 900 for Massachusetts, 675 for Connecticut, 200 for New York, 700 for Pennsylvania, 860 for Maryland, 1,150 for Virginia, 290 for North Carolina and 320 for South Carolina.[16] The fact that the Acadians were sent to these colonies did not mean that they settled there; on the contrary. As will be seen in Chapter 4, hundreds of families and individuals eventually made their way back to the Maritimes. Others travelled southward to Louisiana where they found a new homeland. The itinerary of the 1,150 Acadians who were sent to Virginia, was far more complex. Virginia refused to accept its contingent of "French Neutrals." These Acadians were thus trans-shipped to England as prisoners of war. After the Treaty of Paris in 1763, the survivors were eventually transported to France, primarily to the port cities of Morlaix and St. Malo.

Contrary to popular belief, Acadians were not deported to Louisiana as it was not a British colony. The vast majority of Acadians living on mainland Nova Scotia were shipped to the colonies along the Atlantic coast. However, there were many exceptions. A number of inhabitants of the Cape Sable area, for example, were imprisoned in Halifax and later transported to the port of Cherbourg in France.[17] As late as 1762, there were more than 50 Acadian families imprisoned at Fort Edward—despite the fact that about one thousand people had been removed from the Windsor area in 1755.[18]

Small numbers of Acadians from almost every settlement throughout the entire Atlantic region managed to escape deportation. They either hid or moved to more distant locations. Many Acadians from Nova Scotia, Ile Royale (Cape Breton) and Ile Saint-Jean (P.E.I.) took refuge along the Restigouche and Miramichi Rivers and along the shores of the Bay of Chaleur in what is now northern New Brunswick. Others escaped to the Gaspé Peninsula and the French islands of Saint-Pierre and Miquelon. The entire French-speaking population in the Atlantic region was shattered and dispersed. For some it meant deportation, for others a few years in hiding, and for others almost 50 years of wandering.

In English, the deportation is referred to as the Expulsion. The Acadians, on the other hand, call it the *Grand Dérangement* or the Great Upheaval.

After the fall of Louisbourg in July of 1758, the majority of the Acadians living on Ile Royale and Ile Saint-Jean were repatriated to France. Along with French officials who had served in Louisbourg, these Acadian refugees, as they were called in France, became wards of the state and received pensions from the French government.[19] A small percentage of these refugees settled permanently on Belle-Isle-en-Mer off the coast of Brittany and inland, near Châtellerault, in the old province of Poitou. The vast majority of the refugees, however, spent over twenty years in Saint-Servan, on the outskirts of St. Malo, a large French seaport located a few hours by boat from the Isle of Jersey. As will be seen in Chapter 4, the Robin Company from this tiny Channel island was to play a significant role in encouraging the Acadian refugees to return to the Maritimes. By 1785, on the eve of the French Revolution, most of the Acadians had left France and made their way back to the New World. As a general rule, the Acadian refugees clustered in the ports of Britanny sailed from St. Malo to various locations in eastern Canada, whereas the ones who had attempted to settle in Poitou made their way down the Loire River to the seaport of Nantes whence they sailed to Louisiana.[20]

Despite the fact that the Acadians had been scattered over a vast territory and forced to wander for years, it is astonishing that by the beginning of the 1800s, more than 70 percent of the estimated 23,400 Acadians were located in the Maritimes and Quebec. About 17 percent were living in Louisiana.[21] The story of the return of the Acadians is a story of the tenacity of a people and the profound attachment to ancestral lands.

There are no letters or diaries to provide individual testimonies of the tragic events of the Great Upheaval. In the vast repertoire of Acadian folk music, there is not a single ballad or song that tells of the Deportation.[22] The stories of individual families have become part of the collective memory that, in written terms, can only be pieced together from the occasional petition to civil authorities and from the records of baptisms, marriages and funerals chronicled in church registers.

A number of documents has survived which enables one to imagine the pathetic existence which the deportees suffered in the towns and seaports where they were distributed. In 1756, for example, Claude Bourgeois petitioned the Council of Massachusetts for financial support to prevent two of his daughters from starving to death. The transcript of his testimony gives an indication of the abject conditions in which the Acadian deportees found themselves.

In reading the various petitions, it becomes obvious that the

Acadians could not speak English and that they had great difficulties in finding work or even in obtaining payment for work they did perform. From the details provided in Claude Bourgeois' petition, one can deduce that he was deported from Port Royal and that, contrary to many other cases, he and his immediate family were not split up during the deportation. Since they were able to salvage some flax or wool from their farm near the Annapolis River, one can assume that they were able to take a few possessions with them. Like most of the Acadians who made requests to the civil authorities in Massachusetts, Claude Bourgeois was illiterate.

To the Honorable His Majesty's Council of the Province of Massachusetts Bay. May it Please your Honours.

Claude Bourgeois, your Petitioner, one of the late French inhabitants of Nova Scotia, was sent with his family to Amesbury by order of the General Court, where he has resided constantly with his wife and six children; and begs leave to represent to your Honours, that about four weeks ago ten or twelve men came and took away from him two of his daughters, one of the age of 25 years and the other of 18, that his daughters were at that time employed in spinning for the Family, the poor remains of the Flax of wool which they had saved from Annapolis. Your Petitioner having fetched his Daughters home again, the Town have withheld their subsistence so that fourteen Days past he has received nothing at all to prevent them from starving, and the owner of the house where he lives threatens that he shall pay the rent of it by his children's labour. Your petitioner prays your Honours to relieve him under these circumstances, and your Petitioners shall ever pray, etc.

The mark of + CLAUDE BOURGEOIS
Boston, May 4th, 1756.[23]

Many of the Acadian deportees changed their names and over a period of several generations assimilated to a greater or lesser extent into the American culture: LeBlanc became White, Aucoin became Wedge, Poirier became Perry. Many others, however, preferred to make their way north, by boat or by land, in the hope of finding a better life back in the country their ancestors had farmed for over a century. Several of the petitions to the authorities in the colony of Massachusetts reflect in individual terms this gradual migration northward.

Magloire Hébert, for instance, was deported in 1755 to Carolina. By the summer of 1756 he and his wife and three children had managed to reach the town of Attleboro, south of Boston. As the following request for help indicates, Magloire could barely feed and clothe his small family on the meagre wages he was being paid.

To the Honourable his Majesty's Council of the Province of the Massachusetts Bay.

The Petition of Magloire Hebert humbly shewith.

That your Petitioner is one of those former Inhabitants of Nova Scotia, who soon was stopped by this Government in returning from Carolina, and was placed with his family in a Town called Attleboroug, where he was abode ever since July 1756.

That he received sustenance from the selectmen [elected councillors] *but four weeks from his first coming among them, and then was obliged to work by the selectmen for what sustenance they allowed him, and ever since by his labour has paid for what has supported his family, being himself, his wife and three children, by doing which he has had nothing left to provide clothing and prevent his family from being naked.*

That now the selectmen will find him neither work nor Provisions, so that he and his family are in the greatest distress and must perish unless, your honours will give him orders for their Relief. This he humbly requests your Honours would be pleased to do, and that your Petitioner may have the same allowance that other of his countrymen in the same circumstances are allowed in other Places, when he sees they live contented and are well taken care of and your Petitioner shall ever pray.

MAGLOIRE HEBERT

Boston, May the 2nd, 1757.[24]

Many Acadian families were able to resettle in Nova Scotia, although not on their ancestral lands. By the mid-1760s, for example, the government had redistributed all the Acadian farmland of Grand Pré and the Annapolis Valley to Protestant colonists from New England, known as the Planters. Thus within a decade the most flourishing area of Nova Scotia had been emptied of one population and replaced with another.

NOTES

1. Winthrop P. Bell, *The "Foreign Protestants" and the Settlement of Nova Scotia*, second edition: Acadiensis Press and Mount Allison University, 1990.
2. Leslie F.S. Upton, *Micmacs and Colonists: Indian-White Relations in the Maritimes, 1713-1867*, University of British Columbia Press, 1979, pp. 40-45.
3. Enticed by Abbé Le Loutre, most of the Acadians in Beaubassin moved across the Missaguash River. Their houses, the church and the chapel were burned by the Micmac perhaps also influenced by Abbé Le Loutre. See: *L'abbé Le Loutre et les Acadiens*, J. Alphonse Deveau, Société canadienne du Livre, 1983, pp. 52-53.
4. Leslie F.S. Upton, op. cit., Abbé Gaulin to Governor St. Ovide, 17 November 1719, p. 35 and p. 198.
5. Leslie F.S. Upton, op. cit., pp. 30-37.
6. N.E.S.Griffiths, "The Acadians," *Dictionary of Canadian Biography*, Vol. IV, Toronto, University of Toronto Press, 1979, p. xxi. The author quotes the Treaty: "to be subject to the Kingdom of Great Britain" and "to enjoy the free exercise of their religion according to the usage of the Church of Rome as far as the laws of Great Britain do allow the same."
7. Ibid., p. xxii. For a sample of an oath showing signatures and marks, see the 1727 oath taken at Chignecto (MG11, CO217, vol. 5, fol. 65, P.A.N.S.).
8. *Report concerning Canadian Archives For the Year 1905*, Vol. 2. Ottawa, King's Printer, Appendix D, pp. 77-80. "Oath of Allegiance Taken and Subscribed By the Acadians of Minas District, Cobequit, Piziquid and Beaubassin, in April 1730". The names of the 591 signatories are given. Details re Philipps taken from Guide's Manual, Grand Pré Historic Site.
9. The wording in English varies slightly from one author to another. See: Jean Daigle, "Historical Synthesis, 1604-1763" in *The Acadians in the*

Maritimes, op. cit., p. 37. See also: N.E.S. Griffiths, *The Acadian Deportation: Deliberate Perfidy or Cruel Necessity?, Issues in Canadian History,* Toronto, The Copp Clark Publishing Company, 1969, p. 22, p. 26.

10. N.E.S. Griffiths, *The Acadians: Creation of a People,* Toronto, McGraw-Hill Ryerson, 1973, p. 27.

11. J.S. McLennan, *Louisbourg,* Toronto, The Bryant Press Limited, Fourth Edition, 1979, pp.125-126.

12. Re Governor Shirley's fears, see his message to the Council and House of Representatives quoted in N.E.S. Griffiths, *The Acadian Deportation: Deliberate Perfidy or Cruel Necessity?,* op. cit., pp.53-55.

13. Charles Lawrence was appointed Lieutenant-Governor of Nova Scotia in 1754. He did not actually become Governor until 1756. He died in 1760. Jean Daigle, *The Acadians in the Maritimes,* op. cit., p. 45. See also: N.E.S. Griffiths, *The Acadians: Creation of a People,* op. cit., pp. 54-55; For a succinct analysis of the Deportation, see: John Reid, *Six Crucial Decades,* Halifax, Nimbus Publishing Limited, 1987, pp. 43-51.

14. Extract from the *Journal of Colonel John Winslow of the Provincial Troops While Engaged in Removing the Acadian French Inhabitants from Grand-Pré.* Nova Scotia Historical Society *Collections,* Vol. 3, Halifax, 1883, pp. 94-95.

15. A.H. Clark, op. cit., pp. 214-216. See also: Brenda Dunn, "European Settlement of Minas to 1765, An Overview," Parks Canada, A.R.O., 1981 (manuscript on file at Public Archives of Nova Scotia).

16. Robert G. LeBlanc, "The Acadian Migrations," *Canadian Geographical Journal,* July 1970, vol. 81, No. 1; Muriel K. Roy, "Settlement and Population Growth" in *The Acadians in the Maritimes,* op. cit., pp. 152-155; Canadian Parks Service (Environment Canada) bilingual booklet: *The Deportation of the Acadians,* 1986.

17. Père Clarence d'Entremont, "Histoire de Pubnico" in *Les régions acadiennes de la Nouvelle-Ecosse,* Publication du Centre Acadien, Université Sainte-Anne, 1982, p. 50.

18. Fort Edward National Historic Site, brochure published by Canadian Parks Service. For further details on the prisoners at Fort Edward see Régis Brun's article entitled: "Listes des prisonniers acadiens au fort Edward, 1761 et 1762" in *La Société historique acadienne* vol. 3, No. 4 1969, pp. 158-164.

19. For the story of the Acadian refugees in France, see: Ernest Martin, *Les exilés acadiens en France au XVIIIe siècle et leur établissement en Poitou,* Paris, Hachette, 1936. See also: J.S. McLennan, op. cit., p. 291. The author relates the story of the wife of a French officer who received a pension until she died in 1784. For details on the Acadians deported

from Prince Edward Island, see Georges Arsenault. *The Island Acadians*, translated by Sally Ross, op. cit. pp. 33-36.

20. Albert J. Robichaux, *The Acadian Exiles in Saint-Malo*, 1758-1785; Hebert Publications, P.O. Box 31, Eunice, Louisiana 70535, 1981.

21. Robert G. LeBlanc, see note 16.

22. Marguerite Maillet, *Histoire de la littérature acadienne*, Moncton, Editions d'Acadie, 1983, pp. 48-49; Georges Arsenault, "Chanter son Acadie," in *Vie française*, Le Conseil de la vie française, Québec, 1984, p. 105.

23. Sessional Papers 18, Canadian Archives, Vol. XL, No. 7, 1906, p. 103.

24. Ibid., p. 112.

Part II

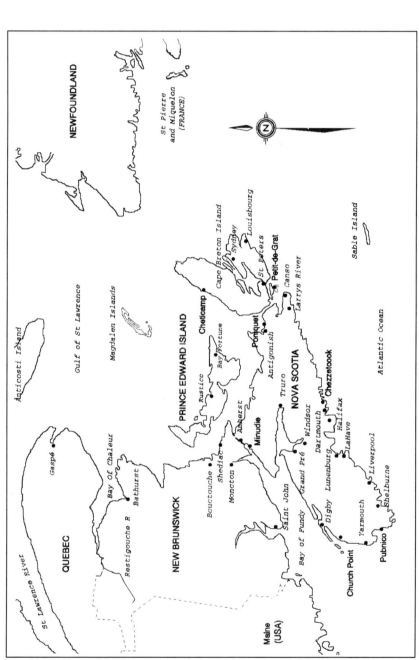

Map of Atlantic Region (Courtesy: Atlantic Direct)

CHAPTER 4

The Return: The Acadians Start All Over Again

The French empire in North America gradually crumbled. The fall of Louisbourg in 1758 meant that France no longer controlled either Ile Royale (Cape Breton) or Ile Saint-Jean (Prince Edward Island). The fall of Montreal in 1760 signalled the end of the French regime in the colony of Canada. According to the Treaty of Paris in 1763, France lost all her territories in North America except the islands of St. Pierre and Miquelon, which were given back to her by Great Britain on the condition that they be used as a haven for French fisherman but without any military fortifications. Although the Treaty of Paris provided the French inhabitants of Canada with a number of guarantees including the right to practise their religion, there were no such provisions made for the Acadians.

The Acadians living in Nova Scotia—those who had escaped deportation and those who had been imprisoned—were scattered over a vast territory that stretched all the way from Cape Breton to the Bay of Chaleur. In 1760, for example, 170 Acadian families were settled temporarily along the Restigouche River in what is now northern New Brunswick. In Cape Breton, on the eastern edge of the colony, about ten Acadian families from Port Toulouse (St. Peters) were leading a nomadic existence, more or less in hiding, in the general vicinity of Isle Madame.[1] Official records in 1764 indicate that on peninsular Nova Scotia an estimated 1,500 Acadians were grouped in four main locations: Halifax, Windsor (Fort Edward), Annapolis Royal (Fort Anne), and Fort Cumberland (formerly Fort Beauséjour).[2]

In 1764 Acadians were given permission to return to Nova Scotia provided they took the oath of allegiance and settled in distant parts of the colony. This decision was primarily the result of vigorous efforts on the part of Jacques Robin, a Huguenot fish merchant from the Isle of Jersey in the English Channel. Robin was anxious to use Acadian labour in the permanent fishing posts he was establishing in Cape Breton and on the Bay of Chaleur. The Acadians were of particular value to him because of their knowledge of the region and their special relations with the Micmac who could provide furs to supplement the fisheries.[3] The following letter dated May 15, 1764, from the Colonial Office in London to Governor Wilmot in Halifax, indicates very clearly the link between the development of the fisheries and the decision to allow Acadians to return to Nova Scotia. The letter also shows that, despite the peace treaty signed in Paris, the British still considered the Acadians a security risk. As one can see, the decision to permit Acadians to resettle was certainly not very enthusiastic.

The account you give in your letter of the 10th of December last of the extraordinary and unwarrantable proceedings of Mons. Robins in presuming to give public invitation to the Acadians to return and settle in Nova Scotia with assurances of protection from Government and the free exercise of their religion, has induced us [...to state that...] we do not think it proper or consistent with the public safety and interest that he should be permited to make any establishment of the nature and in the situation he proposes; the dangerous tendency of which is very justly remarked in your letter.

We desire therefore you will take the first opportunity of signifying to that gentleman the sense we have of the impropriety of his conduct [...]; and you are under no account, without his Majesty's further Order, to encourage any of the Acadians to return and settle in the province under your Government from which the public security made it necessary to expell them at so great an expense, but if any of them should in consequence of Mons. Robin's unwarrantable proceedings return and be desirous of settling in the province, we see no objection to their being accommodated with small lots of land amongst the other settlers, provided they take the Oath of Allegiance and that great care is taken to disperse them in small numbers that it may not lie in their power to disturb and annoy that Government, which was in its first establishment obstructed and brought into so great danger by their rebellious and turbulent disposition.[4]

It is often assumed that this general permission resulted in the sudden influx of hundreds of deported Acadians.[5] In fact, the return from exile took place very slowly. Quite apart from the lingering climate of mistrust, Britain was attempting to populate her colonies with Protestants. Until June 1768, one of the conditions of land grants in Nova Scotia stipulated that a person who received a grant had to settle his land with "Protestant inhabitants within ten years from the date of the grant, in the proportion of one person for every hundred acres." It seems obvious that Acadians would be reluctant to return if their religion prevented them from obtaining land. After the authorities had declared that the statutes of Great Britain that prohibited Catholics from receiving or purchasing land did *not* extend to the colonies, some Acadians began to return to Nova Scotia. The following statement, for example, constitutes a more reassuring message: "...there is no legal obstruction to the granting of lands in fee to the Acadian subjects."[6] It should be noted, however, that the law prohibiting Roman Catholics from owning or inheriting land was not actually struck from the statutes of Nova Scotia until 1783.

By the time the Acadians started returning to Nova Scotia, the lands they had once occupied were already taken by British settlers. As was noted in the previous chapter, New England Planters were quickly established on the rich marshland farms around Grand Pré and elsewhere in the Annapolis Valley. Only in two areas of Nova Scotia were the Acadians able to obtain land where they had lived prior to 1755: in Pubnico, in the southwestern corner of Nova Scotia, and on Isle Madame off the south coast of Cape Breton.

Partly influenced by the availability of land and the development of the fisheries, the Acadians settled in seven main regions in the territory covered by present-day Nova Scotia. These are not the only areas or localities where Acadians were able to establish roots but they are the most important centres of Acadian population from a demographic and cultural point of view.

- Argyle (Yarmouth County)
- Clare (Digby County)

- Minudie, Nappan and Maccan (Cumberland County)
- Chéticamp (Inverness County, Cape Breton)
- Isle Madame (Richmond County, Cape Breton)
- Pomquet, Tracadie, Havre-Boucher (Antigonish County)
- Chezzetcook (Halifax County)

The re-establishment of the Acadians did not take place in the same way or at the same time in each of these areas, nor did the culture evolve in a uniform manner. In communities like Maccan, Nappan, and Minudie, the French language has not survived the pressures of the majority culture. There are no young Acadians in Chezzetcook today who speak their ancestral language. On the other hand, conditions in the district of Clare and in Chéticamp, for example, were and are much more conducive to the preservation of French. Many factors contributed to the survival of the Acadian culture in distant corners of Nova Scotia including the way land was granted and the ethnic composition of the communities. As will be seen throughout this chapter, the settlement pattern as it unfolded during the latter part of the eighteenth century has had a determining influence on the Acadians of today. Each region has evolved differently and has its own special characteristics which are clearly identifiable even in speech habits and accents.

Deported or exiled Acadians began returning to Nova Scotia in the mid-1760s and continued to arrive in small numbers until the late 1820s. The aim of this chapter is not only to follow these migrations as they affect the formation of predominantly Acadian communities, but also to stress the development of regional differences. It would be impossible to relate here the history of every Acadian village or parish. The seven portraits which follow are designed to provide an outline of the emerging Acadian identity during the hundred years following the Deportation, as it relates to present-day realities.

Argyle

In modern terms, Argyle is the name of a municipality in Yarmouth County and it is generally used when referring to Acadian communities located in the southwestern tip of Nova Scotia. Before the Deportation, the region was called Cape Sable. Most, but not all of the Acadians who still speak French, live in West Pubnico, Surette's

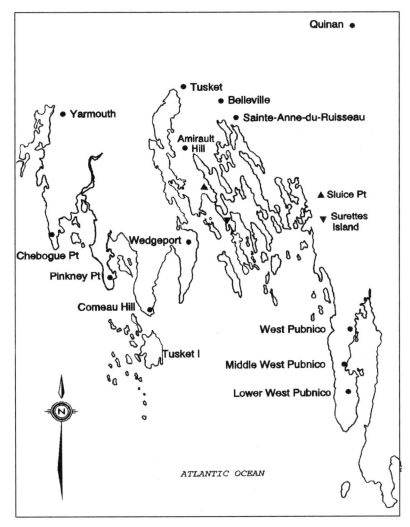

Map of Argyle (Courtesy: Atlantic Direct)

Island, Sluice Point (or Pointe Sault), Amirault Hill (or Butte Amirault), Sainte-Anne-du-Ruisseau (formerly Eel Brook), Belleville, Quinan, Wedgeport (formerly Tousquet), and Pinkney Point. With the exception of the tiny inland community of Quinan, these villages are nestled along an extremely indented and jagged coastline and are much closer by water than by land.

From the 1620s to the late 1750s, there were Acadian settlements interspersed over a much longer section of coastline that stretched all the way from Cape Fourchu, near Yarmouth, to Port Razoir (Shelburne). However, these settlements never attained the importance or the population density of Port Royal, Grand Pré and the other communities along the Bay of Fundy.

The first truly permanent settlement in Cape Sable dates back to 1653. Pubnico (or Pombomcoup as it was originally called) was founded by Baron Philippe Mius d'Entremont, his wife Marie Hélie and their daughter Marguerite who were brought to the New World by Charles de La Tour. Other family names associated with the early development of this region are Amirault and Pitre.

Before the Deportation the most populated settlement in this area was Tébok (Chebogue Point). Founded in the 1740s by eight families from Port Royal, Tébok is the only early settlement along this coast with a marshland environment typical of the Acadian heartland. In fact, Tébok is the Micmac name for "grand-pré" or large meadow. After the Deportation, these fertile lands were quickly taken up by British farmers.[7]

The Acadians in this corner of Nova Scotia were not deported in 1755 like their compatriots in the heartland. There were two raids on the people of Pubnico. The first took place in Le Passage (Barrington Passage) a fishing outpost where families from Pubnico spent the summer. Colonel Prebble attacked this settlement in 1756 and deported 72 men, women and children to Boston. Pubnico itself remained untouched until September 1758 when it was destroyed by Major Roger Morris, acting on the orders of Colonel Monckton. The inhabitants were able to escape before the arrival of the troops, but they were later captured and taken prisoner. Their presence in Halifax is recorded in June 1759 whence they were transported to Cherbourg, France, in November 1760.[8]

It would appear that the Acadians in this corner of mainland Nova Scotia were among the last to be deported, but they were the first to return. After about ten years in exile, nine families returned to Pubnico in 1766, arriving by boat from Boston. Most of the inhabitants in the Pubnicos today are descendants of these families whose names were d'Entremont, Amirault, Belliveau, Mius and Duon (now spelt d'Eon). By 1767 the Government of Nova Scotia had granted 1,012 hectares (2,500 acres) to about 20 families on either side of Pubnico Harbour. There were a few Irish families with names such as Larkin, Murphy, and Goodwin. Most of the d'Entremonts and the Duons settled on the west side of the harbour and the Amiraults and the Belliveaus on the east side. The English-speaking settlers established themselves mainly at the head of the harbour. Gradually more land became available for returning Acadians and for other settlers.

By the early 1780s the Acadian migrations into this region of Nova Scotia had come to an end. The coastal communities of Sainte-Anne-du-Ruisseau, Wedgeport and Tusket were now all well-established. At the turn of the century, and about 40 years after the first land grants in Pubnico, there were approximately 400 Acadians living in Argyle.[9] The geography and the allotment of land grants did not facilitate the development of a string of Acadian villages as was to be the case in the district of Clare or in northern Cape Breton. As the French and English-speaking settlements of Argyle evolved side by side, neither culture remained isolated from the other.

Some of the Acadians who arrived in Argyle between 1764 and 1784 were descendants of the d'Entremonts, the Miuses and the Amiraults who had settled this area in the mid-1600s. But others, like the LeBlancs, the Pothiers and the Doucets, originated from distant parts of Acadie such as Pisiquid (Windsor) and Beaubassin (Amherst).

It is difficult to find a common element among the Acadians who eventually acquired land in Argyle, as the itinerary of different families during the Deportation years varied considerably. Family connections seem to have played a great part in the final destination. This is obvious, for example, in the case of Dominique Pothier and his family. Dominique was born near Beaubassin. He married Anne Surette in Petitcodiac and then they moved to Pré-d'en-Haut, near Memramcook, where their first son was born. The family fled to Cocagne and then to Bouctouche during the Deportation. In 1760 they gave themselves up to the British at Fort Cumberland (formerly Fort Beauséjour). Dominique Pothier's name appears on the list, next to several Surettes, of prisoners at Fort Edward in 1761. Records show that five years later they were in Chezzetcook across the harbour from Halifax. In 1775 Dominique Pothier settled a land grant in Sainte-Anne-du-Ruisseau. His sons,

Sylvain and Charles-Amand, took land in Wedgeport a few years later. All the Pothiers in Yarmouth County today are descendants of this family.[10]

The early settlers had farms to supply many of their needs. For many generations, farming practices were unchanged. Until relatively recently, for example, oxen were used to till the rough and uneven ground.

In 1860, almost a century after the first families re-settled the area, a well-known French historian, Edme Rameau de Saint-Père, visited this part of Nova Scotia. He talked with members of several families, including the Bourques, whose grandparents had escaped deportation and spent time in Shediac or even in Cape Breton before settling in Sainte-Anne-du-Ruisseau. Being unable to obtain a stagecoach, this distinguished Frenchman decided to walk from Sainte-Anne-du-Ruisseau to Pubnico. It took him almost six hours! He was particularly knowledgeable about farming techniques in France, and as he walked he observed the houses and gardens along the rough road. He was struck by the old well-kept orchards and by the rocky ground "that made the use of the plough almost impossible" (TR)—even a comparatively large acreage could not support more than "four cows and a team of oxen." (TR) Rameau de Saint-Père noted in his diary that the homes of the English looked more prosperous than those of the Acadians but that their crops and gardens were similar, "always potatoes, hay, and a few patches of oats and barley." (TR) In Pubnico, he was pleased to notice that the inhabitants were attempting to enrich the soil by using seaweed as a fertilizer. Seaweed and kelp were also gathered to serve as a winter supplement for the many "wild-looking" sheep that ran free and that were raised mainly for their wool.[11] For a man accustomed to the orderly farms of France and convinced that the survival of any people depended on agricultural expansion, Rameau de Saint-Père was not very impressed by the century-old subsistence farming he observed!

Given the infertility of the land, the economy of Argyle was never based on agriculture. Fishing, shipbuilding, and the coasting trade very early on formed the basic pillars for survival. Easy access to the fishing banks and to the Boston markets and a ready supply of good timber meant that, until the early part of the twentieth

Until fairly recently oxen were used to till the rough and uneven ground. Photo taken by Helen Creighton in West Pubnico in 1948. (Courtesy: Public Archives of Nova Scotia)

The home of Charles Amand Babin in Belleville. Photo taken by Siffroi Pothier, c. 1895. (Courtesy: Public Archives of Nova Scotia)

century, all the communities in Argyle depended directly or indirectly on the sea. In 1885 Father Henri-Raymond Casgrain, a nationalist from Quebec, spent several days exploring the coastal communities of Pinkney Point, Comeau Hill, Wedgeport, the Tusket Islands and Pubnico. Father Casgrain was particularly pleased to be able to find Acadians who, in the space of three generations, had overcome the hardship endured by the Deportation and who had become models of industry and success. He was very impressed by the large fishing and shipping enterprise owned and operated by the Pothier brothers of Wedgeport. He examined their "enormous and costly mackerel net" off Murder Island. His description of their establishment provides a glimpse of the bustling activity of a people whose livelihood came from the sea:

The Pothier Brothers are shipowners from Wedgeport with a truly American daring… They own a fleet of eleven sailing ships, not counting the ones they rent each year, seventy dories and smaller vessels for codfishing all manned by hundreds of Acadian seamen and fishermen. They export an average of one hundred and fifty thousand dollars' worth of goods annually to the West Indies.

The entrepreneurial spirit of the Pothiers is equalled only by their generosity and zealousness in everything related to good works and religious interests.[12] (TR)

Given the long-standing trade links with Boston, the Acadians in this corner of the province probably began building boats in the late 1600s. The first official registers indicate that 26 sailing vessels were built in Pubnico between 1800 and 1852, however, during the second half of the century, the golden years of shipbuilding throughout the Maritimes, no less than 130 ships were crafted there. In a book dedicated to his father, Désiré d'Eon (born in 1905) has transcribed many of the old traditions. In the following passage, he describes the cooperative and communal spirit of the Acadians in the Age of Sail:

The building of a boat was a real event. Today we often use the term cooperation in the sense of working together for the common good. Our ancestors knew exactly what that meant. Cooperation was a necessity. Normally a vessel was divided into sixteen shares. One man could have shares in more than one boat.

It usually took two winters to build a sailing vessel. It would take one winter to cut and hawl the wood… There was no shortage of good wood for everything from the mast to the keel. Three types of wood were used: spruce, tamarack and yellow birch…

All sixteen of the shareholders or members of their families would help with the cutting and hauling. Oxen and sleds were used to hawl the wood to the spot where the boat was to be built. The wood was left to cure during the spring and summer. Construction would begin in the fall and usually last all winter. In the early days all the work was done by hand, including the sawing…

During all this activity, the only person who received a wage was the foreman or the "builder". All the other labour was provided free of charge by the shareholders… According to tradition, the best boat builders from those days were Anselme Amirault, Rémi Amirault and Louis LeBlanc, all from the east side of the harbour. Louis and Anselme could build the entire boat, including the ironwork and the sails, and even sail it to the West Indies…[13] (TR)

Although the sea and the nearby forest enabled the Acadians in Argyle to enjoy a relative prosperity, spiritual and educational structures were slow to develop. Unlike other ethnic groups, Catholic or Protestant, who arrived in Nova Scotia after 1763, the Acadians did not have an educated elite, nor could they call upon a mother country to provide them with clergymen or teachers—as was the case for the Scots who settled in Pictou County, for example.[14] For many years the Acadians had to be content with the services of missionaries sent from Quebec. Not until 1799 did they receive a resident priest who was able to attend to their spiritual and educational needs on a permanent basis. The priest, Father Jean-Mandé Sigogne, played a major role in the advancement of the Acadians in southwest Nova Scotia. Like many other priests, Sigogne fled France during the Revolution and took refuge in England for several years before coming to the New World. For many years, he was the only Catholic priest in the whole of Yarmouth and Digby counties. When Father Sigogne arrived in Sainte-Anne-du-Ruisseau, where he lived for a short time before moving to Church Point, there was a small chapel, built in 1784. Under his direction a new church was constructed in 1808. The parishioners in West Pubnico did not have their own church until

1815. A chapel was built in Wedgeport in 1822, but the other Acadian communities of Argyle had no church until the end of the century.[15]

Partly due to laws preventing Catholics from establishing schools and partly due to a lack of teachers, Acadians in Nova Scotia did not begin to receive any formal schooling until the early 1800s. In a number of Acadian villages, not only in Argyle, the first lay teachers were Frenchmen who arrived in Nova Scotia during the Napoleonic Wars. Such was the case of François Lambert Bourneuf who taught in Pubnico during the winter of 1812-1813. In his diary, Bourneuf writes very enthusiastically of his life as a teacher and of the warm welcome he received in Argyle:

I taught in the house where I boarded, and the children loved me like their own father. I felt as if I were in paradise, after having spent three years on warships and three years as prisoner of war. Everybody made me feel at home, young and old, women and girls. I couldn't have been happier, not even with my own family and friends in France. Sometimes I visited other Acadian villages, and was welcomed wherever I went.[16] (TR)

Having existed for so many generations without schools, the degree of illiteracy amongst the Acadians was high. It is not surprising that the first descriptions of the Acadians after the Deportation are not written by Acadians themselves, but by outsiders. Even prominent citizens appear to have lacked the skills one would normally associate with their position. The following description by Bourneuf no doubt contains a grain of truth:

In the spring of 1813, Benoni d'Entremont, Justice of the Peace, came to see me. He had visited me many times before, to have me write papers for him and to ask me all kinds of questions. He hardly knew how to sign his name, but as he had been Justice of the Peace for many years, the people of Pubnico feared him as much as they feared the King of England.[17] (TR)

Acadians were disadvantaged both with regard to education and to politics. Like all Roman Catholics they were not able to run for political office unless they took the Test Oath, which meant renouncing their faith. Nova Scotia abolished this oath in 1827 and

Church bazaar in West Pubnico, c. 1895. Saint Peter's Church was built in 1891. (Siffroi Pothier Collection, Public Archives of Nova Scotia)

was the first province in the Maritimes to do so. The most outspoken defender of the political emancipation of Catholics was Thomas Chandler Haliburton, member for Annapolis in the Legislative Assembly and close friend of Father Sigogne.

Haliburton defended the right of Catholics generally and the Acadians in particular (many of whom were located in his riding) to participate in the political process. In his famous speech to the House of Assembly, Haliburton stated, "Every man has a right to participate in the civil government of that country of which he is a member, without the imposition of any test oath… After all, who created the Magna Carta? Who established judges, trial by jury, magistrates, sheriffs, etc? Catholics."[18]

Simon d'Entremont from Pubnico and Frédéric Armand Robichaud from Meteghan were the first Acadian members elected in the Maritimes.[19] Simon d'Entremont began his term of office in 1837 and served in the House for three years. He had no formal education but thanks to his own determination and to Father Sigogne he could write and speak French, English, Latin and Micmac.[20] Unfortunately, Acadian representation from Argyle was short-lived due to changes in the electoral divisions. As will be seen, political empowerment of the Acadians in Yarmouth County was not guaranteed until very recently.

As the political process did not ensure a voice for Acadians, and certainly not a voice in French, each Acadian region in Nova Scotia tended to develop its own social structure or institution in order to bring the community together and to enhance communication. The form of this institution varied from one region to another depending on the specific context and on the energies and talents of various individuals. The most important Acadian institution that developed in Argyle was the weekly newspaper, *Le Petit Courrier*, founded in 1937 by Désiré d'Eon.

The first French-language newspaper established in Nova Scotia was *L'Evangéline* founded in 1887 by Valentin Landry. This weekly was published first in Digby, then in Weymouth, under the motto *Unir et instruire* (unite and educate). In 1905 Valentin Landry decided to move his paper to Moncton where he would be closer to a larger Acadian population base. *L'Evangéline* continued to be published in Moncton for almost one hundred years. Although it focused on southeast New Brunswick, *L'Evangéline* provided regular news items on the Acadians throughout the Maritimes.

To a certain extent, *Le Petit Courrier* was designed to fill the gap after *L'Evangéline* moved to New Brunswick. After a short career in teaching, Désiré d'Eon decided to found a weekly newspaper that would serve to unite Acadians at a local level, and in particular the Acadians of southwest Nova Scotia. Désiré d'Eon, one of eleven children, was born in West Pubnico in 1905. Like all Acadians he is identified through his paternal lineage: he is the son of "Charles à Augustin à Mathurin à Augustin à Abel à Jean-Baptiste d'Eon" (seven generations of d'Eons). The first edition of *Le Petit Courrier* was published on February 10, 1937. When he first started, Désiré d'Eon had to drive up to Digby to have the newspaper printed. He ran the paper as a volunteer vocation while he worked full-time at the Caisse populaire (Credit Union) in West Pubnico. He attributes his determination to keep the paper alive to all the Acadians who sent him news on a regular basis.[21]

For three decades the *Petit Courrier* was published as a local

Désiré d'Eon founded *Le Petit Courrier* in 1937.
(Courtesy: *Le Courrier de la Nouvelle-Ecosse*)

news bulletin, but in 1972, it was transformed into a provincial newspaper designed to link all the Acadian communities of Nova Scotia. With the help of federal government funds, a newly formed publishing house, Imprimerie Lescarbot, bought the weekly and later renamed it *Le Courrier*. For the first time, the Acadians of Nova Scotia had a newspaper through which they could communicate with one another.

Désiré d'Eon remained a shareholder and Cyrille LeBlanc became the new editor. Over a period of 15 years the paper expanded considerably. The staff was increased from two to ten. By 1984 the circulation had reached 3,400 copies.[22] Unfortunately, the expansion of *Le Courrier* both in size and distribution did not result in a financially viable newspaper, and it was forced to undergo another major restructuring in 1987. The newspaper is operated by the Société de la presse acadienne with the help of a trust fund created with monies from the Secretary of State and the provincial government. Richard Landry, a native of Isle Madame, served as editor until 1992.

The difficulties encountered by *Le Courrier* over the past 15 years are a legacy of history. Because the Acadians were forced to relocate after 1763 in distant corners of the province, their communities are isolated from each other and have evolved differently. Even in the days of modern communication, direct contacts between the different communities are time-consuming and costly. In the past, educational facilities in French varied considerably from one region to another. Along with economic factors, the quantity and quality of French-language education affects the motivation to read and write in the French language. To a certain extent, *Le Courrier* is struggling against the consequences of history which for the Acadians in Nova Scotia is characterized by geographic isolation and assimilation.

Clare

Clare is a municipality in Digby County and it is the largest Acadian region in Nova Scotia both in size and population density. Generally the name refers to the Acadian villages that form an almost unbroken line along the shores of St. Marys Bay. Older generations used to call this string of villages *la Ville française*. In English, the area is usually referred to as the French Shore. In comparative terms for the all the Acadians of southwest Nova Scotia, Clare is *par en-haut* (up) whereas Argyle is *par en-bas* (down). Unlike Argyle, Clare was not settled by Acadians before the Deportation.

The earliest record of an Acadian presence along this shore dates back to 1755-1756 when a small group of refugees led by Pierre "Piau" Belliveau spent the winter on an island off present-day Belliveau Cove. Many of the members of the group died and were buried on the island. In memory of that winter, Piau's Island was used as a burial ground from 1771 to 1791 by the first permanent Acadian settlers. A commemorative chapel was erected on the site in 1890 and is still maintained.[23]

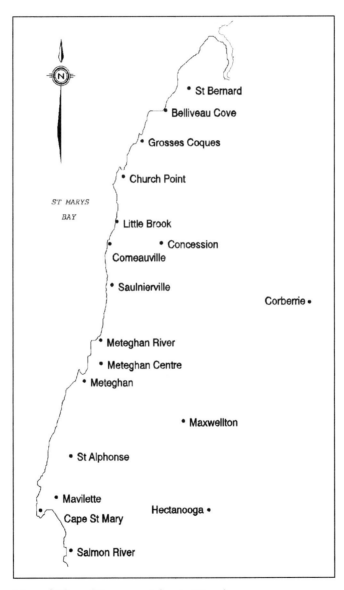

Map of Clare. (Courtesy: Atlantic Direct)

Responding to earlier requests made by groups of Acadians, in July 1768, Lieutenant-Governor Michael Francklin authorized the Deputy Surveyor of Nova Scotia to divide a large tract of land into lots to be granted to Acadians who were living as transients in the vicinity of Annapolis Royal, Windsor and Halifax. The surveyor, John Morrison, was assisted by an Acadian from Annapolis Royal by the name of John Bastarache. The first section of land, about 14 kilometres long, stretched from the Bastarache Line, in present-day St. Bernard, to Little Brook. It included the villages known today as Belliveau Cove, Grosses Coques and Church Point. The area surveyed was called the Township of Clare and now forms part of the municipality of Clare.[24] The Acadians were provided with "licences of occupation" for the lots of their choice. As was common throughout the province, the settlers had to occupy their land for several years before they actually received titles. The size of the lots varied according to the size of the household: the head of the family received 80 acres plus at least 40 acres for each member of his family. All the grants had water frontage, a marsh lot which provided a supply of hay and a large section of woodland.

According to genealogical records and other historical documents, most of the Acadians who were granted land in the township of Clare had lived in the Annapolis Valley before 1755. Many of them were actually born and brought up in the vicinity of Annapolis Royal (formerly Port Royal) and some of them were living there in 1768 when land became available along St. Marys Bay. Other families who settled in Clare had made their way back to Nova Scotia by land or by sea from Massachusetts where they had been deported. The settlement of the St. Marys Bay area took place fairly quickly. By the mid-1770s, about 30 founding families had established themselves in the first section of lots granted along this coastline.

Prudent Robichaud is a typical example of one of the founding fathers of Clare. Born in Port Royal, he escaped deportation and spent the winter of 1755-1756 with Pierre "Piau" Belliveau. Prudent was eventually captured; his name, along with five dependants, appears on the list of prisoners in Fort Edward in 1761. After he and his wife and family were released, they must have made their way back to their native region because the marriage of their daughter Marie-Josephe to Joseph Dugas took place in Annapolis

Royal in 1763.[25] This young couple were the first to take advantage of the offer of land along St. Marys Bay.

In all likelihood Joseph had already learned something about Piau's Island through his father-in-law, Prudent Robichaud. In the summer of 1768 Joseph and Marie-Josephe Dugas moved from Annapolis Royal to the area now known as Belliveau Cove. Their son Joseph, born on September 25, was the first Acadian child born in this area. They were joined the following year by Marie-Josephe's father and several other families who had also been living near Annapolis Royal. Their names, like those of most of the founding families, have become synonymous with St. Marys Bay: Francis Comeau, Joseph Gaudet, Prudent Robichaud, Jean Belliveau, René Saulnier, Pierre Melanson, Yves Thibeau. (With the exception of Saulnier, all of these family names appear in the first census of Port Royal taken by Father Laurent Molins in 1671.)

As mentioned previously, other Acadians who settled in Clare had been deported to Massachusetts in 1755. The village of Church Point, for example, was founded in 1772 by Pierre LeBlanc and François Doucet and their families. They arrived by boat from Salem, Massachusetts. As had been the pattern in Belliveau Cove and Grosses Coques, once several families were established they encouraged their relatives to join them.

This network of family ties is particularly apparent in the case of Pierre Doucet. He was born in Port Royal on May 16, 1750 and was five years old at the time of the Deportation. At the age of 23 he married Marie Madeleine LeBlanc in Salem. After 20 years in exile, Pierre Doucet sailed back to Nova Scotia in 1775 with his wife and children and settled in the Township of Clare where his cousin, Amable Doucet, was already well-established. Amable himself was Prudent Robichaud's cousin and godson. By the time Pierre Doucet and his family landed on the shores of St. Marys Bay, the Acadian migrations into Clare were drawing to an end.[26]

Further expansion along the coast took place after 1785 by which time the sons of the founding families wanted their own land. The present villages of Comeauville, Saulnierville, and Meteghan were thus founded by the second generation of Acadians. The last stretch of coastline—from Mavilette to Salmon River— was transferred to the descendants of pioneer families in 1804 and

1805. Thus by the beginning of the nineteenth century the foundations had been laid for the Acadian communities on the French Shore.

Since more land was made available specifically to Acadians along the shores of St. Marys Bay, more families were able to establish themselves than in Argyle. Consequently, from the very beginning, Clare benefitted from a larger and more uniformly Acadian population base. In 1803, when the Bishop of Quebec, Monseigneur Denaut, made his first pastoral visit to Nova Scotia there were 1,080 Acadians living in Clare and approximately 400 in Argyle.[27]

It was this difference in population that motivated Father Jean-Mandé Sigogne to move from Sainte-Anne-du-Ruisseau in Argyle to Church Point where he lived until his death in November 1844. Although authoritarian by nature, Father Sigogne was a very talented and well-educated priest who provided strong and continuous leadership in both spiritual and temporal matters for 45 years. After he was appointed Justice of the Peace in 1810, he also served as legal counsellor for his parishioners and, being fluent in both French and English, acted as their spokesman in dealings with government. He was fluent in the Micmac language and negotiated on numerous occasions on behalf of the Micmac whom he served with profound affection.[28]

Although the soil in Clare did not match the fertility of the land in the Annapolis Valley, it was better than in Argyle. There were marshes to be reclaimed and a ready supply of excellent timber. Whereas the Acadians in Argyle always relied on fishing and shipping, the Acadians living on the shores of St. Marys Bay benefitted from a more diversified economy. Like their compatriots from *par en-bas*, the inhabitants of Clare participated in the so-called triangular trade that characterized Nova Scotia for several generations. Not long after returning from exile in 1775, Pierre Doucet, for example, established a lucrative shipping business which he operated until the 1790s. Records of his transactions show that he traded raw materials such as boards, planks, salt fish, and potatoes from the area for sugar, molasses, salt, and rum from the West Indies and manufactured goods and textiles from Boston. On at least one occasion, he transported slaves from

Aerial view of Saulnierville and St. Marys Bay, c. 1960 (D.B. Field Collection, Centre Acadien, Université Sainte-Anne)

Jamaica to Havana.[29] In the early 1800s François Lambert Bourneuf, who had left Pubnico to settle permanently in St. Marys Bay, was also involved in shipping and participated in the coastal trade across the Bay of Fundy. His diary provides additional clues on the agricultural produce of Clare.

In April 1817, I took command of a small schooner. I sailed to Saint John every two weeks to trade eggs, potatoes, butter, and other products for merchandise that I sold through Joseph Joppé LeBlanc and Charles à Michaud Melanson. I did well all summer, and this was really the beginning of my business.

In the fall, I sold at cost a small schooner that I had bought during the summer. In the winter of 1817-1818, I had wood cut to build a larger ship, which I sold the following fall for fourteen hundred dollars, four hundred dollars more than it cost me...[30] (TR)

It is often assumed that until the twentieth century the Acadians lived in isolation with few outside contacts. It is obvious, however, that the coastal trade that began in the 1770s resulted in a number of cultural exchanges. The men from Clare who worked on the schooners that regularly sailed across the Bay of Fundy, for example, had ample opportunity to observe customs among the English. It is known that they brought back gifts for their sisters and their wives because, according to an incident that occurred in 1810, two young women decided to wear fashionable hats, bought in Saint John to church. This was considered to be a manifestation of outrageous and scandalous behaviour in the eyes of Father Sigogne. The young women were severely admonished in public for having succumbed to the vice of vanity and for having dared abandon the traditional Acadian kerchief that rimmed the face and covered the head.[31]

Although the shipping trade constituted an important aspect of life in Clare for several generations, the lumber industry dominated the economy. In fact, the proliferation of sawmills along the rivers and streams of the region gave rise to the observation that before the Deportation, the Acadians were farmers, but when they arrived in St. Marys Bay they became woodsmen and lumberjacks.[32] For more than a century, the Acadians in this part of Nova Scotia concentrated on the resources of the forest. Writing in about 1900, Father Pierre-Marie Dagnaud, parish priest and Superior of Collège Sainte-Anne, stated that the forest had always been "the inexhaustible gold mine" of Saint Marys Bay. The many beautiful churches that dot the landscape of Clare are monuments to the Catholic faith but they are also the legacy of a long line of woodworkers and masterbuilders. With the highest wooden steeple in North America, St. Marys Church in Church Point is the largest and most spectacular building in the entire region. It was constructed in 1905 by one of Clare's most famous carpenters, Léo P. Melanson, born in Little Brook and known as Léo à Pierre à Charles. Melanson had no formal education and yet was able to design an enormous structure that still resists the hurricane force winds that sweep the coastline. In addition to building churches, Léo P. Melanson also carved all the intricate woodwork for the interior of the churches at Concession, Church Point, Plympton, Salmon River and St. Bernard.[33]

The fishing industry developed much later in Clare than in Argyle. At the turn of the century, Father Dagnaud observed that whereas fishing was "almost the only resource of the Acadians in Cape Sable," the Acadians in St. Marys Bay were just "beginning to realize that fishing might become their most stable source of

A group of boatbuilders in Salmon River, c. 1900. (Robicheau Collection, Centre Acadien)

income."[34] With the advent of motor boats in the early 1900s and improvements in refrigeration techniques, the commercial fishing industry gradually outstripped the lumber industry. Belliveau Cove, Church Point, Comeauville, Saulnierville, Meteghan and Cape Saint Marys became increasingly important fishing ports.[35]

Like most pioneers in the early 1800s, the Acadians did not always see the necessity for education. As was noted in the section on Argyle, Father Sigogne was the first person in southwestern Nova Scotia to begin the struggle against illiteracy. Soon after his arrival in Church Point, Father Sigogne established a school and began teaching reading and writing to a tiny group of children. As paper was scarce, the young pupils were forced to practise their skills on the backs of old letters and envelopes.[36] Exasperated perhaps by his parishioners' indifference towards the education of their children, Father Sigogne used stern and critical words in order to shame them into accepting their parental responsibilities. The following passage from one of his sermons illustrates both his conviction and his style. The stern pastor might well have entitled his sermon "Ignorance Is a Vice."

Christians, for many years, I have deplored the ignorance that reigns here, ignorance that I have attempted in vain to eradicate. I have often lacked the means and my approach has been totally unsuccessful. Is it due to indifference on your part, the stubbornness of your children or the prevailing circumstances? I do not know the cause but I have noticed that barely half the children who attend catechism are able to answer any questions...

As you know, ignorance is a vice; a vice which places you in an inferior position with regard to educated people...

Having received some assistance for a teacher, I have decided to open a school for three hours on Sundays... The children will be taught reading and writing. Arrangements have been made with the schoolmaster so that catechism and reading will be free whereas writing, which requires special material, will cost a small amount.

I strongly urge young people to attend these classes and I invite parents to promote this school as best they can. You will only have yourselves to blame for your ignorance if you disregard the means of instruction which is being offered you. I will supervise the classes myself in order to ensure proper discipline.[37] (TR)

Until his death in 1844, Father Sigogne promoted the importance of education. As a result of his tireless efforts, the Acadians along St. Marys Bay fared better than their compatriots elsewhere in the province. No other parish in Nova Scotia benefitted from the leadership of a French-language priest for such an extended period of time in the early days of resettlement.

Despite Father Sigogne's efforts, schools developed very slowly. French-language teachers were scarce, financial support from the province was minimal and parents could not always afford to educate their children. Under the Education Act of 1841, the government provided financial assistance for elementary schools throughout the province and granted equal status to English, French, Gaelic, and German. In other words, they could be used as languages of instruction—a privilege that was gradually eroded.

In 1845, one year after Father Sigogne's death, there were 150 pupils and seven Acadian teachers in Clare.[38] By 1867, there were several public elementary schools in the region along with two convent schools for girls run by the Sisters of Charity, one in Church Point and one in Meteghan. However, there were no

Meteghan Centre school, c. 1930. (Robicheau Collection, Centre Acadien)

facilities beyond Grade 9 for Acadian boys. Consequently, they were forced either to continue their French education at Collège Saint-Joseph in Memramcook, New Brunswick, or to enroll in an English-language academy or high school.[39] This situation was not remedied until the foundation of Collège Sainte-Anne in November 1890. The Eudist Fathers who established and ran the college also took over the responsibilities of the parish. Over the years, Collège Sainte-Anne graduated a number of future doctors, teachers, and politicians, among them Edouard Alfred LeBlanc, the first Acadian from Saint Marys Bay to become a priest and, in 1912, the first Acadian bishop in the Maritimes.

The arrival of the Eudist Fathers represented a major step in the preservation of French not only in the sphere of education but also within the framework of the Church. It should be noted that until this time, English-language priests of Irish or Scottish descent dominated the Catholic parishes of Nova Scotia. No other Acadian region in Nova Scotia was guaranteed service by French-language parish priests.[40]

Faced with extremely stiff competition from six anglophone

universities in a small province where the knowledge of English in the workplace is an absolute necessity, the francophone college founded by the Eudist Fathers has always encountered difficulties in attracting students. In 1952, for example, out of a total of 188 students, 100 were from Nova Scotia, 45 from Quebec, 35 from New Brunswick and 8 from the United States.[41] These figures represent only male students as women were not admitted into the college until 1961. Québécois constituted a significant percentage of the enrolment until the late 1960s but after the major educational reforms that took place in Quebec during the Quiet Revolution, Collège Sainte-Anne lost this clientele. With a reduction in the number of students, the future of the college was in danger. A debate took place as to whether the institution should be moved to a larger population centre like Yarmouth and transformed into a community college. However, in 1970 the newly-elected provincial government decided to support the development and expansion of Collège Sainte-Anne as a bilingual university. The following year the administration was secularized and Louis R. Comeau became the first lay president. In 1977 the name was changed to Université Sainte-Anne.

By the time of its centenary year, in 1990, the university was unique for being the only bilingual university in the Maritimes and the only post-secondary Acadian institution in Nova Scotia. In the past ten years Université Sainte-Anne has expanded considerably in the areas of French Immersion and continuing education for part-time francophone students. With a total enrolment of about 350 full-time students in 1990, it is the smallest university in the province. Over the years, it has served not only as an educational institution but also as an important cultural centre for the Acadians in Clare. For example, Les Araignées du Boui-Boui, the university-based theatre company has entertained local audiences and received both provincial and national recognition.

Université Sainte-Anne now offers programs in co-operation with the Université de Moncton and the Université de Montréal. There is also an important resource centre for francophone teachers and the Centre Acadien which houses a large archival collection of Acadian manuscripts, newspapers, tapes and photographs. During its first century of existence, Université Sainte-Anne has provided

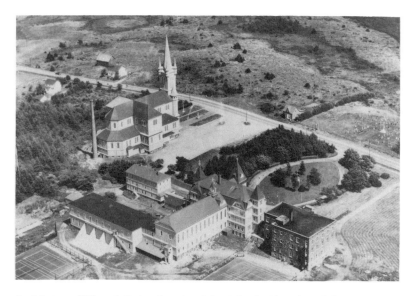

Aerial view of Church Point showing Saint Mary's Church and the Université Sainte-Anne, c. 1960 (D.B. Field Collection, Centre Acadien)

post-secondary education in French for hundreds of young Acadians and for this reason alone it represents much more than a symbolic French presence in southwestern Nova Scotia.

In some ways, Clare has been more fortunate than other Acadian regions in Nova Scotia. To a certain extent this is due to Lieutenant-Governor Francklin's decision in 1768 to designate a large tract of land specifically for the resettlement of Acadian families. This decision ultimately resulted in the development of a series of adjoining villages populated almost exclusively by Acadians, thus creating a geographic region with a francophone majority. There is no doubt that the consequences of this development have touched almost every aspect of life in Clare, from voting practices to the way the inhabitants speak. One of the most important consequences of this solid population base is the fact that since 1836 the Acadians of St. Marys Bay have had a representative in the provincial Legislative Assembly. No other Acadian region in Nova Scotia has had the same degree of political representation—at the provincial, federal or municipal level. The homogeneous and relatively compact population base has also affected the survival and preservation of the French language. Recent research, for example, has shown that of all the Acadian regions in Nova Scotia, the St. Marys Bay area has preserved the largest range of features from seventeenth-century French.[42]

Minudie, Nappan and Maccan

At the head of the Bay of Fundy lie the three communities of Minudie, Nappan, and Maccan. Although Acadian settlers returned to this part of Nova Scotia in the late 1760s, at about the same time the township of Clare was being settled, the fate of the Acadian culture and the French language in the Cumberland Basin region stands in marked contrast with that of the communities along St. Marys Bay.

After 1763, in order to encourage the development of the province, it was not uncommon for the British government to reward military officials by granting them large tracts of land. Under these conditions Joseph Frederick Wallet Desbarres obtained prime farmland in Falmouth (near Windsor), Minudie, Nappan, Maccan, Tatamagouche, and Memramcook (now in New Brunswick).[43] Desbarres, a distinguished cartographer who carried out a detailed survey of the coast of Nova Scotia and Cape Breton Island, was appointed as the first lieutenant-governor of Cape-Breton in 1784. He was born in Switzerland although his family came from the Protestant stronghold of Montbéliard in France. In order to exploit his newly acquired estates, Desbarres was obliged to look for settlers to cultivate the land. In the case of the 8,100 hectare (20,000 acre) grant in Tatamagouche, he was only allowed to install Protestant settlers. For this reason, he invited a number of the so-called Foreign Protestants from Lunenburg to move to Tatamagouche.

As Tatamagouche was the only grant with religious restrictions, Desbarres was able to call upon Acadians as a source of labour on his other holdings. Not only were the Acadians experienced farmers but, before the Deportation, they had dyked and cultivated sections of all the tracts of land that Desbarres received. For example, the Minudie estate or the Elysian Fields, as it was called, consisted of 2,800 hectares (7,000 acres) of which 1,200 hectares (3,000 acres) were dyked lands, cleared upland and orchards.[44]

Some of the Acadians who settled in the Cumberland Basin

region made their way from the Restigouche and Miramichi areas where they had taken refuge between 1755 and 1763. Others had been incarcerated in various prisons, including Fort Edward. Acadian names associated with the Minudie, Nappan, and Maccan estates were Bourg, Melanson, Babin, Forest, Léger, Leblanc, Comeau, Brun, Gallant, Gautreau, and Vautour.[45] Each family was allotted 81 hectares (200 acres) but without being given title to the land. In other words, the settlers became tenant farmers. In addition to a percentage of the livestock, they were obliged to give one-third of their grain harvest and one-quarter of the proceeds from the grist mills to the Desbarres manor on each estate. Although these conditions were not considered to be harsh in the late 1700s, they obviously did not constitute an incentive for efficient farming.[46]

In 1795 Captain John MacDonald visited the Cumberland region and sent a report to Desbarres about the Acadians living on the Minudie estate. He describes the one-roomed houses where they "all sleep, eat, cook, smoke and wash." He was more impressed with their barns which were larger and "more sumptuous" than their houses. Captain MacDonald also observed that the Acadians kept to themselves and that they had "customs of their own, of which they are tenacious, some of which are worse and some better than our customs." In his report MacDonald criticizes the intolerance of English-speaking settlers with regard to their Acadian neighbours.

They readily see the Imperfections on the part of the Acadians as the British in Canada do of the Canadians [French Canadians], *because we are a Saucy Nation too ready to despise others—because we have happened to be the Conquerors. We are of a different origin, Religion, etc. etc. Having taken them in an early stage, we have destroyed them and the course of their prospective Improvement in their own way, and all that has succeeded since we proudly attribute to ourselves instead of giving any credit for the unavoidable Improvement and growth in America of 36 Years more time. While we do not perceive the faults on our own Sides, because they are ours. Sure I am* [that] *we are not more virtuous or happy than they are and I fear we have made them worse men and less happy than they have been.*[47]

After spending about twenty years as tenant farmers, several Acadian families manifested their dissatisfaction by leaving Minudie. They moved across the Isthmus of Chignecto in 1788 into the newly created province of New Brunswick where they were able to obtain land grants. However, the most significant wave of out-migration took place between 1800 and 1808, a few years after Captain MacDonald's visit. Desbarres' son William, who was married to Hélène Melanson, was in charge of the Minudie estate. After his accidental death in 1800, a bitter family feud began between Desbarres' legitimate and illegitimate children with the result that many of the tenants on the Desbarres estates were evicted.[48] Along with other tenants, several hundred Acadians were thus forced to leave their farms in the Cumberland Basin region. The Acadian families who left Minudie were granted land in Shemogue, Cap-Pelé, and Scoudouc in the southwest corner of New Brunswick.

By 1812, there were only about 15 Acadian families left in Minudie. Limited in number and isolated from the French parish of Memramcook, the Acadians in the Cumberland region were absorbed into the English culture very quickly. As petitions from Minudie dating from the early 1800s indicate, the Acadian men were illiterate.[49] Only the continuing presence of French-language institutions, including schools, could ensure the shift from an oral to a written culture.

Although the Cumberland area is not considered an Acadian region today, one can still find many of the family names associated with the resettlement on the Desbarres estates in 1768. This can be explained by the fact that not all Acadians migrated elsewhere in the early years of the nineteenth century and by the fact that, in the late 1800s, descendants of some of the Minudie families came back to the region to work in the grindstone quarries at Lower Cove and in the coal mines at Joggins and River Hebert.

Ironically, the Cumberland Basin region was the only area in present-day Nova Scotia where the Acadians were able to resettle on the fertile land they had dyked and farmed before the Deportation. In other words, only as tenants on the Desbarres estates were they able to carry out the type of agriculture they had practised from the 1636 to 1755. Although the communities of Minudie, Maccan, and Nappan hardly qualify as an Acadian region, they do represent a revealing and significant chapter in the history of the Acadians of Nova Scotia. In comparison to Argyle and Clare, none of the mechanisms that served to protect the Acadians as a distinct cultural and linguistic group fell into place.

Chéticamp

Cape Breton played a key role in the economy of France until the fall of Louisbourg in 1758. Located close to the Grand Banks and on the same latitude as the major French ports of La Rochelle and Rochefort, Cape Breton was a very convenient destination for ships sailing from France, and an essential land base for the cod fishery. As French maps from the mid-1700s show, almost all the fishing stations were situated along the Atlantic coast of Cape Breton. In comparison with the east coast, the west side of the island appears unexplored.

Although there were no permanent settlers in Chéticamp before 1782, records indicate that it was one of the few locations on the west coast to be used as a temporary fishing station in the seventeenth century.[50] Nicolas Denys, who explored the entire coastline of the island during the 1650s, provides the first written description of Chéticamp or Le Chadye. Denys left his establishment in Saint-Pierre (St. Peters) in the southern part of Cape Breton and sailed up the east coast, around the north tip of the island which he called Cap de Nort (Cape North). Then he headed down the west side and arrived at a deep harbour called Le Chadye.

From Cap de Nort there are about fifteen to sixteen leagues. All this coast is nothing but rocks covered with Firs, intermingled with some little Birches. There are found some sandy coves into which hardly a boat can enter. This coast is dangerous. Le Chadye is a great cove which has about two leagues of depth. In its extremity is a beach of sand intermingled with gravel which the sea has made behind which is a pond of salt water. This cove is bordered with rocks on both shores. The Cod is very abundant in this bay, and this attracts vessels there, although they are often lost because of the little shelter is affords.[51] (TR)

After the Treaty of Paris in 1763, fishermen from France were forced to withdraw from the Gulf of St. Lawrence. Merchants from the English Channel Islands were quick to establish themselves in areas previously fished by the French. Most of these merchants were Huguenots whose families had fled France after 1685 and who had settled on the Isle of Jersey. The most famous of these Jerseymen was Charles Robin who established permanent fishing stations, first on the Gaspé coast and along the Bay of Chaleur and then at Arichat on Isle Madame in 1765. A few years later he founded an outpost in Chéticamp.[52] In the past, fish companies had brought out fishermen from France on a seasonal basis, but Charles Robin built his enterprises using a permanent labour force. As noted earlier, Robin actively encouraged Acadians to return and settle in Nova Scotia. He and other Jersey merchants were well acquainted with the plight of the Acadian families in exile near St. Malo.[53] The Isle of Jersey is only a few hours distance from this French port. And so many families, along with their descendants, became an integral part of the Robin empire for more than a century.

By the time the Acadians began moving into the Chéticamp area, the Robins owned a choice section of land and had built sheds and wharves. The Acadian migrations into the northern part of Cape Breton started in 1782—almost 20 years after Clare and Argyle were settled—and came to a close when the last group of settlers arrived in 1829. The migrations into this area also took place over a much longer period of time than in either Clare or Argyle.

Pierre Bois and Joseph Richard appear to be the first Acadians to have landed in Chéticamp. They sailed from the Bay of Chaleur where they had fled from Arichat in 1780 after raids by American privateers. Joseph Richard soon moved to Tracadie, Nova Scotia. Two groups of families, some of whom were related to Richard and Bois, arrived in 1785. They too had spent time in the Bay of Chaleur region where they undoubtedly heard about Robin's establishment in Chéticamp. The following year they were joined by another group of families who came over from Bay Fortune in eastern Prince Edward Island where they had been unable to obtain titles to their land.[54]

The island of Cape Breton was politically separate from Nova Scotia between 1784 and 1820. The granting of land took place very slowly until 1790 after which time it was discontinued for

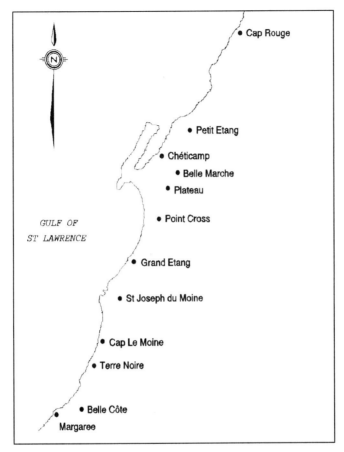

Map of Chéticamp. (Courtesy: Atlantic Direct)

several years. Throughout the island, it was not uncommon for settlers to establish themselves and then petition for title to the land they had been occupying for many years. In this way, 14 Acadian pioneers and their families were granted 2,800 hectares (7,000 acres) in Chéticamp by the government in Sydney in 1790.[55]

Contrary to the way the land was granted along St. Marys Bay, this large tract of land was not divided into lots. It was left to the members of the group to parcel out the land. The men mentioned in the land grant, named the "Charter of 1790," are considered to be the founders of Chéticamp and are referred to as *Les Quartorze Vieux* or the Fourteen Elders. There are two monuments commemorating the Fourteen Elders, one was erected in 1955 on the site of the first church and the other in 1985 to celebrate the bicentenary of Chéticamp.

As with Clare and Argyle, the foundations of Chéticamp are based on a network of family ties. The following list (showing both husbands and wives) illustrates how marriage linked the small group of pioneer families.[56] The list also gives an indication of the most common names that can be found in Chéticamp today.

After the Deportation most of these individuals and their parents had travelled over immense distances—much greater distances than the founding families of Clare who were not exiled in France. The itinerary of each of the families is quite different. Isabelle Boudrot, for example, was born near St. Malo, France, in October 1763. Her brother, Joseph, was born in August of 1768, also near St. Malo. Their parents had been deported to England in 1758 from Virginia where the Acadians had been refused entry. They survived several years in English prisons and were eventually transported to St. Malo in May 1763, at the end of the Seven Years' War. After spending ten years in France, the Boudrot family returned to the Maritimes in 1773 with a group of Acadians, including Pierre Aucoin and Grégoire Maillet who are also listed among the Fourteen Elders. Grégoire Maillet's itinerary was different in that he had left Grand Pré in the 1750s and immigrated to Ile Saint-Jean (Prince Edward Island). Along with hundreds of other Acadians on the Island, he was transported to St. Malo in 1758. He arrived in Chéticamp with Anne LeBlanc, his third wife.[57]

The Fourteen Founding Families of Chéticamp

1. *Pierre BOIS*
2. *Raymond POIRIER married to Marie BOIS*
3. *Augustin DEVEAU married to Rose RICHARD*
4. *Anselme AUCOIN married to Rose CHIASSON*
5. *Paul CHIASSON married to Louise BOUDROT*
6. *Basile CHIASSON married to Adélaïde ARSENEAUX*
7. *Jean CHIASSON married to Isabelle BOUDROT*
8. *Joseph GAUDET married to Marie-Anne RICHARD*
9. *Pierre AUCOIN married to Félicité LEBLANC (and later to Marie DOUCET)*

10. *Joseph BOUDROT married to Anne CHIASSON*
11. *Lazare LEBLANC married to Modeste CHIASSON*
12. *Joseph DEVEAU*
13. *Joseph AUCOIN married to Marie HEBERT with adopted son Cyriac ROACH*
14. *Grégoire MAILLET married to Anne LEBLANC*

Acadian settlers continued to arrive in the Chéticamp area over a period of almost 50 years. Most of them had spent at least a decade in France. They made their way to Cape Breton from various locations including the Magdalen Islands, St. Pierre, and Miquelon. After struggling for many years with the injustices of absentee landlords on Prince Edward Island, more Acadians decided to join their friends and relatives in Chéticamp and Margaree. Thirty-six families, for example, came across from Rustico in 1822 and another five families as late as 1829.[58] In addition, Chéticamp also became the home for a number of seamen from France who arrived between 1800 and 1815 under various circumstances during the Napoleonic Wars. These men are the ancestors of all those in Chéticamp who bear the names Lefort, Luidée, Chapdelaine, Camus, and Fleuri. Several agents from Jersey married into the Acadian community, one of whom was Jean Lelièvre.

By 1830, Acadian settlements in northern Cape Breton covered a stretch of coastline about 40 kilometres long. From north to south down the coast, Acadians were settled in Cap-Rouge, Petit-Etang, Chéticamp, Belle-Marche, Plateau, Point Cross, Grand-Etang, Saint-Joseph-du-Moine, Cap-le-Moine, Terre-Noire, Belle-Côte, and Magré (Margaree). In the latter part of the nineteenth century these villages eventually formed three parishes that were part of the diocese of Antigonish: Saint-Pierre (Chéticamp), Saint-Joseph-du-Moine, and Saint Michael (Margaree). Although this part of Inverness County is comprised of a number of villages, it is normally referred to as Chéticamp—the name of the oldest and largest community. Like the string of villages along St. Marys Bay, the villages in the Chéticamp area formed an homogeneous Acadian population, with the exception of Belle-Côte and Margaree where a number of Scottish families settled.

In comparison with Argyle and Clare, Chéticamp was much

more isolated. Except for the fishery, contacts with other centres of population were not only limited but very difficult. In the early days of Chéticamp, between 1787 and 1801, the settlers were served by Catholic missionaries appointed by the Bishop of Quebec. The following lines from the correspondence of the missionary priest, Father Lejamtel, give a vivid picture of the perils involved in reaching these distant missions of northern Cape Breton:

I always try to take care of these missions early, for navigation is always dangerous on these shores about the time of the equinoctial wind and afterwards. I risked my life several times in my early years when I was not acquainted with the place, and for 14 years past, on 25 or 26 September 1799, when I had set out with renewed vigour, I took the resolution never again to embark in the autumn unless it were to save my life from some other menace.[59] (TR)

As was the case in Clare and Argyle, the first resident priest did not arrive until the end of the eighteenth century. And like Father Sigogne, the first resident priest in Chéticamp had fled the French Revolution. Father Gabriel Champion arrived in 1801 after spending the winter with the Acadians in Bay Fortune, Prince Edward Island. Like many of the priests who came during the first half of the nineteenth century, his stay in Chéticamp was brief.

One of the longest serving and most influential priests in Chéticamp was Father Pierre Fiset, from Ancienne-Lorette, Quebec, who was ordained in Antigonish. He was professor of French at St. Francis Xavier University and then pastor at Havre-Boucher before going to Chéticamp in 1875 where he served as parish priest until his death in 1909. Father Fiset was responsible for the construction of St. Peter's Church in 1892 and the convent in 1900. The French religious order of the Filles de Jésus directed the convent, which still exists today. Father Fiset, both a priest and an entrepreneur, made innumerable contributions to the economy of Chéticamp—in many cases designed to break the monopoly of the Robin empire. Thanks to his initiative, for example, a regular steamboat service was established in 1886 between Chéticamp and Pictou, thus connecting the region to the railway.[60] As Father Sigogne had done over half a century earlier in southwestern Nova Scotia, Father Fiset offered the continuing and energetic leadership of a

Wharf and fish houses of Father Fiset, c. 1900 (Courtesy: Nova Scotia Museum)

priest who promoted the French language. Virtually all the parish priests who served in Chéticamp over the years were French-speaking, as opposed to the Irish and Scottish priests who ministered to the Acadians in Margaree and in the southern part of Cape Breton. In 1953 the Eudist Fathers took over the pastoral care of the Chéticamp parish and remained in charge until 1988.

Chéticamp was founded as a fishing station and its economy has always revolved around fishing and the marketing of cod and other species. The hilly terrain and the poor soil meant that the people of this part of Cape Breton never relied entirely on agriculture, but from the early days of settlement until the 1940s, most families had subsistence farms, or as one elderly resident of Chéticamp recalls: "Every home had a cow or two; they all had a pig, and always ten or twelve chickens, a horse and a wagon."[61]

If the inhabitants were able to obtain a degree of independence in farming, this was certainly not the case with regard to the fishing industry. From the 1770s to the 1890s the financial lifeline of Chéticamp was controlled and dominated by the "Jerseys" or the Charles Robin Company.[62] The effect of this monopoly on the fishermen, the fish workers and their families was economically devastating. Basically the company had a stranglehold on the catching, buying, selling, and processing of fish. Boats and fishing gear belonged to the company to whom the fishermen paid a rental fee representing one-tenth of their catch. Employees were not paid in money. They were paid either in supplies like meat, salt, flour, molasses, and peas or in credit which meant that they always had to buy at the company store.[63] This system stands in marked contrast to the way the shipping and fishing industries evolved in Clare and Argyle. The possibilities for individual enterprise such as Father Casgrain had admired in Argyle were non-existent. Milton Aucoin, who was 75 years old in 1984, describes the life of the fishermen as it was explained to him by his grandfather.

[The Jerseys] *used to hire them. The people had nothing. But the Jersey people had a fishing point at the Chéticamp Island. The Jerseys owned everything. The boats belonged to the Jerseys. And they would pay so much for the catch. Never in cash. They'd have to buy at the store for whatever they caught.*[64]

Needless to say, this system gave rise to generations of poverty and bitterness. But it is also partly because they were exploited for so long that the inhabitants of the Chéticamp region developed one of the strongest co-operative movements in Nova Scotia. The first sales co-operative in Chéticamp was founded in 1915 by a group of fishermen.[65] Mrs. Ida Delaney, who organized co-operatives and credit unions for many years, explains why the shift from private to co-operative ownership became necessary in Chéticamp.

In the first place, some of the [fishermen] *hardly saw any cash at all, because they sold their fish to the merchants—the Jerseys, the Robin-Jones and the Lawrences. That's the sad part. They controlled these people for years and years. There wasn't a fisherman among them. Of course the Fisets came later on. I don't think they were exploiters. Anyway, the fishermen sold their fish to these merchants and they bought what they needed for the house from them. So at the end of the year, you balanced the books. They were always in debt. Then they had to borrow to get something for the winter. After the co-ops, they got rid of the exploiters.*[66]

Generally the co-operative movement in Nova Scotia is associated with Antigonish County and Cape Breton. Given the orientation towards Christian socialism that developed in the Catholic Church at the end of the nineteenth century, the strongest proponents of the co-operative movement were to be found amongst the

Laurette Deveau, Executive Director of the Co-op Council, an umbrella group for all the co-operatives in Chéticamp. (Courtesy: Société Saint-Pierre)

Catholic clergy.[67] The active promotion of fishermen's organizations began as a result of the Royal Commission Investigating the Fisheries of the Maritime Provinces and of the Magdalen Islands that was set up by the federal government in 1927. Reverend Moses Coady, professor at St. Francis Xavier University, was appointed by the government to organize an educational campaign amongst fishermen with the aim of forming co-operatives throughout the Maritime Provinces. During the 1930s Father Coady's Antigonish Movement helped found numerous co-operative lobster factories and co-operatives for processing and marketing fish.[68] Although the first co-operative in Chéticamp was formed as early as 1915, the growth of co-operatives in the region was directly related to the economic realities in the fisheries and the influence of the Antigonish Movement.

In no other Acadian region did co-operatives become as

popular as they did in Chéticamp. Co-operatives still form an essential part of life. As Yvon Deveau, president of the Co-op, stated in 1984: "Co-operation is not just a credit union, a store or a factory, it is a way of life."[69] (TR) There are seven co-operatives in the region today and, according to membership statistics, most people belong to more than one. By contrast, the only co-operative movement that became firmly established in Argyle and Clare was the credit union, known as the "caisse populaire." However, credit unions in the Chéticamp area have considerably more members than in Clare and Argyle combined.[70] As the Acadians of Inverness County have only been represented twice in the Legislative Assembly (Moise J. Doucet and Hubert AuCoin) and have had very little impact at the municipal level, the co-operative movement has a special role and certainly constitutes a form of empowerment which political structures have not provided.

In 1936, the federal government expropriated lands in Cap-Rouge, an Acadian settlement north of Chéticamp, for the creation of the Cape Breton Highlands Park.[71] Designed to stimulate the economy of northern Cape Breton, the park coincided with the beginning of leisure travelling by automobile, and Chéticamp, located at the western end of the park, became the only Acadian region integrated into the Nova Scotia tourist industry. (Accessible by rail, Grand Pré became famous in the late 1800s—but Grand Pré ceased to be an Acadian settlement in 1755.) Of the thirteen motels located in the Acadian regions of Nova Scotia today, nine are in Chéticamp.

For its hooked rugs, Chéticamp has undoubtedly gained an international reputation. This cottage industry was started in 1922 by Lillian Burke, an American friend of the Alexander Graham Bell family residing in Baddeck. Through her influence, hooked mats that had been made in Chéticamp before this, were transformed with fine wool, and dyed in soft, contrasting colours that became the trade-mark of the cottage industry. In 1936, on the instigation of the well-known leader in the co-operative movement, Alexandre Boudreau, some of the women who were supplying rugs to Lillian Burke in New York decided to form their own group so they could market their rugs at a fairer price.[72] The Co-opérative artisanale, founded in 1963, provided a formal structure for the

The tourist industry began in Chéticamp after the creation of the Cape Breton Highlands National Park in 1936. (Courtesy: Nova Scotia Information Services)

production and sale of hooked rugs. The production has expanded considerably since the 1920s and in the 1980s the industry represented an annual income of over half a million dollars to the economy of Chéticamp, significantly increasing employment, especially for women at home.[73]

To a large extent the geographical isolation of Chéticamp contributed to the preservation of the French language and culture. Of all the Acadian regions in Nova Scotia, it has suffered the least from assimilation.[74] With a homogenous Acadian population in a limited territory, it has benefitted, like Clare, from a relatively strong tradition of French-language instruction in the local schools. The presence of French, Québécois and then Acadian priests gave French-language continuity to the Church, the dominant spiritual and social institution. The Acadians of Chéticamp form about 21 percent of the total population of Inverness County. Unlike their compatriots in Clare who form about 45 percent of the population of Digby County, the francophones of Inverness County have not had a representative voice in the Legislature.

Isle Madame

Isle Madame is the name of the largest island in an archipelago situated off the southwest coast of Cape Breton. Until recent years, well over half the population of Richmond County lived on this island. Arichat, the most important town on Isle Madame, is also the capital of Richmond County. Like Pubnico in Argyle, Petit-de-Grat on Isle Madame was settled by Acadians before the Deportation.

Fishermen have frequented the waters off Isle Madame and the south coast of Cape Breton Island for more than three centuries. The first Frenchmen to settle in this area, at least on a temporary basis, were brought out in the 1640s by Nicolas Denys who founded the short-lived fishing station of Saint-Pierre (later called Port-Toulouse, now known as St. Peters), located on a narrow stretch of land separating the Atlantic Ocean and the Bras D'Or Lakes.[75]

When France lost Acadie in 1713, it founded the colony of Ile Royale (Cape Breton) which was protected by the immense fortress at Louisbourg. It was the cod fishery, and not agriculture, that formed the economic basis of the new colony. In order to populate the island, France tried to entice Acadians to leave their fertile lands along the shores of the Bay of Fundy. For various reasons, very few of them were tempted by these invitations. In fact, recent research has shown that only 67 Acadian families moved to Cape Breton between 1713 and 1734 and even some of these families eventually moved back to mainland Nova Scotia.[76] The Acadians settled in the two main outports of Cape Breton—Port-Toulouse and Petit-de-Grat—and became involved in coastal trade with Louisbourg.

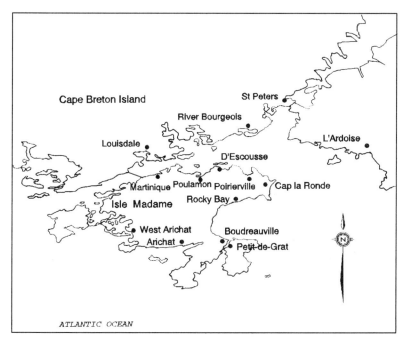

Map of Isle Madame. (Courtesy: Atlantic Direct)

Almost every Acadian in Richmond County today can claim descent from the cluster of families who immigrated to Cape Breton in the early part of the eighteenth century. Their family names are Coste, Petitpas, LaForest, Boudrot, Dugas, Boucher, Vigneau, Fougère, Langlois, Marchand, and Samson.[77]

By the time the Frenchman, Sieur de la Roque, carried out his detailed census of all the settlements on Ile Royale in 1752, there were about 35 Acadian families settled on Isle Madame along with several families from France. Sieur de la Roque provides the following description of life on the tiny island:

The nature of the soil is not suitable for cultivation, as in addition to the fact that fogs are constantly prevalent during the whole of spring, the quality of the soil can only be described as a mixture of earth largely composed of clay, and an infinite number of rough stones heaped upon the top of another…

The settlers on this island follow various callings, in order to secure a livelihood. Those who are not engaged in the cod fisheries, are employed in navigation during the summer, whilst in the winter they make cord wood, which they sell at 9 livres a cord, delivered at the coast, whilst as a general rule all the settlers endeavour to add to their earnings by finding keep for a few head of cattle. The whole coast is practicable for small vessels, and a landing can be very easily effected at almost any point...

Petit Degrat is suitable only for the codfishery. None of the people who are settled there have any other occupation. Fish are very abundant and none finer are found at Ile Royale...

The harbour of Grand Nerichac [Arichat] makes one of the finest ports that there is in the country. A survey shows that it is well fitted for those carrying on the codfishery by means of vessels.[78] (TR)

Hundreds of Acadians took refuge on Cape Breton, especially in Louisbourg, during the early 1750s. The majority of them were loaded onto ships and transported to France in 1758 after the fall of Louisbourg. A few of them, however, were able to escape this deportation and, along with the older Acadian families, went into hiding or fled to the French islands of St. Pierre and Miquelon. They gradually made their way back to the region they had once occupied. For example, in 1765 both Charles Martell and Homer Mombourquette, originally from Louisbourg, were living on the south coast of Cape Breton in the community of L'Ardoise.[79]

Several documents lead one to conclude that Isle Madame was not quite deserted between 1758 and 1763. There were Acadian families already established on Isle Madame when Charles Robin founded his fishing establishment in Arichat in 1765.[80] Normally the Jersey merchants returned to their native island in the late fall, but in 1768 Charles Robin decided to spend the winter in Arichat. In his diary, he refers to several Acadians including Rhéné LeBlanc, Simon and Charles Fougère, Claude Dugat, Rhéné Therriau, and Anselme Bellefontaine. In the following entries, for example, he gives an idea of the friendly relations he established with his neighbours with whom he conversed fluently in French.[81]

Tuesday
Feb. 21st
Geo. Bichard sewing a main sail for Rhéné Therriau's schooner, as we have nothing to do and Therriau is a good neighbour and has a great

Aerial photograph showing the Co-op buildings and the village of Petit-de-Grat in 1979. (Courtesy: Nova Scotia Information Services)

deal of work to do against the spring which made me offer him to get that job done for him.
Tuesday
April 11th
Early this morning went to the village and soon after came back with Anselme Bellefontaine's wife and her sister, as they promised yesterday to come and see me, being the last time they will venture over the ice this spring, after dinner went with them to the village.

In 1768 Lieutenant-Governor Francklin prepared a list of the inhabitants on Cape Breton Island who had made improvements to their land and who therefore should have been eligible for land titles. Seven names were mentioned with regard to Petit-de-Grat: Charles Fougère, Charles Dugas, Louis Boudreau, Joseph Boudreau, John Peters, Peter Fougère, and Joseph Gaudin.[82] The census of 1774 indicates that there were 400 inhabitants on Isle Madame, most of whom were concentrated in Petit-de-Grat and Arichat. According to the first resident missionary on Isle Madame, Father William Phelan, there was a chapel in Arichat when he came in 1786. Unfortunately the next 50 years of parish records for the whole of Isle Madame were lost when the presbytery in Arichat was destroyed by fire in 1838.[83]

Unlike the township of Clare, land was not made officially available to the Acadians who wished to settle in Richmond County and on Isle Madame in particular. The distribution of land throughout Cape Breton took place more haphazardly than on mainland Nova Scotia. As a result, the majority of settlers lived on Isle Madame for a long time, often more than 20 years, before they obtained titles to their land. As the amount of habitable land and water frontage was limited, Acadian migrations to Isle Madame came to an end by the early 1800s. In 1811, for example, there were approximately 1,200 inhabitants, 90 percent of whom were Acadian. The same census also indicates a surprisingly large number of livestock considering the poor soil: nearly a thousand sheep, about 500 head of cattle and around a dozen horses. Following the coastline around the archipelago, the main settlements of Isle Madame were D'Escousse, Rocky Bay, Petit-de-Grat, Arichat Harbour, Arichat, and West Arichat. Acadians also settled along the south coast of mainland Cape Breton in two main localities: L'Ardoise and River Bourgeois which lie a few kilometres on either side of the former French settlement of Port-Toulouse. By 1824, for instance, there were about 30 Acadian families living in River Bourgeois with surnames like Landry, Samson, Bourque, Boucher, Fougère, Pitre, and Babin.[84]

When settlers applied for titles to their land, they were often asked their age, where they were born and how long they had they had been living in Cape Breton. By selecting a few representative cases from the Cape Breton Land Papers, one can see that Isle Madame was resettled not only by descendants of families who had immigrated to Ile Royale in the early 1700s, but also by Acadians who had lived in exile for many years.[85] The following examples show the complex fabric of resettlement in Richmond County:

Charles Landry
- *requested title to his land in 1810*
- *he was 70 years old, had 9 children, 7 of whom were living in Cape Breton*
- *he was born in the territory of present-day New Brunswick in 1740*

- *he had been living in Arichat since 1780*

Nicholas Petitpas
- *requested title to his land in 1815*
- *he was 60 years old and had 9 children*
- *he was born in Louisbourg in 1755*
- *he had been living in D'Escousse since 1785*

Moses LeBlanc
- *requested title to his land in 1809*
- *he was 44 years old*
- *he was born in St. Malo (France) in 1765*
- *he had been living in Arichat since 1784*
- *he took the oath of allegiance in Arichat 1793*

Paul LeBlanc
- *requested title to his land in 1815*
- *he was 46 years old and had a wife and 2 children*
- *he was born in Belle-Isle-en-Mer (France) in 1769*
- *he had been living in Cape Breton (presumably Arichat) since 1775*

Cyprian Samson
- *requested title to his land in 1815*
- *he was 51 years old and had 12 children, all living with him*
- *he was born in Cape Breton in 1764*
- *he had been living in Petit-de-Grat since 1785*

Marie Babin
- *is one of the very rare women whose name appears in a petition for land*
- *she petitioned Governor Ainslie in 1818 for title to 140 hectares (340 acres) located in West Arichat for herself and her children, Joseph, Peter Paul, Abraham, Susan and Madeleine*
- *her husband, Pierre, died after receiving title to a lot of 90 hectares (230 acres) in 1803*
- *she was granted the land immediately*
- *Marie and Pierre Babin appear to have met and married in Arichat. Marie was born in Port-Toulouse and Pierre was born in the Grand Pré region and deported to Massachusetts with his family in 1755.*

As was the case elsewhere, Acadians were permitted to resettle provided they signed the oath of allegiance to the British monarch. Many Acadians on Isle Madame appear to have taken the oath in Arichat in 1793. This is no doubt due to the fact that between 1792 and 1793, several hundred Acadians who had taken refuge on the islands of St. Pierre and Miquelon, returned to Cape Breton, mainly to Isle Madame. They decided to leave the French islands because they refused to take an oath under the new constitution of France instituted in 1792 after the Revolution.[86] Such was the case of Father François Lejamtel who left Miquelon with about one hundred Acadians. As noted earlier by his own account, Father Lejamtel risked his life visiting the isolated missions of Cape Breton. For most of the 22 years he served Cape Breton, he was the only priest.

As with Chéticamp, the Acadians were attracted to Isle Madame because the Robin Company offered employment in the fishery. For a number of reasons, however, the company did not become a monopoly on Isle Madame, and consequently the fishery evolved differently from Chéticamp. First of all, Charles Robin suffered a setback in 1775 when his stores were burned by his American competitor, John Paul Jones. Several other fish merchants moved to Isle Madame partly as a result of Robin's weakened position, but mainly because of its location with respect to the fishing banks and the international trade routes. One of these companies belonged to the Janvrin family, also from Jersey. They were granted the large island off Arichat, now called Janvrin Island.

Another company was owned by Laurence Kavanaugh of Irish descent who expanded his operation from St. Peters to Isle Madame in the 1790s.[87] His father had originally established his business in Louisbourg in 1760. Kavanaugh was the first Catholic elected to the Legislative Assembly—several years before the abolition of the Test Oath. It would appear that government officials were more interested in his considerable fortune and influence than in the fact that he was of the Catholic faith!

The Jersey families associated with Isle Madame and Richmond County are Robin, Janvrin, Bourinot, Jean, Malzard, Hubert, Gurcy, LeViscount, LeLacheur, Fixott, Briand, and Mauger.[88] Despite the fact that they represented a very small percentage of the population, these families occupied virtually all the important judicial, governmental and military positions in Richmond County until the mid-1800s. This reflected not only the economic and political power of Protestant merchants but also the educational disadvantage of the Acadians. The Jersey families who first settled on Isle Madame were bilingual, well-educated and they had the distinct political advantage of belonging to the Church of England.

The Jersey merchants and the Kavanaughs were all dependent on Acadian manpower. The majority of Acadian men on Isle Madame were fishermen and sold their catches to these companies. However, unlike the situation in Chéticamp, the Jersey merchants did not own all the fishing vessels on Isle Madame. A large number of schooners were built, owned and operated by Acadians. Some of the most famous Acadian names associated with the shipping business throughout the 1800s were Thomas LeNoir, Charles Boudreau, Isidore LeBlanc, Benjamin Gerroir, Elias Boudreau, Mellam Poirrier, Simon Babin, and Dominique Girouard.[89] The Jersey companies did, however, maintain their monopoly in the area of equipment and supplies—including commodities like salt, indispensable for curing fish.

Monseigneur Plessis, Bishop of Quebec, made two pastoral visits to Nova Scotia, the first in 1812 and the second in 1815. He visited Arichat on both occasions and was particularly impressed by the activity and appearance of the port in 1815. The following entry in his diary gives an idea of the export trade and the growing prosperity of Isle Madame. Bishop Plessis approved of the trades in the fishery and shipbuilding, but he considered the coasting trade immoral and dangerous, because it often implied smuggling the "demon rum."

In the midst of these spiritual dangers, Arichat has assumed an entirely different aspect materially. Even within the last three years there is a notable difference and a considerable betterment. The houses are more attractively constructed, and the people dress better. They eat better food, such as bread (which the Acadians know so well how to do without); not that their fields produce more grain, for they do not cultivate them, but because they have money enough to buy flour.

There is also much more activity in the harbour. Many more ships come and go, and stiff bargains are made. Some of these ships carry coal from Sydney, and others plaster from Antigonish. Some even go to the

Strait of Belle Isle to gather from its rocks eggs of sea-gulls, starlings,
magpies, cormorants and other sea birds...[90] (TR)

The economic growth of Arichat attracted a number of Irish,
English and Scottish immigrants during the 1820s. As a result of
this influx of English-speaking settlers, the relative percentage of
Acadians in Arichat, where almost half the population of Isle
Madame was concentrated, dropped from 90 percent in 1811 to
66 percent in 1838. These new migrations into the area had much
less impact in other parts of the island. Petit-de-Grat, West Arichat,
Poulamon and D'Escousse were still Acadian and French-language
strongholds in the 1880s.

Because of its thriving economy and its central location for
travel by water, Arichat was chosen as the seat of the new diocese
that was created to serve the eastern counties of Nova Scotia where
thousands of Scottish Catholics had immigrated in the 1790s and
early 1800s. The parish church of Notre Dame l'Assomption in
Arichat became a cathedral when the first Bishop of Arichat was
ordained in 1844. Although the seat of the diocese was transferred
to Antigonish in 1880, Arichat was an important political and
educational centre.

Several elementary schools were established on Isle Madame
by the late 1820s although all the teachers were English-speaking.
The major advances in education were made during the 1850s
under the influence of the second Bishop of Arichat, Rt. Rev.
Colin Francis MacKinnon. As soon as he took office, Bishop
MacKinnon expressed his eagerness to establish an institution in
Arichat that would serve as a seminary and classical college for lay
students and future priests. Most of the students who attended
Bishop MacKinnon's Seminary-College were Scottish although
there were a few Acadians. In 1855 after only two years of
operation on Isle Madame, the Seminary-College was moved to
Antigonish where, in 1866, it became a co-educational institution,
St. Francis Xavier University.[91]

By the 1850s Acadian leaders throughout the Maritimes were
emerging to spearhead the movement for educational and linguistic
rights for French-speaking citizens. One of these leaders was Father
Hubert Girroir. He began his ministry in Arichat in 1854. Father
Hubert Girroir was the first Acadian born in Nova Scotia to become

The church of Notre Dame l'Assomption became a cathedral in 1844 when the first bishop of Arichat was ordained. Photo taken by E.G.L. Wetmore in 1953. (Courtesy: Nova Scotia Museum)

a priest. A native of Tracadie, he served in Arichat, Chéticamp and Havre-Boucher. For almost 30 years he fought for French-language instruction in schools frequented by Acadian children—not an easy task in a diocese dominated by Scottish priests who, like the Irish, believed in the future of an English-language Church.[92]

An academy or high school continued to function in Arichat under Father Girroir's direction. He succeeded in obtaining members of the French-speaking order of the Christian Brothers from Montreal to run the school from 1860 to 1866, but they were obliged to leave as a result of Charles Tupper's Free School Act of 1864 which placed certain stipulations on the qualifications of headmasters of schools receiving public funds. In an attempt to enable the Christian Brothers to stay and thus ensure the existence of a French secondary school on Isle Madame, Father Girroir addressed the following letter to the Premier of Nova Scotia, Sir Charles Tupper:

It seems that there is a fatality attached to the Acadian race: for since thirteen years that I have been in public life, I have worked like a man at my post, beggared myself for the education of the country, and, the moment that matters were assuming a fair state of existence, here comes a death blow that blasts all my anticipations. It seems that, whenever an Acadian community is on the point of taking position among others, there must be something to thwart the efforts of many years. God help us! Nevertheless, my confidence in you makes me hope that you, Hon. Sir, will come to our rescue by granting us what we justly expect.[93]

Neither Father Girroir nor any of his successors were able to obtain members of a French-language religious order to take over the Arichat Academy. As a result, it continued to function with lay teachers, several of whom were Acadian graduates of St. Francis Xavier, including Rémi Benoit, a native of D'Escousse. Young girls were more fortunate to the extent that a convent school was opened in Arichat in 1856 under the direction of the Sisters of the Congregation of Notre Dame of Montreal. A second convent school was opened later in West Arichat. According to a prospectus at the end of the 1870s the convent in Arichat offered a full "course of instruction in the French and English languages."[94]

The first Acadian from Cape Breton to sit in the Legislative Assembly was Henry Martell, elected in 1840. For 19 consecutive years he represented the riding of Arichat Township and when this seat was abolished in 1859, he sat as a member for Richmond County until 1863. Only ten Acadians, all residents of Isle Madame, have been elected to represent Richmond County in the Legislative Assembly. Judging from the Debates and Proceedings of the House of Assembly, one of the most influential and outspoken of these politicians was Isidore LeBlanc who sat from 1878 to 1886. Twenty years after Father Girroir's efforts in Arichat, Isidore LeBlanc was still struggling to obtain French-language instruction. On April 17, 1879 he addressed his fellow members in French— a unique event in the history of the Legislative Assembly— requesting that a bonus be given to French-language teachers so that Acadian children could receive instruction in their mother tongue. He stressed the enormous difficulty of acquiring knowledge conveyed in the English language, a language with which the children were unacquainted.

The annual ceremony of the blessing of the fleet. Petit-de-Grat, 1989. (Courtesy: Fédération acadienne de la Nouvelle-Ecosse)

By the time Isidore LeBlanc was elected to the Legislative Assembly the economy of Isle Madame had already begun a slow decline. Perhaps one of the hardest blows to the economy was the construction of St. Peters Canal begun in 1854 and completed in 1869.[95] Within a few years the flourishing trade that had characterized Arichat since 1815 was shifted through the Bras D'Or Lakes to the Sydneys. The extension of the railway on the mainland from

New Glasgow to Mulgrave in 1880 and then on Cape Breton from Point Tupper to Sydney in 1891 also diverted traffic away from the harbours of Isle Madame. When Father Casgrain visited Cape Breton during his famous pilgrimage to the Maritimes in 1885, he travelled to Baddeck via St. Peters Canal. He also visited Arichat but was struck by the dilapidated state of the houses and the almost deserted port.[96] The steam ferry linking the island with mainland Cape Breton had been destroyed by fire in June 1885. In an effort to provide better communication with Cape Breton, on March 19, 1886, Isidore LeBlanc spoke to the Legislative Assembly in favour of the construction of a bridge across Lennox Passage. The drawbridge was not built until 1916.

Although the golden age of shipping and shipbuilding had come to an end on Isle Madame, the fisheries continued to play an important role especially with the development of lobster canning factories and the gradual modernization of fish processing. Like Chéticamp, Isle Madame benefitted from the co-operative movement in the 1930s and it is still an integral part of the life of the community. Fish plants continue to be the main source of income, although for many generations young Acadians have been forced to leave Isle Madame in search of employment. Presently more and more Acadians are employed in the heavy industries of Port Hawkesbury where English is the language of work.

Despite the economic factors that have accelerated the assimilation rate in recent decades, there are two French-language schools on Isle Madame. There are numerous socio-cultural associations that operate in French and that are affiliated with Acadian provincial associations. The Société historique acadienne de l'Ile Madame, for example, has actively promoted the creation of an Acadian Village that would not only stimulate the economy but also provide tangible proof of the very important role that Isle Madame once played in the history of Nova Scotia.

Pomquet, Tracadie and Havre-Boucher

Three harbour locations, Pomquet, Tracadie, and Havre-Boucher, situated along the shores of St. Georges Bay were colonized by returning Acadians and several French immigrants between 1772 and 1790. As one can detect from the names, a number of the

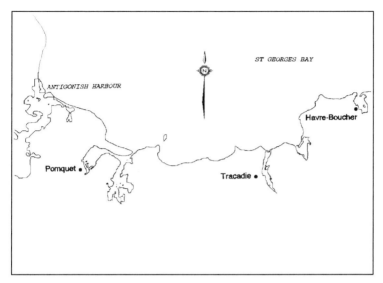

Map of Pomquet, Tracadie and Havre-Boucher. (Courtesy: Atlantic Direct)

families were descendants of the Acadians who immigrated to Ile Royale in the early 1700s.

Of the three communities, Tracadie appears to be the oldest.[97] Pierre Benoit and his family moved from Arichat to Tracadie around 1772. He was later joined by the Fougère brothers, also from Arichat. Other families arrived in the mid-1780s. These included the Girroirs and the Bonnevies from Chezzetcook and the Deslauriers family, originally from Quebec.

Havre-Boucher was founded in the 1780s by Claude Decostes and family from Arichat. Other families who had spent years in exile in St. Malo arrived in Havre-Boucher via the Robin Company establishments in Arichat and Bonaventure, in the Gaspé region. Family names associated with this group of settlers were Fougère, Daigre, LeBlanc, Dugas, Côté, and LeParou.

The first Acadian families to settle in Pomquet arrived from St. Malo in 1772, and like their compatriots they appear to have arranged passage back to the New World with the merchants from the nearby Isle of Jersey. The surnames of the founding families of Pomquet were Broussard, Duon, Doiron, Lamarre, and Vincent. These families were joined in the 1780s by another group of

Acadians who had also made their way from St. Malo. As was often the case, these families were related by marriage to the founding families. This second group included Broussards, Landrys, Boudrots, and Melansons, and Rosia who all received land grants situated along Pomquet Harbour and Taylor Creek.

Over the years, these three villages have been linked to Arichat and to Chéticamp, both economically and culturally. Until the construction of the Canso Causeway in 1955, the Strait of Canso separating mainland Nova Scotia and Cape Breton Island constituted a natural trade route to the Atlantic Ocean. Throughout the nineteenth century, lumber, shingles, and barrel staves were shipped from Pomquet and Tracadie to Arichat.

From the days of the first resident priest, Father Amable Pichard in 1803, until 1863, all three villages formed part of the Tracadie parish. A number of priests served the Acadians of both Antigonish County and Cape Breton: Father Fiset ministered for ten years in Havre-Boucher before going to Chéticamp; Father Hubert Girroir spent the last 14 years of his life in Havre-Boucher, a few miles from his native village of Tracadie; Father Charles P. Martell (brother of Henry Martell, the first elected Acadian representative from Cape Breton) served as parish priest of Tracadie from 1860 to 1877. Given the proximity of St. Francis Xavier University, it is not surprising that the influence of the Antigonish Movement extended to Havre-Boucher, an important fishing centre, where a co-operative was formed in 1932.

Unlike the communities along St. Marys Bay and in the Chéticamp region, Havre-Boucher, Tracadie and Pomquet are not adjacent to one another, nor were they settled exclusively by Acadians. As a result, many of the Acadians in Antigonish County were assimilated very quickly into the culture of the majority. For example, in 1876, Pascal Poirier met at least one Acadian family in Tracadie who no longer spoke French in the home. Pascal Poirier, a native of Shediac, New Brunswick, was a well-known advocate of the right of the Acadians to take pride in their language and heritage. He became a prominent member of the Société nationale l'Assomption, the interprovincial association that spearheaded the conferences held in the 1880s at which the Acadian flag and national anthem (*Ave Maris Stella*) were chosen. (The Société still

exists today under the name of the Société nationale des Acadiens).
Pascal Poirier also visited Pomquet and Havre-Boucher where he
met with Father Hubert Girroir. In the account of his travels in
eastern Nova Scotia and Cape Breton, Poirier describes several
insidious and blatant forms of racism that Acadians were forced to
endure and that certainly did not contribute to the preservation of
their language and culture. One of the incidents he relates took
place in Pomquet. In describing the event, Pascal Poirier expresses
his anger and outrage, but he also provides a positive role model of
pride and conviction.

*On the road to Pomquet I met a farmer whom I invited to climb into
my carriage. As we drove along, we chatted.*
*— If you're going to see the priest, he said, you'll have to enter the
presbytery through the back door.*
— Why's that?
*— Because us French folk have to go through the kitchen when we go to
see him.*
— And what about other people?
— Oh well, the English are allowed in the front door.
I was filled with indignation.
— We'll see about that, I said to him.
I headed straight for the presbytery.
*— I wish to see the parish priest, I said in French to the plump young girl
who answered the door.*
— All right. Go by the other door, she said in English.
*— I will enter through the same door as the Christians, and not through
the back door with the dogs, I responded in a loud voice. At this point
the priest appeared and said in English:*
— You want to see me, Sir.
— Oui, Monsieur, I replied.
*— Entrez, alors, he said in very good French. All the priests in the
Maritimes attend the Seminary in Montreal or Quebec where they
learn to speak our language.*[98] (TR)

As was the case in other dispersed and ethnically mixed
communities, the position of the French language in this region of
Nova Scotia was considerably weakened with each passing generation. Today, of the three communities, only Pomquet with a

population of 427 in 1981 has a school where classes are taught in French. In recent years, Pomquet has celebrated its Acadian heritage by holding an annual winter carnival in February. One of the seven regional offices of the Fédération acadienne de la Nouvelle-Ecosse is located in Pomquet.[99]

Chezzetcook

The Halifax-Dartmouth area constitutes the largest urban centre in the Atlantic region. Because of a lack of employment opportunities, over the years many rural inhabitants, including Acadians, have been forced to leave their communities and move to the urban and industrial centres of Canada and the United States. Acadians form the majority of the estimated 7,000 francophones scattered throughout the Halifax-Dartmouth metropolitan area. In the vast majority of cases, English has, by necessity, become the dominant language of these Acadians—both with regard to schooling and the workplace.

Quite apart from the thousands of individuals who have migrated to the metropolitan area in the twentieth century, there is a small Acadian population in Halifax County that dates back to the 1760s, if not earlier.[100] These Acadians live in the neighbouring communities of West Chezzetcook and Grand Desert about 30 kilometres from Dartmouth on the Eastern Shore. Although few of their inhabitants under the age of 60 speak their ancestral language today, the villages retained many of their Acadian customs and traditions until the 1950s.

As was noted with regard to Dominique Pothier who settled in Sainte-Anne-du-Ruisseau, several hundred Acadians were brought to Halifax as prisoners between 1758 and 1762. Some were deported and some were permitted to resettle in various parts of the province. A certain number of these former prisoners made their way across Halifax harbour to Chezzetcook—perhaps because of the marshlands, but more likely because it was a Micmac settlement known to French missionaries for many years.[101] Family names, still common today in West Chezzetcook and Grand Desert, which can be traced to these former prisoners are Boudreau, Bellefontaine, Lapierre and Wolfe. Despite the appearance, the latter name is French. Augustin Wolfe was born in Alsace, France, in 1721 and appears as a colonist in Halifax in 1751. He seems to have become sympathetic to the French cause in 1752 and after various travels was taken prisoner in 1761.

In addition to these former prisoners, there was another group of Acadians, all of whom had been living in Cape Breton, who were granted permission by Governor Lawrence to settle in Chezzetcook as a gesture of "indulgence for their past Services to the English Government."[102] This group included names like Petitpas, Bonin (now Bonang), Roma, Manet, and Mayet. Chezzetcook also became the home for the Breau and the Bonnevie families from the French island of Miquelon and for Simon Julien, a deserter from the Napoleonic wars. By the beginning of the 1770s there were about 12 Acadian families in Chezzetcook and when Monseigneur Plessis, Bishop of Quebec, made his last pastoral visit to Nova Scotia in 1815, there were 47 families.

The first lay person to bring the Acadians of Chezzetcook to the attention of the public was the American writer, Frederic S. Cozzens, who visited Nova Scotia in 1856. His book entitled *Acadia; or, a Month with the Bluenoses*, published in New York, is considered to be the first travel guide to Nova Scotia. Cozzens came to this province because he, like countless others, was profoundly moved by Henry Wadsworth Longfellow's epic poem called *Evangeline* which first appeared in 1847. This famous American poet used the tragedy of the expulsion of the Acadians from Grand Pré as a backdrop for the story of a fictitious Acadian by the name of Evangeline Bellefontaine. Almost instantly Evangeline became a symbol of the Acadians and a folk heroine who embodied the romantic ideals of purity, courage, and faithfulness.

To a certain extent, Cozzens exploits the extraordinary popularity of *Evangeline* in order to captivate his own readers. Despite his enthusiasm for Longfellow's poetry, Cozzens makes a clear distinction between fiction and reality. In his introduction, for example, he explains the origin of the two ambrotypes (improved version of the daguerreotype photograph) included at the beginning of his book. As Cozzens states in the following lines, the two women from Chezzetcook in the ambrotypes are no doubt the first Acadians ever to have had their picture taken:

It may interest the reader to know that these [ambrotype photographs] *are the first, the only likenesses of the real Evangelines of Acadia. The women of Chezzetcook appear at daybreak in the city of Halifax, and as soon as the sun is up vanish like the dew. They usually have a basket of fresh eggs, a brace or two of worsted* [woolen] *socks, a bottle of fir-balsam to sell.*[103]

After having discovered and photographed these modern "Evangelines" at the market in Halifax, Cozzens and his travelling companion decide to visit Chezzetcook; on their way, they meet two more Acadians:

We are re-reading Evangeline *line by line. And here, at this turn of the road, we encounter two Acadian peasants... As we salute the pair, we learn they have been walking on their way since dawn from distant Chezzetcook: the man speaks English with a strong French accent; the maiden only the language of her people on the banks of the Seine...*[104]

Cozzens arrives at his destination and writes:

Meanwhile let us open our eyes again upon the present, just below us lies the village and harbour of Chezzetcook...

Occasional little cottages nestle among these green banks, not the Acadian houses of the poem, "with thatched roofs and dormer windows projecting", but comfortable, homely-looking [simple or plain] *buildings of modern shapes, shingled and unweather-cocked.*[105]

Perhaps because of the interest generated by Cozzens' book and perhaps due to the proximity to Halifax, the Nova Scotia Museum possesses the oldest existing traditional Acadian costumes. All the items in this unique collection originate from Chezzetcook and date, for the most part, from about 1850 or earlier. Several of the pieces, including a bridal cap, a large black kerchief, a cotton-print jacket and a striped homespun skirt, were worn by Marguerite Bellefontaine who was married in 1843 and who died in 1910. The long black and white homespun skirt was worn by Madame Bellefontaine on Sundays and holidays. On ordinary days, at least until the early 1900s, the Acadian women of Chezzetcook would usually wear a black kerchief over the head and a plain grey homespun skirt. The Nova Scotia Museum also has in its collection the white waistcoat worn on festive occasions by Marguerite's husband, Charles Bellefontaine (1816-1902). Normally the men

An Acadian woman from Chezzetcook in 1856. Lithograph based on ambrotype photograph. (*Acadia; or, a Month with the Bluenoses* by F.S. Cozzens; Public Archives of Nova Scotia)

from Chezzetcook wore a grey homespun coat and trousers and a home-knitted white sweater with blue spots.[106]

Numerous visitors to Nova Scotia, including Bishop Plessis, commented on the sobriety and simplicity of the traditional Acadian costume.[107] Until the late 1800s, pressures within the communities tended to prevent men and especially woman from adopting new styles. As was seen in the case of the two young women in Church Point at the beginning of the nineteenth century, it was Father Sigogne who discouraged any new frivolous items of clothing. By the end of the century, however, it is quite clear that some young Acadian women "rebelled" against the traditional dress of their mothers. The following incident took place around 1885 in a train between Yarmouth and Digby. It is related by Father Henri-Raymond Casgrain in his travel book entitled *Un pèlerinage au pays d'Evangéline*. In this case, the old and the new sit side by side. The pressures to "modernize" and the pressures to respect tradition are all operating at the same time; they relate to the choice of clothing, the choice of language and even to the choice of life-style.

Speaking of this obsession to anglicize, one of my colleagues told me about a stern lesson he was obliged to give not long ago. He was an Irish priest from an Acadian parish who was travelling from Yarmouth to Digby. Two young girls, both with good Acadian names, got on the train dressed in the latest styles from the United States and they were talking to each other in English. All of a sudden they saw two young Acadian women wearing the "cape normande" or black kerchief on their heads.

— Look at those two French women! How ridiculous! said one of them in English. And they proceeded to burst into laughter.

The good priest, whom they had not noticed, turned to them indignantly, scoured sternly and said in a voice loud enough for the other passengers to hear:

— What, are you not ashamed of yourselves. You, Acadians, your nationality makes you blush! As a matter of fact, I happen to know you. You are certainly not worth these two good women that you are making fun of. I also happen to know them and they are excellent mothers, the pride of their parish. As for you... [108] (TR)

Photo taken by Paul Yates of Acadian women from Clare in 1923. (Courtesy: Public Archives of Nova Scotia)

NOTES

1. Michel Poirier, *Les Acadiens aux îles Saint-Pierre et Miquelon 1758-1928*, Les Editions d'Acadie, 1984, p. 20; Stephen A. White, "The Arichat Frenchmen in Gloucester: Problems of Identification and Identity" in *The New England Historical and Genealogical Register*, Vol. CXXXI, April 1977, p. 84.

2. John Reid, *Six Crucial Decades*, op. cit., p. 50.; See also Colonial Office Records, CO 217, Vol. 4, doc. 230, 1764, P.A.N.S.; Captain John Knox notes in his journal of 1757 that 48 Acadian families who had been living along the Annapolis River managed to escape to the mountain. *Knox Historical Journal of the Campaigns in North America*, The Champlain Society, Toronto, 1914, vol. I, p. 114, P.A.N.S.

3. Mason Wade, "After the Grand Dérangement: The Acadians' Return to the Gulf of St. Lawrence and to Nova Scotia," *The American Review of Canadian Studies*, Vol. 5, No. 1, Spring 1975.

4. Letter dated May 15, 1764 from the Colonial Office to Montague Wilmot, Governor of Nova Scotia (C.O. 218, pp. 416-418), P.A.N.S.

5. Lieutenant-Governor Michael Francklin permitted the Acadians to return to Nova Scotia and obtain land by Order-in-Council, September 28, 1764. (see: Alphonse Deveau, *Along the Shores of St. Mary's Bay*, Imprimerie de l'Université Sainte-Anne, 1977, vol. I, p.40).

6. Re Protestant inhabitants, see letter dated December 15, 1763, from Colonial Office to Governor Wilmot, (C.O. 218, p. 257), P.A.N.S.; Re "no legal obstruction," see Hillsborough, Secretary of State in Whitehall to Lieutenant-Governor of Nova Scotia, C.O. 218, vol. 25, 1768, P.A.N.S.

Argyle

7. Father Clarence d'Entremont, "Le Cap Sable: ses établissements acadiens avant la dispersion," *La Société historique acadienne*, cahier 14, vol. II,

No. 4, 1967, pp. 167-172.; *Histoire du Cap-Sable de l'An mil au Traité de Paris (1763)*, Herbert Publications, 1981, Vol. 2, p. 670; Vol. 3, pp. 1043-1972; Vol. 4, pp. 1910-1927.

8. Father Clarence d'Entremont, "Le Cap-Sable: ses établissements acadiens avant la dispersion," op. cit., pp. 169-170; *Histoire du Cap-Sable de l'An mil au Traité de Paris (1763)*, op. cit., Vol. 4, p. 2081; "Histoire de Publico" in *Les régions acadiennes de la Nouvelle-Ecosse: histoire et anecdotes*, Centre Acadien, Université Sainte-Anne, 1982, p. 50.

9. Neil Boucher, "Les Acadiens du Sud-Ouest de la Nouvelle-Ecosse 1760-1850," *Les Cahiers de la Société historique acadienne*, Vol. 21, No. 4, 1990, p. 79.

10. Father Clarence d'Entremont, *Histoire de Wedgeport*, p.20, P.A.N.S.; See also Régis Brun, "Liste des prisonniers acadiens au fort Edward," *Les Cahiers de la Société historique acadienne*, vol. 3, No. 4, 1969, pp. 158-164. See also: Joan Bourque Campbell, *L'Histoire de la paroisse de Saint-Anne-du-Ruisseau*, Ed. Lescarbot, 1985.

11. "Voyage de Rameau de Saint-Père en Acadie 1860," in *Les Cahiers de la Société historique acadienne*, vol. 37, 1972, pp. 303-306.; For a series of photos taken in forties see: John Durant, "Acadia Utopia," *Saturday Evening Post*, April 19, 1947, P.A.N.S.

12. L'abbé H.-R. Casgrain, *Un pèlerinage au pays d'Evangéline*, Paris, Libraire Léopold Cerf, 1890 (4th ed.), p. 333.

13. Désiré d'Eon, *Histoires de Chez-Nous, Faits et anecdotes d'un temps qui n'est plus*, Yarmouth: L'Imprimerie Lescarbot Ltée, 1977, pp. 10-11.

14. Campbell and MacLean, *Beyond the Atlantic Roar: A Study of Nova Scotia Scots*, McClelland and Stewart Ltd., 1974, p.121.

15. Samuel P. Arsenault, "Geography and the Acadians," in *The Acadians of the Maritimes*, op. cit. p.113 and p.123.

16. *Diary of a Frenchman*, edited and translated by J. Alphonse Deveau, Halifax: Nimbus Publishing Ltd., 1990, p. 71.

17. Ibid., p. 73

18. Beamish Murdoch, *A History of Nova Scotia, or Acadie*, Halifax, James Barnes Printer, 1867, p. 576.

19. Neil Boucher, *The Development of an Acadian Village*, Editions Lescarbot, 1974, pp.45-47.

20. Philippe Doucet, "Politics and the Acadians," *The Acadians in the Maritimes*, op. cit., p.229.

21. *Le Courrier*, May 10, 1989.

22. *Le Courrier*, June 27, 1990; Jan. 4, 1989; Oct. 7, 1987; Nov. 9, 1991. See also: *Les Héritiers de Lord Durham*, document prepared by the Fédération des Francophones hors Québec and made public May 1977, Section on Nova Scotia, p. 29; *La Vie acadienne en Nouvelle-Ecosse*, Université Sainte-Anne, 1985, vol. 2, p.73.

Clare

23. J. Alphonse Deveau, *Along the Shores of Saint Mary's Bay*, op. cit., Vol. I, p.39.
24. Ibid., p. 40; Father P.M. Dagnaud, *Les Français du Sud-Ouest de la Nouvelle-Ecosse*, Librairie Centrale, (Besançon, France), 1905, p.5.
25. J. Alphonse Deveau, "Histoire de la Baie Sainte-Marie" in *Les régions acadiennes de la Nouvelle-Ecosse*, op. cit., pp. 24-25; see also Régis Brun, "La liste des prisonniers acadiens au fort Edward," *Les Cahiers de la Société historique acadienne*, vol. 3, No. 4, 1969, pp. 158-164;
26. J. Alphonse Deveau, *Les personnes éminentes*, Editions Lescarbot, 1988, pp. 87-89, pp. 74-77.
27. Neil Boucher, "Les Acadiens du Sud-Ouest de la Nouvelle-Ecosse 1760-1850" in *Les Cahiers de la Société historique acadienne*, vol. 21, No. 4, 1190, p. 79. It should be noted that 400 may be too low since Denaut refers only to Tousquet or Wedgeport.
28. G. P. Gould, A.J. Semple, *Our Land: The Maritimes, The Basis of the Indian Claim in the Maritime Provinces of Canada*, St. Anne's Point Press, 1980, p. 44.
29. J. Alphonse Deveau, *Les personnes éminentes*, op. cit., p. 87. See also: Neil Boucher, "Les Acadiens du Sud-Ouest de la Nouvelle-Ecosse 1760-1850" in *Les Cahiers de la Société historique acadienne*, Vol. 21, No. 4, 1990, p. 82.
30. *Diary of a Frenchman*, op. cit., p. 93.
31. Father P. M. Dagnaud, *Les Français du Sud-Ouest de la Nouvelle-Ecosse*, Librairie Centrale, (Besançon, France), 1905, p. 133.
32. J. Alphonse Deveau, *La Ville Française*, Les Editions Ferland, 1968, p. 79.
33. J. Alphonse Deveau, *Les personnes éminentes*, op. cit., pp. 130-132.
34. Father P. M. Dagnaud, *Les Français du Sud-Ouest de la Nouvelle Ecosse*, op. cit,, pp. 255-256.
35. J. Alphonse Deveau, *La Ville Française*, op. cit., pp. 105-107.
36. Neil Boucher, "Les Acadiens du Sud-Ouest de la Nouvelle-Ecosse 1760-1850," op. cit., p. 87.
37. Father P. M. Dagnaud, *Les Français du Sud-Ouest de la Nouvelle-Ecosse*, Librairie Centrale, (Besançon, France), 1905, pp. 167-168.
38. Neil Boucher, "Les Acadiens du Sud-Ouest de la Nouvelle-Ecosse," op. cit., p. 87.
39. J. Alphonse Deveau, *La Ville Française*, op. cit., p. 144, p. 167.
40. Léon Thériault, "The Acadianization of the Catholic Church in Acadia (1763-1953)," in *The Acadians of the Maritimes*, op. cit., pp. 272-339.
41. René LeBlanc and Micheline Laliberté, *Sainte-Anne: collège et université 1890-1990*, Université Sainte-Anne, 1990, p. 302, pp. 297-330; see also: *The State of Minority-Language Education in the Provinces and*

Territories of Canada, The Council of Ministers of Education, 1983, pp. 190-192; J. Alphonse Deveau, *La Ville française*, op. cit., pp. 167-177; Edith (Comeau) Tufts, *Acadienne de Clare*, Edith Tufts, 1977, p.86.

42. Karin Flikeid, "A Comparative Study of Nova Scotia Acadian French," Final Report, SSHRCC Grant, p. 4; "Unity and Diversity in Acadian Phonology: An Overview Based on Comparisons among the Nova Scotia Varieties," in *Journal of the Atlantic Provinces Linguistic Association*, vol. 10, 1988, pp. 63-110.

Minudie

43. For details on the original grants and subsequent acquisitions, see: John Clarence Webster, *Joseph Frederick Wallet Desbarres*, Shediac, 1933, pp. 64-65. See also: A.H. Clark, op. cit., p. 109, pp. 221-222., pp. 347-349.

44. Mason Wade, "After the Grand Dérangement: The Acadians' Return to the Gulf of St. Lawrence and to Nova Scotia," *The American Review of Canadian Studies*, Vol. 5, No. 1, 1975, p. 61.

45. Régis Brun, "Un brin d'histoire de Menoudie, Nappan et Maccan," *La Société historique acadienne*, Cahier 13, pp. 90-99.

46. G.N.D. Evans, *Uncommon Obdurate: the Several Public Careers of J.F.W. Desbarres*, University of Toronto Press, 1969, p. 36.

47. Mason Wade, "After the Grand Dérangement: The Acadians' Return to the Gulf of St. Lawrence and to Nova Scotia," op. cit., pp. 61-62.

48. Lois Kernaghan, "J.F.W. Desbarres and Mary Cannon: a man and his mistress," *Acadiensis*, Fall 1981, p. 35. See also the *Desbarres Papers*, Section 5, pp. 4111-4127 and pp. 4136-4142, P.A.N.S.

49. Judging from the signatory marks on the notes, bonds and leases in the *Desbarres Papers*, the Acadian men were illiterate in 1800. See, for example, Section 5, p. 4137.

Chéticamp

50. Surveyors Franquet in 1752 and Holland in 1768 quoted in Father Anselme Chiasson, *Chéticamp: History and Acadian Traditions*, translation of updated 1962 French edition, Breakwater, 1986, p. 24. See also: B.A. Balcom, *The Cod Fishery of Isle Royale: 1713-58*, Ottawa, 1984, p.7.

51. Nicolas Denys, *Description and Natural History of the Coasts of North American (Acadia)*, translated and edited by William F. Ganong, Toronto: The Champlain Society, 1908, pp. 185-186.

52. Harold A. Innis, *The Cod Fisheries: The History of an International Economy*, Toronto: Ryerson Press, 1940, pp. 277-279, pp. 190-192; Mgr. Donat Robichaud, *Le Grand Chipagan: Histoire de Shippagan*, Mgr. Donat Robichaud, 1976, pp. 166-167; Father Anselme Chiasson, op. cit., p.26.

53. See letter from Philippe Robin to Simon Comeau intercepted by the

French authorities in 1772, quoted in Ernest Martin, *Les exilés acadiens en France au XVIIIe siècle*, Paris: Librairie Hachette, 1936, p. 90.

54. Father Anselme Chiasson, op. cit., pp. 26-27; Georges Arsenault, *The Island Acadians*, translated by Sally Ross, Ragweed Press, 1989, pp.56-59.

55. Father Anselme Chiasson, op. cit., pp. 32-35, pp. 291-294;

56. Father Anselme Chiasson, op. cit., pp. 26-27; Father Anselme Chiasson, "Les Quartoze Vieux de Chéticamp," speech given in 1980 by Father Chiasson, published by the Société Saint-Pierre, 1981.

57. Father Charles Aucoin, centennial calendar 1985: Le Bicentenaire de Chéticamp.

58. Father Anselme Chiasson, op. cit., 103-104; Georges Arsenault, op. cit., pp. 56-59.

59. A.A. Johnston, *A History of the Catholic Church in Eastern Nova Scotia*, St. Francis Xavier University Press, Antigonish, 1971, Vol. I, p. 171.

60. Father Anselme Chiasson, op. cit., pp. 130-135.

61. Laura Sadowsky, "The Chéticamp Waltham Connection: A Study of Acadian Ethnic Identity," unpublished Master's thesis, Université Laval, 1987, p. 31.

62. Father Anselme Chiasson, op. cit., p. 65. The title of the company changed over the years: Philippe Robin and Company, Charles Robin and Company, Charles Robin, Collas and Company, Robin, Jones and Whitman and Company; see also: Harold A. Innis, op. cit., p. 428.

63. Father Anselme Chiasson, op. cit., pp. 66-68; see also: Harold A. Innis, op. cit., pp. 282-283.

64. Laura Sadowsky, op. cit., p. 27.

65. Father Anselme Chiasson, op. cit., p. 71.

66. Laura Sadowsky, op. cit., p. 30.

67. Jean Chaussade, *La pêche et les pêcheurs des Provinces Maritimes*, P.U.M., Montreal, 1983, p. 236. See also: Chapters 1 and 2 of *Une force qui nous appartient: la Fédération des caisses populaires acadiennes, 1936-1986* by Jean Daigle, Ed. d'Acadie, 1990.

68. Harold A. Innis, op. cit. pp. 438-441.

69. *La Vie Acadienne en Nouvelle-Ecosse*, Université Sainte-Anne, Centre de ressources pédagogiques, 1985, vol. 2., p. 53.

70. Ibid., pp. 52-53.

71. Father Anselme Chiasson, op. cit., p. 88; see also: Réjean Aucoin, *Cap-Rouge: sur les traces des habitants, Chéticamp*, Les Amis du Plein Air. Aucoin gives the names of the 15 families expropriated and the history of the settlement founded around 1821.

72. Father Anselme Chiasson, op. cit., pp. 87-89.

73. Father Anselme Chiasson and Annie-Rose Deveau, *L'histoire des tapis*

"hookés" de Chéticamp et leurs artisans, 1985, pp. 80-81, pp. 48-50, pp. 132-139.

74. *Les Héritiers de Lord Durham*, document published by the Fédération des francophones hors Québec, made public in May 1977, section on Nova Scotia, p. 46.

Isle Madame

75. A.H. Clark, op. cit., p. 269. see also: Father Clarence d'Entremont, *Nicolas Denys*, op. cit., p. 340. Nicolas Denys was granted exclusive fishing rights in the region.

76. Bernard Pothier, "Les Acadiens à l'Ile-Royale (1713-1743)," *Cahiers de la Société historique acadienne*, Vol. III, No. 3, 1969.

77. Stephen A. White, "The Arichat Frenchmen in Gloucester: Problems of Identification and Identity" in *The New England Historical and Genealogical Register*, Vol. CXXXI, April 1977, p. 84.

78. Census of Sieur de la Roque, Canadian Archives, Sessional Paper No. 18, 1906, P.A.N.S.

79. Calendar of Cape Breton Land Papers 1787-1848, Year 1816, Nos. 1428, 1435, P.A.N.S.

80. See Governor Wilmot's concerns in 1763 re trade between Acadians on Isle Madame and St. Pierre, Canadian Archives Sessional Paper No. 19 for 1906, Appendix J, p. 210, P.A.N.S.; Thomas Pichon, *Lettres et Mémoires pour servir à l'Histoire naturelle et Civile et Politique du Cap Breton*, written in 1758, published in 1760, pp. 39-43, P.A.N.S; Ronald Labelle, "L'histoire orale et l'identité culturelle chez les Acadiens de la Nouvelle-Ecosse," *La Société historique acadienne*, Dec. 1984, p. 144.

81. "Journal of Charles Robin (1767-1787)," photocopy of original document available at the Centre d'études acadiennes, Université de Moncton. Robin wrote in English and French with equal fluency and eloquence. Most of his diary is written in English.

82. Richard Brown, *A History of the Island of Cape Breton*, originally published in 1869, new edition: Belleville, Ontario, 1979, p. 368.

83. A.A. Johnston, op. cit., Vol. I, p. 104.

84. Ephrem Boudreau, *Rivière-Bourgeois*, Les Editions Lescarbot, 1984, p. 25.

85. Calendar Cape Breton Land Papers 1787-1848, See: 1809, 1810, 1815, 1818, P.A.N.S; original land grants available at Dept. of Lands and Forests, Provincial Crown Lands Record Centre (Dartmouth). Stephen White provided genealogical information re the Samson and the Babin families.

86. A.A. Johnston, op. cit., Vol. I, pp. 154-155. Aside from the abolition of the monarchy, one of the consequences of the Revolution was the separation of the Church and the State.

87. Ibid., pp. 450-452. Laurence Kavanaugh Jr. was the first Catholic elected to the Legislative Assembly. He was elected in 1820 but did not take his seat until 1823. He was not forced to take the Test Oath.

88. Paul A. Touesnard, "Growth and Decline of Arichat: 1765-1880," unpublished M.A. thesis in Economics, Dalhousie University, 1984, p. 137. The author provides many useful statistics on the population of Arichat.

89. Gabriel LeBlanc, "Histoire de l'Ile Madame," in *Les Régions acadiennes de la Nouvelle-Ecosse, Histoire et anecdotes*, op. cit., p. 35.

90. A.A. Johnston, op. cit., Vol. I, p. 278.

91. A.A. Johnston, op. cit. Vol. II, re: Seminary-College, see: pp. 296-304. For early schools, see: RG 14, vol. 57, 1829-1881, School Papers, P.A.N.S.

92. Ephrem Boudreau, "Un évêché au Cap-Breton", *Les Cahiers de la Société historique acadienne*, Vol. V., No. 3, 1974. "L'abbé Hubert Girroir 1825-1884," *Les Cahiers de la Société historique acadienne*, Vol. VI., No. 2, 1975.

93. A.A. Johnston, op. cit., Vol II, pp. 427-431.

94. Ibid., Vol. II, p. 514.

95. Tony E. Walker, Manuscript Report No. 214, "St. Peter's Canal: a Narrative and Structural History," Parks Canada, 1973.

96. H.-R. Casgrain, op. cit., p. 443.

Pomquet, Tracadie and Havre-Boucher

97. For all the genealogical information in this section we are indebted to Stephen A. White, Centre d'études acadiennes, Université de Moncton. Other sources for information on these three villages: *Place-Names and Places of Nova Scotia*, pp. 284-285, pp. 538-539, 678-679; see also: A.A. Johnston, op. cit. Vol. I, pp. 125-126; see also: Réal Daigle, "Histoire de Pomquet" in *Les Régions de la Nouvelle-Ecosse*, op. cit., pp. 37-43; see also: *The State of Minority-Language Education in the Provinces of Canada*, op. cit., p. 188.

98. "Mémoires de Pascal Poirier," in *Les Cahiers de la Société historique acadienne*, Cahier 23, Vol. IV, No. 3, 1971, p. 108.

99. The elementary school in Pomquet was not granted Acadian status by the Department of Education until November 1992. The other offices of the FANE are located in Petit-de-Grat, Chéticamp, Sydney, Saulnierville, West Pubnico and Halifax.

Chezzetcook

100. A.H. Clark, op. cit., p. 225.

101. Ronald Labelle, *La vie acadienne à Chezzetcook, Nouvelle-Ecosse*, special

edition of *Les Cahiers de la Société historique acadienne*, Vol. 22, Nos. 2-3, 1991.

102. Ibid., p. 23. Ronald Labelle's analysis is based on the genealogical research of Father Frédéric Melanson.

103. Frederic S. Cozzens, *Acadia; or, a Month with the Bluenoses*, New York, Derby and Jackson, 1859, p. iv.

104. Ibid., p. 34.

105. Ibid., pp. 52-53.

106. Information taken from the "Report on the Provincial Museum for 1934-35" by Harry Piers, pp. 28-29 (provided by Scott Robson).

107. Jeanne Arsenault, "La survie du costume traditionnel français en Acadie," in *La vie quotidienne au Québec*, Presses de l'Université du Québec, 1983, p. 253. See also photos taken by Helen Creighton in 1948, Helen Creighton Collection, P.A.N.S.

108. H.-R. Casgrain, *Un pèlerinage au pays d'Evangéline*, op. cit., pp. 324-325.

CHAPTER 5

Choices and Challenges:
Acadians in Nova Scotia Today

By the beginning of the twentieth century, there were approximately 45,000 Acadians living in Nova Scotia.[1] Scattered in closely-knit communities at opposite ends of the province, they represented almost 10 percent of the population. Bound together by their French ancestry, their religion, and a compact network of family ties, the Acadians formed a distinct collectivity within a larger society. On the one hand, they shared with thousands of other Nova Scotians many features of the rural life-style associated with the fishery, the lumber industry, shipbuilding, and subsistence farming. On the other hand, their language, their traditions, and their history gave them a unique identity.

The Catholic Church constituted the single most important spiritual and social framework for Acadians everywhere. Prayers and religious feasts gave meaning to life, punctuating the days and the years with occasions that brought together people of all ages. Léonie Comeau Poirier, a school teacher and journalist, grew up in Meteghan Centre in the 1920s. In the following passage from her book entitled *My Acadian Heritage*, published in 1985, she describes the feeling of camaraderie and the strong sense of belonging that dominated annual celebrations like Mardi Gras.

In the Acadie of my childhood the time for renewal of both body and spirit was the holy season of Lent. Lent was the official harbinger of spring—the time when, the lethargy of winter over, man and nature spring forth to start anew.

In those days, this period of forty days was a time of fasting and

Léonie Comeau Poirier (Courtesy: Léonie Comeau Poirier)

abstinence by everyone with the exception of the very young or those suffering from illness. There were no movies, no dancing parties, or even weddings…

All was not austerity, however. The day before the beginning of Lent was a day to be remembered. It was for fun and frolic. On the Tuesday preceding Ash Wednesday the young people of the community dressed in their finest attire while mother prepared a huge pot of delicious fudge.

It was mardi-gras! Family and friends gathered for a sing-song. The air was filled with music and the aroma of fudge. We sang such favorites as "Partons la mer est belle" and the poignantly beautiful but tragic love story of Evangéline. The joy of mardi-gras was enhanced by the spirit of camaraderie by everyone and our voices sounded sweet in the early spring evening.[2]

The principal feature uniting Acadians and isolating them from other Nova Scotians was their language. At the beginning of the twentieth century, very few Acadians spoke any English. In 1910, for example, there were 87 schools in Nova Scotia where Acadian children arrived "with no knowledge of English."[3] Almost all of these one-room schools were located in Inverness, Richmond, Digby and Yarmouth counties. There were, however, 5 situated elsewhere: 1 in Pomquet and 4 on the shores of Tor Bay in Guysborough County (Port Felix, East Port Felix, Charlos Cove and Larrys River). In addition to these 87 schools, there were 2 others: 1 in Arichat and 1 in Havre-Boucher, where "the majority only come with a knowledge of French."[4] These statistics are important indicators of the strength of the French language in the home and the cohesiveness of Acadian communities in the early 1900s.

Félix Thibodeau, a graduate of Collège Sainte-Anne, was born in Church Point in 1909. He was the first person in Nova Scotia to write an entire work in Acadian, in other words to attempt to capture the sounds of a specific regional accent and the flavour of a very old French.[5] Published in 1974, *Dans note temps avec Marc et Philippe* is composed of about fifty short conversations between two elderly men who reminisce about life along the shores of St. Marys Bay in the early 1900s. In the following dialogue, Marc and Philippe talk about a typical barn-building bee (*une coultine*) that took place late one June. The event was an occasion to celebrate but it also enabled about 50 men and 10 women from the village to share their skills by helping one of their neighbours. At five o'clock, after a hard day's work, the roof (*la couverture*) was ready to shingle (*bardocher*) and the barn could soon be filled with hay (*fouonne*). To mark the birth of the new building, a spruce tree was placed on the peak of the roof. Only after this symbolic gesture could the revelry begin: the priest gave everyone permission to dance, a Micmac fiddler was invited to accompany the traditional reels and cotillons, and Maximin à Léang, the proud owner of the new barn, brought

Félix Thibodeau in his private museum. (Courtesy: Fédération acadienne de la Nouvelle-Ecosse)

out demi-johns of spirits (*eau d'vie*) while the women served rappie pie (*le pâté-à-la-râpure*), the culinary speciality of St. Marys Bay.

In writing a dialect that was heard but never seen in print, Félix Thibodeau ennobled and empowered oral traditions that date back to the early days of French settlement in Port Royal. In transcribing the French language as it is spoken in his region of Nova Scotia, Félix Thibodeau documented and brought to life the communal spirit that united Acadians.

Marc – *Quand que l'monde arrivit là le matin d'la coultine, tout l'bois était paré; Maximin et deux ou trois autres aviont marqué, la longueur, les mortaises et les tenons en tcheu d'arronde, tout câ qu'ça prenait pour une grange.*

Philippe – *C'était le dernier jour de jonne, y avait point qu'une cinquantaine d'hoummes et une dizaine de femmes. Tout c'qu'on avait besoin c'ait une hache et un marteau, puis une douzaine de scies d'travers. Pour dîner on avait des patates et des harangs, tchuits au feu d'hors.*

Marc – *Toute avait été à merveille; à cinq heures la couverture était parée à bardocher.*

Marc – *Ouai, pi juste avant d'hucher pour le pâté-à-la-râpure, Marie d'la Pointe arrivit avec un pruste et elle monta l'attacher au faîte du pignon.*

Philippe – *C'est à c'temps là que Maximin arrivit avec ses deux d'mi Johns d'eau d'vie. Sais-tu que s'avait aidé à souper.*

Marc – *Câ qu'était le pu beau, le prêtre avait dounné la permission d'danser. On avait d'mander au savage de d'nir jouer le violon. Personne était en bière et tout l'monde s'en avait été content.*

Philippe – *Imagine toi av'oir une grange presque parée à mettre le fouonne, toute dans une journée.*

Marc – *Ouai, et persounne s'en avait aperçu et tout l'monde avait été à un pique-nique.*[6]

In his second work, dedicated to his mother who died in 1973 at the age of 97, Félix Thibodeau explores the traditional activities associated with women. Once again he uses conversations and the spoken word to evoke life in the early decades of the twentieth century. In *Dans note temps avec Mélonie et Philomène* the wives of Marc and Philippe chat about the past. They evoke their role in transmitting the Catholic faith to their children and they describe their many household chores, including cooking, house-cleaning, spinning, knitting, weaving, and feeding the chickens. Like women in other pioneer societies, Mélonie and Philomène, were care-givers and healers. In the following exchange, for example, they recall the preparation of home remedies that had been passed on to them from their ancestors who in turn had learned them from the Micmac. Special plants and herbs were gathered, then dried in the attic to be mixed and boiled for cough medecines, poultices and other curative substances. In this particular case, Mélonie remembers how her mother took care of coughs (*toux*) by boiling the bark from a young fir tree (*l'écorce de jeune sapin*). As if to improve on this bitter and strong (*enmar et for*) mixture she would add a touch of ginger (*gingembre*) or a few grains of pepper (*poivre*).

Philomene – Ma mère nous a-t-y point en'oyés d'la fois ramasser des herbages. Su l'en dernier j'savions quoi emporter. Mon père itou, tant qu'y en trouvait au bois, y les emportait au logis. C'était point souvent qu'en servir qu'y étiont verts. On les amarrait en gerbes pi on les mettait au p'tit geurnier. Au besoin, on allait chercher la bounne herbage, on la mettait à tremper ou on la faisait bouillir. Des fois faullait ajouter une portion d'autre chouse qu'on prenait au magasin.

Mélonie – Pour la toux, ma mère faisait bouillir d'l'écorce de jeune sapin. C'était enmar et for toute en même temps. Des fois ma mère mettait du gingembre, des fois y faullait aller à la porte pour prendre son vent. Des fois a mettait des graines de poivre.[7]

Cultural heritage is often described as an invisible treasure that can be transported anywhere and handed down from one generation to the next. In the case of the Acadians, the transmission of this culture was essentially oral and thus unrelated to any type of formal education. Traditions and folklore survived despite illiteracy, despite the Deportation and despite years of wandering. As the quotations from Léonie Comeau Poirier and Félix Thibodeau indicate, music and songs constitute essential elements of the cultural heritage. Catherine Poirier, born in Cap-le-Moine, near Chéticamp, in 1901, has captured in her own compositions the importance of singing as a communal activity.

Like thousands of other young Acadians, Catherine was forced to leave the Maritimes in search of employment. At the age of 21, she moved to Massachusetts where she was able to find work cleaning houses in the Boston area. It was there that she met her first husband, Mosé Roach, also a native of Chéticamp. The couple

Catherine Poirier (Courtesy: Michael Roach)

returned to Chéticamp in 1929 to take care of ailing relatives. After the death of her first husband, Catherine married Jos Poirier. Like most of the women in the village, Catherine was able to contribute to the family income by hooking rugs. Over the years she became well known in the craft of hooking, partly because she had the audacity to break away from the accepted floral patterns.[8] In 1985 a number of her folk-art style rugs were acquired by the McCord Museum in Montreal. In addition to creating original rugs, Catherine Poirier composed several songs in her later years that evoke the joys of community togetherness. In one of her songs she lists the simple pleasures and favourite pastimes that contribute to a sense of community: seeing friends and relatives, young and old, playing cards, singing traditional songs and helping neighbours. She ends her song with these words of wisdom:

La fleur la plus belle
Plaira par sa beauté
Mais l'amitié fidèle
Dure une éternité
Nous avançons en âge
Cela on n'en doute pas
(Translation: The most beautiful flower will please through its beauty, but faithful friendship lasts an eternity, we're growing old, we're sure of that.)

Father Anselme Chiasson, born in Chéticamp in 1911, is unquestionably one of the most prominent folklorists in Canada. While studying with the Capuchin Fathers in Ottawa in 1927, Anselme Chiasson began compiling historical notes on his native village. Over a period of 30 years he returned regularly to Cape Breton, and on each occasion he interviewed elderly members of the community, recording their stories, songs, and legends.[9] In order to ensure the survival of the words and melodies of the folksongs which he had collected in the field, he began publishing the *Chansons d'Acadie* in collaboration with Father Daniel Boudreau. The first three volumes of this collection of about 300 traditional songs were published in the 1940s and the remaining four between 1972 and 1985. Most Chéticamp families today possess a copy of all the volumes in this songbook series.[10]

By 1960 Father Chiasson had moved to Moncton where he participated in the founding of the Société historique acadienne which oversees the publication of the scholarly journal the *Cahiers*. He published his first parish monograph in 1961. It was entitled *Chéticamp, histoire et traditions acadiennes* and was translated into English 25 years later. In 1964 Father Chiasson was appointed archivist at the Centre d'études acadiennes at the Université de Moncton where he worked for over a decade. With the assistance of the experienced rug-hooker, Annie-Rose Deveau, Father Chiasson

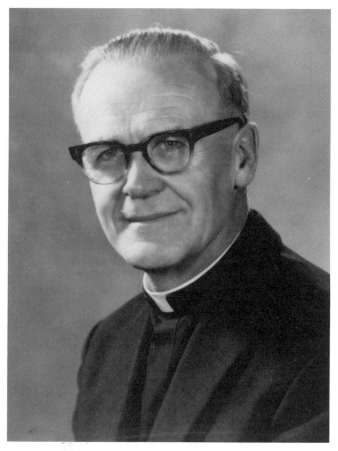

Father Anselme Chiasson (Courtesy: Centre d'études acadiennes, Université de Moncton)

published a second study on his native village focusing on the development of this well-known cottage industry, *Histoire des tapis "hookés" de Chéticamp et de leurs artisans* (1985).[11]

Father Anselme Chiasson's extensive research in Cape Breton, New Brunswick and the Magdalen Islands has provided detailed information on the social and religious customs that have characterized Acadian communities for many generations.

Léonie Comeau Poirier, Félix Thibodeau, Catherine Poirier, and Father Chiasson have all contributed in their own way to the preservation of Acadian culture and traditions. They all have in common the fact that they were born before 1916 and grew up in the days before the isolation of Acadian communities was diffused by cars and radios, at a time when the French language was barely tolerated by the anglophone majority. Official attitudes with regard to the French-speaking minority are obvious in the public education system, for example. In the introduction to his major study on Chéticamp, Father Chiasson states that he was "a victim of a school system claimed to be bilingual where all [his] life [he] suffered from a deficient French teaching, received in grammar school." [12]

The following passage from Léonie Comeau Poirier's autobiographical work indicates clearly that English, not French, was the valued language in school. One can also appreciate the extent to which the primary and secondary education of children depended on the initiative and economic prosperity of their parents.

Meteghan Centre finished building its own school around the year 1920. My father was one of the strong advocates for the establishment of the school. He died in 1921 just after his efforts produced results and closer educational facilities had been constructed for his five children.

The school board consisted of a secretary and three trustees. They hired the teacher and paid her from the taxes collected from the people. Taxes were hard to gather in those days. People had no money. The teacher could not get anything until money came in from taxes. The provincial government, however, sent a bonus in the middle of the term for a hundred dollars or so. Often that's all the teacher had to go on for months. It merely paid her board and room.

Teachers worked hard for the little money they got. Our new school was built with two classrooms: the one downstairs was for the younger children up to grade five and the one upstairs held grades six to ten. Classes were conducted in French during the morning and English in the afternoon...

English began in grade one along with the French reader.

My family was fortunate in having a mother who could not only read and write but, a rarity then, could also speak English. She had been a school teacher in St. Martin, then she worked as a governess in Lynn, Massachusetts, before her marriage to my father.

Some children were not thus favored and they found it difficult to keep up with those who had help at home... [13]

The Nova Scotia Department of Education had tolerated so-called Acadian or bilingual schools since the mid-1800s, not because it was interested in encouraging the use of French or fostering the Acadian identity, on the contrary. The evolution of the public school in the Acadian regions of this province shows very clearly that the authorities wanted French-speaking children to be able to integrate as quickly as possible into the dominant culture. In other words, the prime aim of the education system was to assimilate. In 1902, for example, the Acadian Commission had been appointed by the government to investigate "the best methods of teaching English in the schools situated in the French districts of the province."[14] It was made up of three anglophones and five francophones including Ambroise Comeau, the Liberal Member of the Legislative Assembly for Clare, Father P.M. Dagnaud, superior of Collège Sainte-Anne, and Father Amable Mombourquette of Arichat. The commission made several recommendations all of which were accepted by the educational authorities of the time: a bilingual course would be offered during the summer at the Normal School in Truro to give Acadian teachers special pedagogical training; an Inspector for Acadian Schools would be appointed; a series of French readers would be prepared; and English would become the sole language of instruction as of Grade 5. Except for the crucial matter related to the number of years of schooling in the mother tongue, the Acadian Commission had gained some ground. But it took another 37 years before the Department of Education agreed, in 1939, to allow Grades 1 to 6 inclusive to be taught in French—except for Arithmetic which would be taught in English as of Grade 4. However, these improvements appear to have been too little, too late since the strength of the French language had already been considerably eroded since the beginning of the century. In 1931, for example, 32 percent of the Acadians in Nova Scotia no longer considered French their mother tongue.[15]

In his annual report for 1936-1937, Louis A. d'Entremont, the first Inspector of Schools for the combined districts of Clare and Argyle, provides a rare glimpse of the unrelenting efforts to teach Acadians English. It is obvious from the following comments that schools served as bastions of the English language in the midst of francophone communities.

The question of language is very vital in a large part of this division. The easy and correct use of English and quick and ready understanding are the important aims of all our work with bi-lingual children. With the majority of pupils the only opportunity to hear or use English is confined absolutely to the school, year in and year out.[16]

Over the years, Acadian educators petitioned persistently for improvements that would enable their pupils to receive a better grounding in French. The requests for improvements addressed to the Department of Education focused on three main areas: teacher training, instruction in French, and authorized French-language textbooks. These requests were based on the assumption that an Acadian child could not possibly be well served by a teacher who taught in French from English textbooks and who had no professional training whatsoever in French. As Isidore LeBlanc had already pointed out in the Legislative Assembly back in 1879, Acadian children were doubly disadvantaged: they came to school speaking one language and were expected to learn everything, including reading and writing, in another language. Their mother tongue, the very basis of their culture, was thus placed immediately in an inferior position. Generations of Acadian children became victims of an educational system that left them unable to feel confident in either French or English. This situation continued with minor improvements until the late 1960s when a number of important changes took place in Canada that created a more favourable climate for francophone minorities generally.

There is no doubt that the presence of a large francophone population in eastern Canada has always given strength and encouragement to the Acadians of Nova Scotia. The rise of the separatist movement and the transformations that took place in Quebec society during the Quiet Revolution (1960-1966) had a profound influence on French Canadians generally and on the political structures of Canada. To a large extent the Acadians of Nova Scotia have benefitted from battles won by the francophones of Quebec and New Brunswick. Denise Samson, a prominent young Acadian from Petit-de-Grat who held several important cultural positions before she died of cancer in 1991, expressed this interrelationship in the following manner:

For more than twenty-five years, I feel that the federal government has used us to try to please Quebec. The vision of a bilingual Canada was put forward as a reaction against the dissatisfaction of Quebec. Let's not fool ourselves into believing that the idea of a bilingual Canada was designed to save the francophones outside of Quebec... We became important every time the separatist movement took on strength and managed to stir public opinion in Quebec in favour of independence.

Don't misunderstand me. I don't reproach Quebec for using every bargaining tool at its disposal. I am happy that Quebec has the possibility to reflect and decide which political context will enhance its cultural and linguistic survival. We [Acadians and other francophone minorities] *do not have that flexibility.*[17] (TR)

French is the mother tongue of about one quarter of the population of Canada, approximately 5 million or 85 percent of these people live in the province of Quebec where they form the overwhelming majority. In all the other provinces, except for New Brunswick, francophones form less than 5 percent of the population. As noted at the beginning of the chapter, in the early 1900s virtually all the Acadians of Nova Scotia were French-speaking and constituted about 10 percent of the population. However, in the space of 80 years (two generations), the percentage of francophone Acadians was reduced by one half. The number of francophones that make up the 5 percent in the different provinces obviously varies according to the total population of the province. In Ontario, for example, there were 484,265 francophones in 1981. In Nova Scotia there were 35,810 and in Prince Edward Island there were 6,505. The French-speaking minority in New Brunswick constitutes about one third of the population or 237,570 individuals.[18]

Even with these figures it is possible to see that the political impact of French-speaking citizens varies considerably from one province to another. As a general rule, the survival of the French language in Canada has been closely linked to population numbers and the relative percentage of francophones and anglophones within a specific territory.[19]

In 1963 the federal government founded the Royal Commission on Bilingualism and Biculturalism, presided over by André Laurendeau and Davidson Dunton. This was the first time the relative status of the French and English-speaking people was examined from one end of the country to another. As a result of their findings, in 1966 (on the eve of Canada's centennial celebrations), the commissioners published a series of recommendations designed to redress the inequalities between the two main language communities. The recommendations can be summarized very briefly as follows:

1) that French be firmly established as an official language of the federal government
2) that federal government documents and correspondence be available in both English and French
3) that federal government services be available in French where there is a French-speaking majority or substantial minority
4) that provincial governments make services available in the two languages in areas having substantial minority populations of either tongue
5) that French and English be declared official provincial languages in Ontario and New Brunswick.[20]

Following the proclamation of the Official Languages Act in 1969, the federal government gradually established mechanisms for bilingualism within its jurisdiction. Although the status of French has been greatly improved in the past 20 years within the federal civil service, it still does not mean, for example, that a francophone living in an Acadian region of Nova Scotia can receive services in French from all local federal government departments.[21] On the whole, the principle of linguistic equality is accepted although there are still gaps in the services available in French.

New Brunswick became officially bilingual in 1969—during Premier Louis Robichaud's last term of office. The actual implementation of linguistic duality took place gradually throughout the 1970s while Richard Hatfield was premier. However, it was not until the 1980s that the government of Nova Scotia began to take concrete steps to support the francophone minority in the province. Many factors have helped create a more positive attitude towards the Acadians in Nova Scotia. The political climate both at the federal and the regional level has encouraged affirmative action.

The Council of Maritime Premiers was established in 1971 to facilitate joint undertakings of an economic and educational nature. With New Brunswick being officially bilingual, recognition of the Acadians was a political reality in one of the member provinces, making it more possible for the Acadians in Nova Scotia and Prince Edward Island to benefit from the strong position of their compatriots. The Council sponsored projects in the field of education throughout the 1970s and established the Maritime Provinces Education Foundation in 1982 which acted as a funding agency for the development of learning materials in French and English to be used in schools throughout all three provinces. This pooling of resources has enabled projects that otherwise would have been impossible in a small province like Nova Scotia, especially in the area of Acadian studies.[22] The Nova Scotia Museum (a branch of the Department of Education), for example, carried out a survey of about 40 pre-Deportation sites in the early 1970s along the Annapolis River and the Minas Basin but the research remained at a standstill for over a decade. However, thanks to a renewed interest in Acadian history and to the co-operative approach generated by the Maritime Provinces Education Foundation, major archeological excavations began at Belleisle in 1983. These digs, along with research carried out at other sites in the Maritimes, have provided tangible information on the daily life of Acadians before 1755.

The political and cultural climate throughout the 1970s gave rise to a growing interest in French Canada, and French as a second language was increasingly regarded as a useful asset in the job market. More and more English-speaking parents began sending their children to French immersion schools. The immersion system was introduced in the early 1970s as a logical offspring of the Official Languages Act. Although Nova Scotia was one of the last provinces to establish French immersion schools, the expansion of the enrolment in the past few years has followed national trends. In 1981 there were approximately 865 children enrolled in immersion classes in Nova Scotia. By 1988-1989 there were 4,300 pupils in immersion classes throughout the province and these numbers continue to increase.[23] The popularity of the immersion system is one manifestation of a more positive attitude on the part of the anglophone majority toward the French fact in Canada. One can assume that this attitude will prevail at least as long as both English and French are valued in the federal civil service.

The Official Languages Act not only affected attitudes within the majority culture, but it also gave new support to the francophone minorities across the country. One of the first and most important concrete developments that took place in Nova Scotia was the creation of a province-wide association that enabled Acadians to consolidate their efforts to defend and promote their language and culture. The Fédération acadienne de la Nouvelle-Ecosse, commonly referred to as "LA FANE," was founded in 1968 under the auspices of the Official Languages Program of the Secretary of State.[24] Father Léger Comeau, a well-known educator and defender of the French language, became the first president of the FANE. After graduating from Collège Sainte-Anne in 1940, he moved to Charlesbourg, Quebec, where he studied at the Seminary of the Eudist Fathers. Father Comeau later obtained degrees in theology and philosophy in Rome and at the Université de Montréal and admits that it was only after spending 15 years in the province of Quebec that he came to understand "the value and the depth of the Acadian heritage he had received from his ancestors."[25] (TR) Father Comeau taught at university in both Edmundston and Bathurst before he was appointed head of the Interdiocesan Seminary in Halifax. He later became Director of Continuing Education at Université Sainte-Anne and has played a prominent role in cultural circles both at the provincial and the regional level. An eloquent and inspired speaker, Father Comeau has stated on numerous occasions his firm belief that in order to survive and function in both English and French, "We Acadians must perfect our maternal tongue." (TR) In December 1988, Father Comeau received France's highest honour, the *Légion d'honneur*, for his longtime service and dedication to the French cause.

One of the first accomplishments of the FANE was to facilitate communication between the different regions by transforming *Le Courrier* into a provincial newspaper in 1970 and by establishing the printing and publishing company called the Imprimerie Lescarbot Ltée. With the financial support of the Secretary of State and the collaboration of the extension department of Université Sainte-Anne and the Université de Montréal, the FANE was able to set up a permanent training program in 1976 for "animateurs" or community development officers who were subsequently hired to work in the Acadian regions of the province. Over the years, the "animateurs" helped organize information meetings and various social and cultural events at the grassroots level. Thus, with a permanent staff funded by the Secretary of State, the federation gradually established itself as the main catalyst for cultural development and the mouthpiece and pressure group for the Acadians of Nova Scotia.

Prior to 1968, the Acadians in Nova Scotia did not have a truly representative provincial organization. This was due mainly to the fact that they were scattered at opposite ends of the province, but it was also due to the fact that there were two important sister organizations that grouped Acadians throughout the Maritimes and that defended the French language, the Catholic faith and Acadian traditions. Founded in the 1880s the Société nationale l'Assomption (known today as the Société nationale des Acadiens or the SNA) spearheaded regular meetings or conventions that examined educational and social issues such as the choice of Acadian national symbols, French-language instruction in schools, Acadian representation in the hierarchy of the Church, the appointment of an Acadian bishop, massive emigration of Acadians to the United States, and the role of co-operatives.[26] In 1921 the Société nationale l'Assomption launched a fundraising campaign throughout North America that enabled the construction of the commemorative church in Grand Pré. The second organization which promoted similar ideals was a mutual insurance company founded in Waltham, Massachusetts in 1903. It was called the Société l'Assomption and became better known at the local level especially as it provided scholarships for young people to further their education in French. By the 1920s, for example, there were 14 chapters of the Société (Mutuelle) l'Assomption in Cape Breton and more than 20 on mainland Nova Scotia. Virtually all of these branches were located in Acadian villages.[27] In 1923, the members of this society, the *Assomptionistes*, contributed towards a statue of Notre-Dame l'Assomption, the patron saint of the Acadians, which was placed in the memorial church at Grand Pré. Today, with its headquarters in Moncton, the Assumption Mutual Life Insurance Company constitutes a major financial institution in New Brunswick.

In other parts of Canada, francophone associations developed

In 1968, Father Léger Comeau was the first president of the FANE. Twenty years later, he received the *Légion d'honneur* from the President of France, François Mitterrand. (Courtesy: Father Léger Comeau)

at the provincial level between 1910 and 1926 in order to ensure French-language education. The Association d'éducation des Canadiens-français du Manitoba, for example, was established in 1916 specifically to protest against the suppression of instruction in French in Manitoba. The Acadian association on Prince Edward Island, the Société Saint-Thomas d'Aquin, existed since 1919 and in its early days focused strictly on educational issues.[28] Unlike their compatriots on the tiny neighbouring province, the Acadians in Nova Scotia found themselves in several very different school districts and separated by enormous distances (Cape Breton alone is twice the size of Prince Edward Island). This made the formation of a province-wide association much more complex. The appointment of Acadian school inspectors (which guaranteed a concern for French-language instruction) proved to be less of a hurdle in southwestern Nova Scotia where the population base was relatively concentrated. In Cape Breton, several Acadian inspectors served in

Richmond County, including Rémi Benoit in the 1870s, but the schools in the Chéticamp area were placed under the supervision of the English-language inspectors of Inverness County.

After 1890, the presence of the Collège Sainte-Anne in Church Point provided additional energy and inspiration for educational reforms in Clare and Argyle. As a result, associations that advocated improvements in the school curriculum, in teacher training and in French textbooks were able to develop earlier in southwestern Nova Scotia than in Cape Breton. The teachers of Clare and Argyle formed the Institut Acadien-Français de Clare et Argyle and its first convention was held in May of 1900 in Church Point.[29] Two years later, the government formed the Acadian Commission which resulted in the first concerted effort to reform the so-called bilingual or Acadian schools. Ambroise Comeau, Liberal Member for Digby County from 1890 to 1907, served on the Commission and attended the meetings of the institute on a regular basis.[30]

Except for a period of three years (1917-1920), ever since Frédéric Armand Robicheau took office in 1838, there has always been an Acadian from Clare in the provincial Legislature. There is no doubt that this continuous presence has given the Acadians of St. Marys Bay a political strength and recognition which none of the other Acadian regions have ever been able to attain. After Ambroise Comeau resigned from the House to become the first Acadian senator from Nova Scotia, he was replaced by J. Willie Comeau who served as Liberal Member for Digby County for a total of 35 years, from 1907 to 1948. J. Willie Comeau was one of the first students to enroll in the newly founded Collège Sainte-Anne and thanks to the support of Father Gustave-Marie Blanche, the superior of the college, he was appointed assistant commissioner for Canada at the Paris Exhibition in 1900. Ten years later he became president of the Société nationale l'Assomption. Throughout his political career, J. Willie Comeau applied pressure behind the scenes in order to bring about improvements in the education system for Acadians. He was influential in the adoption of a new curriculum for Acadian schools in 1939 and the establishment of credit courses for teaching-training at Collège Sainte-Anne.[31] Like his predecessor, J. Willie Comeau resigned from provincial politics when he was appointed to the Senate where he served until his death in 1966. The following year, his son, Benoit, was elected to the Legislative Assembly and was thus able to carry on the family tradition. Benoit Comeau played a prominent role in the Cabinet of the Liberal government led by Premier Gerald Regan until 1978 and sat in the Opposition benches until 1981.

As they had no direct political representation and as they were too far away to be effective in an association based in the southwest corner of the mainland, a group of educators in Chéticamp decided to form their own organization. Named after the patron saint of their church, the Société Saint-Pierre was founded in 1947. According to the constitution, quoted by Father Anselme Chiasson, the society gave itself a broad mandate to promote social and educational advancement in a co-operative spirit and defined its goals in the following terms:

To constitute in an association the Acadians of our region, that is to say, eastern Nova Scotia and Cape Breton Island, of developing among them a spirit of solidarity and fraternity, of working to conserve our heritage, of promoting our intellectual, social, and economic interests, and, especially, in encouraging by all possible means, education in subjects of descendance, or of Acadian or French origin, to all those who have the aptitudes and necessary qualifications.[32]

For many years the Société Saint-Pierre concentrated on furthering the cause of French education. It organized annual contests in the Acadian schools, distributed prizes and awarded interest-free loans that enabled Acadians from Cape Breton to continue their education in French-language institutions.

The Société Saint-Pierre is still very active today and thanks to the energetic leadership of the Eudist Father Charles Aucoin has its own cultural centre called Les Trois Pignons (the three gables), constructed in 1978. In addition to the society's offices, the building also houses a collection of over 100,000 genealogical reference cards compiled by Father Aucoin, a library, a small museum, and a permanent exhibit of hooked rugs by the renowned Chéticamp artist, Elizabeth LeFort.

The Association des Instituteurs Acadiens de la Nouvelle-Ecosse was founded in 1948 and the Acadian Education Association was founded the following year. These were the first organizations that grouped Acadian educators at a provincial level and were linked to regional and national associations of a similar nature. Given the presence of Collège Sainte-Anne and the comparative strength of the Clare and Argyle school district, the leadership in these organizations tended to focus on southwestern Nova Scotia. The Acadian Education Association struggled for improvements in the French curriculum and for the introduction of French-language radio in Acadian schools (English-language programs had been introduced in most of the schools by the early 1930s). It also participated in community projects including the upkeep of the commemorative church in Grand Pré until the park was acquired by the federal government in 1957.[33] After the creation of the FANE in 1968, the organization ceased to exist although Acadian teachers have subsequently formed their own association within the Nova Scotia Teachers Union.

One of the major concerns of the FANE throughout the 1970s was the rate at which the Acadians were being assimilated into the anglophone majority. The percentage of persons of French origin whose mother tongue was English had increased dramatically since the Second World War. In 1931, 32 percent of Acadians no longer considered French their mother tongue; by 1971 (one generation later) the figure had jumped to 53.9 percent.[34] There were many factors that had contributed to the breakdown of the linguistic cohesiveness of Acadian communities including the arrival of the radio, the telephone, television and the paving of roads. In an attempt to slow down the assimilation rate, the FANE decided to concentrate its energies on increased French-language curriculum in Acadian schools. Thus, the main solution to the problem of assimilation was seen to lie in the education of future generations. The FANE also lobbied for improved French-language radio and television services which would link Acadians to francophones elsewhere in Canada and add to the cultural framework of the province.

By the early 1970s, many of the requests put forward by Acadian teachers in Clare, Argyle, Richmond, and Inverness had been accepted by the Department of Education.[35] At this time, there were about 6,000 students enrolled in 22 Acadian schools in Nova Scotia.[36] Compared to the 89 bilingual schools in 1910, this reduced number reflects both the erosion of the French language and the consolidation of schools that had taken place throughout the province in the 1950s. The proportion of classes taught in French varied from 100 percent to 50 percent at the elementary level, and from 60 percent to 40 percent at the secondary level.[37] With the exception of Richmond County, English was not introduced before the end of Grade 2. As a general rule, the higher the grade, the lower the proportion of French, indicating clearly that priority was given to English.

In 1971, two years after the Official Languages Act was passed in the House of Commons in Ottawa and the Legislature of New Brunswick had declared the province officially bilingual, the Liberal government of Nova Scotia under Premier Gerald Regan appointed the Royal Commission on Education, Public Services and Provincial-Municipal Relations. The commission was chaired by John F. Graham, Professor of Economics at Dalhousie University, who had become sensitized to the situation of the Acadians while serving on the Byrne Commission set up by Premier Louis Robichaud in New Brunswick in the early 1960s.[38] In its final report, published in 1974, the Graham Commission devoted an entire chapter to the education of francophones in Nova Scotia. The premise on which the commissioners based their recommendations was that Acadians in Nova Scotia need English, but that they have a right to be educated in French and a right to co-ordinate the organization and development of programs and learning materials in their own schools. This represented a totally new approach to education for the francophone minority, very different from the attitudes that had prevailed amongst English-speaking educational authorities in Nova Scotia for over a century. The recommendations that the commissioners made pertaining to Acadian schools constituted the first attempt to adapt and restructure minority language education in Nova Scotia according to the spirit of the Official Languages Act.

In the long term, the Graham Commission had a major impact on the formation of public policies in Nova Scotia. In the short term, however, it had little effect. Not one of the recommendations related to the education of Acadians was acted upon. Leaders in the Acadian community and the FANE responded very positively to the chapter devoted to their schools but were disappointed with the lack of action on the part of the government and with the apathy of Acadian parents concerning increased French-language education. As the following statement indicates, the FANE wanted both the government and Acadian parents to adopt a more assertive position with regard to the value of French for future generations.

Despite the slowness of the Minister of Education to spell out in a Bill the recognition of French as a language of instruction and the definition of an Acadian school, he has recognized, even encouraged, classes in French for Acadians. This recognition is manifested by the presence of a curriculum supervisor for Acadian schools within the Department of Education...

It is imperative that the Minister of Education provide official sanction for the work that is being accomplished by granting legal status to Acadian schools and thus avoid confusion and ambiguity...

Over the past six years [i.e. the early 1970s], *our experience in the field has shown clearly that parents are apathetic and indifferent with regard to education in French for their children. This attitude can be excused partly due to a lack of information. We find ourselves forced to demolish the age-old myth according to which English is the only valid language of instruction.*

In order to combat this apathy which is often at the root of our problems, it is absolutely essential that any information campaign designed for Acadian parents must show clearly the advantages of bilingual training for their children.[39] (TR)

Despite the continuing pressure of the FANE, it was seven years before a number of the recommendations of the Graham Report were actually put into effect in the form of an amendment to the Education Act.

In fact, as has often been the case in the past 30 years, the momentum for change was generated outside the cultural and political arena of Nova Scotia. On November 15, 1976 René Lévesque led the Parti Québécois to victory at the polls in Quebec. One of the direct results of this election was the recognition in English Canada that minority language education was a right. At the First Ministers' Annual Conference in August 1977, "All the provincial Premiers agreed to make their best efforts to provide education in English and French, wherever numbers warrant."[40] A few years later, Minority Language Educational Rights became part of the Canadian Charter of Rights and Freedoms.

Canadian Charter of Rights and Freedoms
Minority Language Rights
Section 23:

(1) Citizens of Canada (a) whose first language learned and still understood is that of the English or French linguistic minority population of the province in which they reside, or (b) who have received their primary school instruction in Canada in English or French and reside in a province where the language in which they received that instruction is the language of the English or French linguistic minority population of the province, have the right to have their children receive primary and secondary school instruction in that province.

(2) Citizens of Canada of whom any child has received or is receiving primary or secondary school instruction in English or French in Canada, have the right to have all their children receive primary and secondary school instruction in the same language.

(3) The right of citizens of Canada under subsections (1) and (2) to have their children receive primary and secondary school instruction in the language of the English or French linguistic minority population of a province (a) applies wherever in the province the number of children of citizens who have such a right is sufficient to warrant the provision to them out of public funds of minority language instruction; and (b) includes, where the number of those children so warrants, the right to have them receive that instruction in minority language educational facilities provided out of public funds.

—Published in 1981, signed by Queen Elizabeth II on April 17, 1982.

In 1978 the Liberal government of Nova Scotia was defeated at the polls by the Conservatives led by John Buchanan. Ironically, when his government amended the Education Act in June 1981, the only Acadian MLA was sitting on the Opposition benches. The amendment, known as Bill 65, marks a turning point in the history of education for Acadians in Nova Scotia. It gave long-awaited legal status to Acadian schools, it set guidelines for the ratio of instruction in French and English, and it ensured the development of a curriculum that would include the history and heritage of the Acadians.

The latter element was particularly significant as a study of authorized school textbooks carried out by Réal Samson and Andrew S. Hughes showed that young Nova Scotians—both anglophone and francophone—were learning nothing about the Acadians that would enable them to deduce that any Acadian communities existed in their own province.[41] In most cases, children in Nova Scotia were only acquiring a sprinkling of facts about Champlain's Habitation at Port Royal and about the Expulsion (often of Evangeline!) at Grand Pré. Thus, according to textbooks used in the 1960s and 1970s, Acadians did not exist in the present and three centuries of their history remained untold. There is no doubt that Bill 65 and other changes that took place during the 1980s in several provincial departments generated new interest in Acadian studies and contributed to the promotion of Acadian communities.

Although Bill 65 was passed on June 15, 1981, the implementation of the reforms took place very slowly and proved to be much more complicated either than the Department of Education or local school boards had predicted. Even though Acadian educators and the FANE had been consulted in order to establish guidelines for the "new" Acadian schools, many parents resisted the proposed changes as they represented an increase in the number of classes to be taught in French. In other words, there was a gap between what the parents felt would be useful for their children and what Acadian educational authorities felt was necessary in order to slow down the assimilation rate. To a certain extent, this gap did not come as a complete surprise; the activities of the FANE at the grassroots level during the 1970s had revealed a definite apathy on the part of Acadian parents with regard to increased French-language education. However, the proposed educational reforms brought out into the open many attitudes that reflect several centuries of domination by an English-speaking majority.

The story of the implementation of Bill 65 is more than the story of a change in the ratio of classes given in French and English. Initially, Acadian parents were concerned that "too much" French might jeopardize the future of their children in an English-speaking province. To understand this reaction, one must remember that Acadian parents whose children were attending school in the early 1980s were between 25 and 40 years old. Consequently they grew up in the 1950s and 1960s, at a time when the English-speaking majority showed little, if any, tolerance for people who spoke French in public (especially if it did not happen to be the so-called "Parisian French"). The school years of these young Acadian parents coincided with the arrival of English-language television—the French network did not reach Nova Scotia until the late 1970s, long after viewing habits were well established. There have never been any French-language vocational or trade schools in Nova Scotia. Integration into the dominant culture of the workplace was therefore an economic necessity for all Acadians. Based on the experience of previous generations, in other words their own parents and grandparents, the average Acadian parent in 1984 had no reason to believe that his or her children would be better off with an education that placed more emphasis on French. The prestige and usefulness of bilingualism was not felt as early or even to the same degree in rural communities as in urban centres like Halifax where most of the federal government offices for the Atlantic region are located.

It was generally assumed by educational authorities that statistics related to growing assimilation would provide sufficient proof of the need for a solid French-language education. However, all parents did not perceive fluency in French and the encroachment of the English language in the same way. Nor did Acadian parents and students have a clear idea of the changes that would be required in the curriculum in order for the school in their community to be designated as an "Acadian school" under Bill 65. Confusion and different perspectives gave rise to considerable controversy in Chéticamp, for example. Innumerable discussions and public debates took place without any knowledge of the guidelines which set the "minimum requirements designed to provide young Acadians with written and oral communication skills in both official languages." Although the long-term objectives of the Department of Education were left undefined, the curriculum guidelines were clearly identified in an information sheet published in September 1983:

1) From kindergarten to Grade 4, all subjects are to be taught in French, except for English which is to be introduced at the beginning of Grade 3.

2) From Grades 7 to 9, students will have a minimum of 10 classes in French, with at least 3 classes in French per year.

3) From Grades 10 to 12, students will have a minimum of 8 classes in French, with at least 2 classes in French per year.[42]

In March 1984, Réjean Aucoin and Jean-Claude Tremblay, former producer and anchorman at Radio-Canada in Moncton, interviewed 15 students enrolled in Grade 10 or 11 at the Ecole Notre-Dame l'Assomption (NDA) in Chéticamp.[43] At the time, there were 292 pupils enrolled in Grades 1 to 6 and 350 in Grades 7 to 12. Sixteen of the pupils in the elementary grades and 98 at the secondary level were anglophones and required separate classes in English. Of the students interviewed, only two knew what the "new" Acadian school meant and were in favour of additional French classes. When asked whether they would like more classes in French, all the other students stated that they were happy with "the way it is now" ("*comme c'est asteur*"). All the students, without exception, felt that they were bilingual although they all admitted that, given a choice, they preferred to write in English because they found it easier than French. The latter point was confirmed by Wilfred Boudreau, the principal of the school. When asked what would be necessary for NDA to meet the requirements of Bill 65, Mr. Boudreau stated that English would have to be introduced six months later, at the beginning of Grade 3; four additional French classes would have to be phased in for Grades 1 to 6; and two French classes would have to be added to the high school curriculum. Given time and appropriate staffing, these changes were not considered insurmountable. However, Mr. Boudreau stressed that public clarifications were urgently needed in order to dispel fears among many parents that NDA would eventually become a unilingual French school.

Unfortunately these fears still existed over a year later when, in July 1985, the Department of Education announced that Notre-Dame l'Assomption would be given the status of "Acadian school." Partly due to a lack of information sessions prior to this announcement, Chéticamp was soon torn apart by discussions over the implications of this new status. All of the major francophone organizations in the region, including the co-operatives, the Société Saint-Pierre and the FANE, endorsed these changes which were perceived as contributing to the preservation of the French language. The Co-op Council, for example, wrote that its members "believe in preserving our culture and heritage. The family and the community have great responsibilities in this matter but the school has been and always will be the key instrument."[44] The main concern of parents who opposed any decrease of English content in the curriculum was that the economic and social mobility of their children would be curtailed. The controversy gradually died down and NDA is now functioning as an Acadian school.

When examining the debate that took place in Chéticamp, one should remember that there are no communities in Nova Scotia where 100 percent of parents with school age children are French-speaking Acadians. The percentage of English-speaking parents—whether they are of Acadian, Scottish or Irish descent—varies from one school district to another. As a large consolidated school, NDA, for instance, receives children from Pleasant Bay and Meat Cove. This mixture of linguistic and ethnic backgrounds obviously means that all the parents whose children attend the school do not have the same point of view with regard to preserving the French language. Not only does this school population represent different cultural priorities, it also produces a difficult learning environment for francophone students. Even among children, the presence of one anglophone in a group of francophones means that the conversation takes place in English. The students interviewed by Jean-Claude Tremblay stated that it was natural in the school yard to switch to English if an anglophone friend was present, or as they put it "*T'as pas de choix.*" Depending on one's position, this switch can be an acceptable or an irritating experience. From a pedagogical point of view, the undeniable pull of English constantly undermines the efforts to improve and enrich the French language in Acadian communities.

According to the text of Bill 65, "the principal language of administration of an Acadian school and communication of an Acadian school with the community it serves shall be French." One of the consequences of this ruling was that all information addressed to parents was to be written in French. After more than a century of schools in which English was the dominant written language, the vast majority of Acadian adults in Nova Scotia read and write English more easily than French. Many Acadians throughout the Maritimes who carry out most of their daily life in French do most, if not all, of their reading in English (newspapers, magazines and books). The only French language newspaper in Nova Scotia, *Le Courrier,* is a weekly and it has only been distributed throughout the province since the early 1970s. By volume alone, the English language dominates the printed word everywhere in the Maritimes. One can understand, therefore, that parents might have felt alienated when their children arrived home from school with a note in a language they were not in the habit of reading.[45]

The main goal of Bill 65 was the promotion of the French language and the Acadian culture. It soon became obvious that the promotion of French could not take place without respecting the linguistic realities of the various Acadian communities in Nova Scotia. The damage of generations of assimilation could not possibly be repaired overnight. The implementation of Bill 65 not only meant working with children, but also with their parents. As Jean-Louis Robichaud, now director of the Centre de ressources pédagogiques at the Université Sainte-Anne, wrote in 1984 in a report commissioned by the Clare-Argyle School Board:

Information destined for parents should be written in both languages, in order to take into account the reality of their daily life, their education, and the presence of English-speaking parents. It is very much in the interest of the school system to ensure that parents know and understand what their children are doing in school.[46] (TR)

Written information from the schools to the parents is thus provided in both languages. As French is the mother tongue and preferred spoken language of the majority of families in the districts of Clare and Argyle, school board meetings take place in French (the two districts were combined under one board in 1982). The Secretary of State provides funding for simultaneous translation services for English-speaking parents. School board meetings in the other Acadian districts take place in English.

A study carried out in 1987 among Acadian teenagers by Betty Dugas-LeBlanc confirmed the inroads English had made into Acadian homes in the space of two generations. These teenagers were between 13 and 18 years old, consequently they were born between 1969 and 1974. The study was sponsored by the Conseil jeunesse provincial, the FANE, and Health and Welfare Canada. Betty Dugas-LeBlanc examined not only language habits but also life styles and leisure activities. Based on information provided by a representative sample of young Acadians in the different regions, the following table indicates the percentage of English and French spoken in the home.[47]

Language Spoken at Home			
Region	French %	English %	Both Languages %
Chéticamp	56	5.2	37.9
Isle Madame	9	18	73
Pomquet	4.5	4.5	90.9
Clare	68.8	6.5	24.6
Argyle	46.7	15.9	34.4
Halifax	13	43.5	43.5

An Acadian school, as defined by Bill 65, is a school in which instruction is given mainly in French and in which the principal language of administration and communication is French. An Acadian school can be created upon the request of a school board in an area in which "there is a sufficient number of children whose first language learned and still understood is French." The ambiguous nature of this definition became fully apparent in 1986 when a group of francophone parents (not a school board) in Sydney requested that a school be formed for their children. This request from the Committee for French Education marked the beginning of what Jocelyne Marchand described as a "roller coaster ride of litigation and negotiation" that lasted for three years.[48] In March 1989 these parents discovered that a total of 50 pupils constituted a "sufficient number" to warrant the establishment of French-language classes, but not an autonomous school.[49] As a result of this ruling by the Appeals Division of the Supreme Court of Nova Scotia, in September 1989 four classrooms were made available for francophones (up to Grade 8) living in Sydney. With funding from the Secretary of State, the Committee for French Education had carried out a survey of all school children in Cape Breton County in 1983. The survey enabled the committee to identify over 600 children who were legally entitled to be educated in French. Given these numbers, the small registration in 1989 was disappointing but understandable. The enthusiasm of many parents had diminished considerably after several years of conflict with the school board and uncertainties as to where the school would be located. In the final analysis, the most peaceful solution was to accept the status quo of English-language education. However, the existence of four classrooms on the second floor of Cornwallis School may provide concrete encouragement for other Acadian parents in Sydney to enroll their children.

During the school year 1988-1989, there were 167,600 school children in Nova Scotia. Of that number, approximately 3,800 pupils were enrolled in minority language schools, in other words, where French is the principal language of instruction, including 13 Acadian schools.[50] It also includes two francophone schools established principally (but not exclusively) for the children of members of the armed forces. One is located in Dartmouth and the other in Greenwood, in the Annapolis Valley. These two francophone schools accounted for about 535 of the total number of pupils in minority language schools. There are now three Acadian schools in Cape Breton: one in Chéticamp (School District of Inverness), Petit-de-Grat, and Arichat (School District of Richmond). In the district of Clare, the Acadian schools are located in Salmon River, Meteghan, Meteghan River, Saulnierville, and Church Point. In the district of Argyle, the Acadian schools are located in Wedgeport, Tusket, Sainte-Anne-du-Ruisseau and West Pubnico. In each of these four districts, Acadian children can now receive schooling in

French from primary to Grade 12. Although it offered most of its classes in French, the elementary school in Pomquet, Antigonish County, was not designated as an Acadian school by the Department of Education until November 1992.

All minority language schools in which 75 percent of the classes are given in French are funded by the federal government. French Immersion classes also receive support from the federal government. As noted earlier, in 1988-89 there were 4,300 pupils enrolled in the French Immersion system in Nova Scotia. These numbers are on the increase because the popularity of immersion programs is still growing. This means that there are now more children (mainly anglophone) taking French Immersion than there are Acadian children attending school in their ancestral language. This phenomenon is not unique to Nova Scotia.[51] It has long been the case in western Canada. Given the size of the Acadian population in Nova Scotia and the drop in the Acadian birth rate, the gap between the enrolment in Acadian schools and French Immersion schools can only become greater. In the light of this trend, it is important to remember that the role of the Acadian school is not only to further the cause of the French language in Nova Scotia, but also to foster the development of the Acadian culture.

Denise Samson, former executive director of the FANE and founding director of the Société de la presse acadienne, had a clear perception of the essential link between language and culture which she expressed very eloquently:

Language without a culture is nothing more than a means of communication. On the other hand, a language that stems from a culture becomes a creative tool for that culture. Culture is the soul of a community. A language transmits that culture from one generation to the next. A language that is linked to a culture expresses a unique way of seeing the world and of solving problems. Language contributes to the development of the creativity that is essential to the survival of a culture through the centuries.

For me, French without a culture has very little meaning. I find English useful as a means of communication, but I do not identify with the English culture. I am an Acadian woman who, on a national scale, belongs to the French Canadian culture.[52] (TR)

The obstacles encountered during the course of the educational reforms need not be regarded in a negative light. On the one hand, they showed that thoughtful consultation with the grassroots is an essential element in change. On the other hand, they illustrated the diversity within the Acadian collectivity of Nova Scotia. The heated discussions, which of course attracted the media, left most anglophones quite bewildered, especially parents who were endeavouring to put their children in French Immersion. Despite the initial uncertainties—often based on rumours rather than facts—the overall effect of Bill 65 has been extremely beneficial. It has given new prestige to the French language in Acadian communities. It has enabled pupils to receive a more solid training in their mother tongue. It has facilitated the creation of study programs suited to the needs of Acadians in Nova Scotia. It has enabled the creation of a special administrative unit within the provincial Department of Education and the appointment of a Director of French-language Programs (Ken Gaudet and subsequently Aubray LeBlanc). It has also resulted in the integration of the pedagogical resource centre at the Université Sainte-Anne and the provincial Department of Education. All of these innovations have consolidated minority language rights in Nova Scotia. In many cases, they constitute structured responses to regular requests that had been articulated by Acadian leaders since at least the 1860s when Father Hubert Girroir sent a letter from Arichat to Sir Charles Tupper, Premier of the province and a Father of Confederation.

Perhaps it is an indication of the growing recognition of the Acadians, but at no point in history has Acadian representation in the Nova Scotia legislature been stronger than it is has been since the late 1980s. Following the September 1988 election, there were three Acadian members in the Conservative government, and one member, Bernie Boudreau (Sydney), in the Liberal opposition. First elected in 1983, the Honourable Guy LeBlanc (Clare) has occupied several senior cabinet positions including, Minister of Community Services, Minister of Fisheries and Minister of Education. He was appointed Minister Responsible for Acadian Affairs in 1988. The Honourable Neil LeBlanc (Argyle) was appointed Solicitor General and subsequently became Minister of Government Services. Leroy Légère (Yarmouth) is also in the Cabinet and currently holds the Labour and Fisheries portfolios. His father, Felton Légère, sat in the House of Commons in Ottawa from 1958 to 1968. In addition to these four elected politicians, there is now an Advisor for Acadian Affairs whose office is situated within the Cabinet Secretariat. Jean-Dennis Comeau was the first person to hold this position designed to coordinate francophone affairs.

Until very recently there has only been sporadic Acadian representation from Argyle. In 1984 the large riding in Yarmouth County was split in such a way as to almost guarantee the presence of an Acadian MLA from Argyle. Although Simon d'Entremont from Pubnico was the first Acadian to actually sit in the Legislature, he was not re-elected in 1840.[53] In fact, it was more than 50 years before another Acadian was elected in Yarmouth County. This second Acadian from Argyle was Conservative Albert A. Pothier, who sat from 1894 to 1897. At the federal level, Argyle has been able to send two representatives to Ottawa: Vincent Pottier, a Liberal from Belleville, who represented the riding of Shelburne, Yarmouth and Clare from 1935 to 1945, and Felton Légère, a Conservative. This is an impressive number, given the fact that since Confederation a total of six Acadians from Nova Scotia have sat in the House of Commons in Ottawa!

The other four federal politicians have all been elected since the late 1960s.[54] The obvious desire for francophone representation is undoubtedly an indirect result of the Royal Commission on Bilingualism and Biculturalism which brought linguistic inequalities to public attention. Louis Comeau, a Conservative, was the first person to represent the new federal riding of South West Nova. He was elected in 1968 and held his seat in the Opposition until 1974. He was replaced by Coline Campbell who sat as Liberal Member for South West Nova for ten years—"a rare honour which few women have known," as Edith Comeau Tufts stated in her book on the Acadian women of Clare.[55] Coline Campbell studied at the Collège Notre-Dame in Moncton and graduated from St. Francis Xavier and Université Laval and holds a law degree from the Université d'Ottawa. She was appointed parliamentary secretary to the Minister of Health and Welfare by Prime Minister Trudeau and in 1975 led the Canadian delegation at the World Conference for the International Year of the Woman. Coline Campbell was defeated in 1984 by Gérald Comeau, a Conservative from Clare, whom she in turn defeated in the federal elections of 1988. Gérald Comeau taught business administration at the Université Sainte-Anne for a number of years. In 1991 he was appointed to the senate by Prime Minister Mulroney, thus continuing the tradition (begun in 1907) of having one Acadian from Nova Scotia in the upper house.

The Acadians of Cape Breton have only recently acquired a voice in federal politics in the person of Francis LeBlanc who was elected to the House of Commons in 1988 as Liberal Member for Cape Breton Highlands—Canso. Their representation at the provincial level has, like that of the Acadians of Argyle, been sporadic. Between 1840 and 1988, only ten Acadians have been elected from Richmond County despite the fact that they have always constituted the majority of the population in the riding. As noted in the previous chapter, on only two occasions have Acadians been able to break through the overwhelming Scottish majority of Inverness County: once in 1897 and a second time in 1925. The two politicians in question, Moise J. Doucet and Hubert M. Aucoin, both held office for a short period of time.

It is obvious that, with the exception of the voters in Clare, Acadians have not been an integral part of the electoral machine in the province. In addition, the diversity of the Acadian regions made it difficult for any one politician to be a spokesman for all the Acadians of Nova Scotia. There is no doubt, however, that the overall political climate in recent years has given more weight to the Acadians currently serving in the government. This support has been translated into concrete projects not only in education, but in tourism, small business, advanced education and job training.

In January 1988, for example, the provincial government inaugurated a policy of French-language grants for public libraries where a minimum of 12 percent of the population is francophone, which in practical terms means libraries in Cape Breton and southwestern Nova Scotia. This initiative constitutes a significant improvement. Until the beginning of the 1950s, libraries in the Acadian regions of Nova Scotia depended almost entirely on private contributions and donations from the Alliance Française (an international cultural organization supported by the French government) for their French-language books. Recent studies of

French-language book circulation indicate that Acadians in Clare and Argyle read much more in French than their compatriots in Inverness and Richmond Counties.[56] Presumably this pattern will change as more French-language books are placed on library shelves and as more students graduate from the three Acadian schools in Cape Breton. In the past decade, the growth of the French-language publishing industry in Canada and the co-operative ventures funded by the Maritime Provinces Education Foundation have enabled the production of a wide variety of books and learning materials. In the Maritimes alone, Les Editions d'Acadie (Moncton) have published more than 150 titles since their foundation in 1972, Les Editions Lescarbot (Yarmouth) have published 50 titles since 1974, and Michel Henry Editeur (Moncton) 12 titles since 1985.[57]

Unlike generations of Québécois since the 1930s, Acadians did not grow up to the sounds of radio programs produced in their own language and relating to their own society. The evolution of both radio and television in Quebec has had a profound effect on the cultural consciousness of every Québécois. Very few Acadians were able to tune into French in the early days of radio. Even their schools received programs in English broadcast from Halifax. However, because of their geographical location the inhabitants of northeastern New Brunswick, western Prince Edward Island, and northern Cape Breton were able to listen to programs from the Quebec station in New Carlisle, Gaspé.[58] The majority of Acadians in Nova Scotia only had access to English-language radio stations until fairly recently. Radio-Canada (the French-language network of the Canadian Broadcasting Corporation) did not establish a station in the Maritimes until February 1954. This station with a production centre is located in Moncton. Trans-mitters were gradually set up in Nova Scotia: in 1960 in south-western Nova Scotia and 1970 in Pomquet and Cape Breton (the quality of the reception has been improved over the years).[59]

In the same way that CBC English-language radio (and televi-sion) in the Maritimes is dominated by Toronto-based productions, French-language Radio-Canada is dominated by Montreal-based productions. Regional content on the French network is limited to about seven hours per day and tends to focus on New Brunswick where 85 percent of Acadians live. Since September 1986, however, a small production centre has been opened in Halifax which produces a morning radio program from 6 o'clock to 9 o'clock specifically designed for Acadians in Nova Scotia. Other than the weekly newspaper, *Le Courrier*, this is the only media link between the various Acadian communities in Nova Scotia.

The French television network of Radio-Canada has only been available in this province from the mid-1970s to the early 1980s, depending on the region. The percentage of material produced in Moncton is very limited and, except for a special event or the occasional news item, there is no Nova Scotian content at all. Since English-language television with some local content has been available throughout the province for more than 30 years, most Acadians in Nova Scotia have not changed their viewing habits in order to watch television in French. Even in New Brunswick, Acadians have not switched over completely to French-language television. The Caplan Sauvageau Report on Broadcasting Policy published statistics indicating clearly that by the mid-1980s viewing of French-language television in the Atlantic Region still formed a small percentage of the total viewing time.[60]

The Caplan Sauvageau Task Force received "brief after brief" from francophones outside of Quebec calling for an end to Radio-Canada's almost total disregard of the regions. The overall message was that the official language minorities (French and English) want more than simply the provision of services in their language, in other words "programming that reflects the culture of [their] community and region."[61] Given the cutbacks in public broadcasting, it would seem unlikely that Acadians in Nova Scotia will receive an increase in services from Radio-Canada in either television or radio. On a strictly local level the province has provided technical and financial assistance recently to community-based programming on a small scale. In *Le Courrier* of December 12, 1990, Richard Landry commented on the cutbacks and the lack of programming designed for Nova Scotians. He titled his editorial "Surviving With Even Less." (TR)

One thing is certain with regard to these cutbacks and the subsequent increase in the so-called national programs from Quebec: Acadian television viewers in this part of the country are going to become less interested in a national French network that talks less and less about them.

There are already too many programs from the national network. They show public figures that few people here have ever heard of and the programs are too "cultured" for the average person who is being encouraged to speak French more often. This type of person will simply turn to American programs that are more appealing even if they are in English. We already know what the consequences [of these viewing preferences] *are. It is unfortunate.*

Yes, once again it's with even less that francophones minorities like ourselves will have to struggle for their cultural and linguistic survival. It's yet another step towards the melting pot. Let's prepare for the worst, there is a fifty million dollar cut predicted for next year. It is up to us to see that our interests are better protected the next time. (TR)

While French-language television and radio services are far from complete, there is no doubt that they have contributed considerably to a climate of self-awareness. In the same way that the proliferation of books since the mid-1970s has enabled Acadians to learn and write about themselves, television and radio programming has shown the richness and diversity of Acadian culture throughout the Maritimes. Acadians can see and hear each other in a way that was not possible in the past. However, the importance of locally produced radio and television programs should not only be measured in terms of the passive listener or spectator. Radio-Canada has filmed and recorded various artistic productions, including plays, festivals, and concerts. It has thus provided a stage and a dynamic means of expression for innumerable artists and musicians.

The National Film Board opened a French-language production centre in Moncton in 1974 and has contributed to the development of artistic talent and cultural awareness. While New Brunswick obviously dominates the content of the majority of Acadian films produced since the late 1960s, Nova Scotian Acadians have been able to see themselves thanks to the work of Phil Comeau. He has made several prize-winning films including *La Cabane* (1978), *Les Gossipeuses* (1978), *J'avions 375 ans* (1982), *Le tapis de Grand-Pré* (1986), and *Au mitan des îles* (1991).[62] All of Phil Comeau's productions illustrate the uniqueness of Acadian com-

Phil Comeau (Courtesy: Phil Comeau)

munities in Nova Scotia. But *La Cabane* and *Les Gossipeuses*, set in the Saint Marys Bay region, are particularly important because they represent the first artistic portrayals of young Nova Scotian Acadians caught between modern and traditional values. With a great deal of humour, Phil Comeau raises a number of serious moral and social issues that remind the spectator that preserving one's heritage and cultural identity in the late twentieth century is not easy. How does one remain Acadian and still be an integral part of society today? Which values destroy the culture? Which ones enable the culture to grow and evolve? Phil Comeau does not provide answers to these questions, nor does he solve the conflict between the generations. Using the modern medium of the film, he does, however, capture and communicate, in an entertaining way, the complexity of choices within Acadian society today.

In his most recent work, filmed over a decade after *La Cabane* and *Les Gossipeuses*, Phil Comeau concentrates not on conflict but on the sense of belonging of a group of people and the continuity of a way of life. *Au mitan des îles* is a documentary on the fishermen who migrate to the Tusket Islands off Wedgeport during the lobster season. For three centuries Acadian families have taken temporary residence in the shanties built along the shores of these islands. In an interview in *Le Courrier*, Phil Comeau explains why he chose to focus his camera on Arthur LeBlanc and his family:

He is a young fisherman. That means that after 300 years this way of life is going to continue. He's 36 years old, that proves that there's a future here. He is typical of the 150 other fishermen who go out on the islands. He's likeable and people like him. Fifteen people live together in his shanty. It's very moving. [63] (TR)

From a visual and a linguistic point of view, *Au mitan des îles* provides a very specific portrait which forms part of a series of documentaries on the Acadians and the sea. The theme-song was composed especially for the film by Eric Surette, one of the best known musicians from Argyle.

During the first ten years of its existence, the FANE co-ordinated activities related to almost every aspect of cultural and educational development. An office was set up in each of the Acadian regions. As the different dossiers expanded and became more complex, more specialized associations were formed. The Association des Festivals acadiens de la Nouvelle-Ecosse was founded in 1979 to co-ordinate the existing Acadian festivals. It became a federation and hired its first director, Dave LeBlanc, in 1983. From then on it was referred to as "la FéFANE" and over the years took on more and more responsibilities in the field of tourism and culture. In May 1989 the FéFANE was replaced by a more comprehensive cultural organization called the Conseil culturel acadien de la Nouvelle-Ecosse under the co-ordination of Ronald Bourgeois, the well-known singer-composer from Chéticamp. With the exception of the winter carnival in Pomquet and the Festival Acadien d'Halifax-

Dartmouth, all of the festivals including the Acadian Days at Grand Pré, take place during the summer. These festivals serve as tourist attractions, but also a way of involving Acadians of all ages in their heritage. Barbara LeBlanc and Laura Sadowsky link these modern-day festivals to the tradition of the parish picnic which developed as a social event in the late 1800s. These folklorists provide the following description of the *Escaouette* festival which takes place in the Chéticamp area:

The entire community participates in the week-long festivities. Emphasis is placed on Acadian history and heritage. The activities include: concerts of traditional music, song and dance; story-telling; historical skits; reenactment of traditional tasks such as fullery; a parade with historical floats; and the choosing of the hosts of the festival, Evangeline and Gabriel who symbolize the expelled Acadians. The costumes, which the local bank and shop clerks wear, contribute to the historical atmosphere.[64]

In each region the festival has a special flavour and features local talent. In Clare, for instance, one can normally enjoy the music of the well-known group called the Tymeux de la Baie and a perform-ance by the young women of the Baie en Joie, a dance troupe founded by Anne-Marie Comeau. Each festival constitutes a mo-ment in the year when young and old can participate and take pride in being Acadian.

The Acadian Games or the Jeux de l'Acadie also encourage active participation of young people. They have been in existence since the mid-1980s and take place at the provincial and the regional level. Over the years, the Games have enabled Acadian children to discover the diversity of their culture throughout the Maritimes. Chéticamp hosted *les Jeux* in 1989 and for the first time, only young Acadians who were prepared to speak French throughout the games were allowed to participate.[65] Preservation of the ancestral language requires determination and a firm commitment even at a very young age. With English everywhere and so accessible—especially on the television at home—it is harder than ever before for young people not to be drawn totally into the dominant culture.

Given the changes that have taken place in the cultural and political sphere over the past 20 years, one might assume that it

Members of the dance troupe, La Baie en Joie. Photo taken at the Grand Pré National Historic Site in 1989. (Courtesy: Fédération acadienne de la Nouvelle-Ecosse)

The Acadian Games in Chéticamp, 1989. (Courtesy: Société Saint-Pierre)

would easier for the young Acadian today to speak (and to want to speak) French than it was for the Acadian who grew up in the 1950s or 1960s. One might think that the structures that now provide support for the francophone minority in Nova Scotia could counteract the forces of assimilation. The French-language school system is now well-established and protected by Article 23 of the Charter of Rights and Freedoms. A provincial federation and a number of affiliated associations now protect and foster the Acadian culture. Since the early 1980s the provincial government has demonstrated a firm commitment to the Acadian community. Radio, television, books, films and many services are now available in French. Dave LeBlanc, administrative director of *Le Courrier*, sees all of these initiatives as essential but still not enough to guarantee the survival of the Acadian language and culture without the personal conviction and commitment of every individual.

The fact that we have Acadian schools does not mean that our future is guaranteed. Institutions and organizations like the Université Sainte-Anne and the Fédération acadienne give us hope. But it is the personal conviction of the people that count...

It is only within the last twenty years that technology has tripled. Our ancestors did not have to face that problem. However, it is our problem now... What are we going to do about it?[66] (TR)

Despite all the support structures that have been put into place since the late 1960s and despite individual energy and goodwill, the pressures of the mainstream culture are overwhelming. Three hours of radio programming with a Nova Scotian Acadian content cannot compete with the expansion of the home video industry, for example. In the past few years, hundreds of American films on videocassette have become available in almost every village throughout Nova Scotia, including Acadian villages. Television programs from Montreal and Moncton cannot compete with the dozens of English-language channels brought into the home by the privately owned satellite dish. The Acadian may have a different language and a different culture, but he or she is just as much a North American as any other inhabitant of Nova Scotia. In fact, the Acadians have a history of being resolutely North American: many Acadians who found themselves in France after 1755 and

Three young Acadians celebrate their heritage during the 1989
festival in Clare. (Courtesy: Fédération acadienne de la Nouvelle-
Ecosse)

who had the opportunity to settle in France preferred to return to
the New World.

The videomachine and the satellite dish became part of the
cultural landscape in the 1980s. These advances in communication technology make the role of the Acadian school and the
attitudes of the anglophone majority even more important. If
Acadian school children do not receive a solid education in French
which values the language, in all its diversity, the traditions and the
history of their people, then who will participate in the Acadian
festivals of the future?

The Catholic Church no longer constitutes the unifying and

protective force than it once did. The Church has undergone profound changes since the Second Vatican Council of 1962. The values and life-style of individual Acadians have also changed. Since the mid-1960s, for example, at least one out of three Acadians in Nova Scotia have married non-Acadians. Recent demographic studies show that English becomes the language spoken at home for about 90 percent of these couples. As a general rule, the smaller the minority (at the level of the province or the region), the greater the likelihood of mixed marriages and of English becoming the language of the children.[67] Forty years ago, social and religious pressures would have made marriages outside the faith and ethnic group almost impossible. For a long time, relative isolation, the language barrier and the influence of the parish priest meant that marriages with Irish or Scottish Catholics were fairly infrequent. Even with regard to marriage, young Acadians of today have more freedom of choice than their parents or their grandparents.

In May 1989 the Federation of Acadian Parents of Nova Scotia, known as "la FPANE," held its fifth annual general meeting. The motto was *Nos enfants, notre avenir* or "Our children, our future."[68] This federation now holds the responsibility for educational concerns. After having carried the flame for 15 years, the FANE is thus no longer directly involved in francophone education. The existence of this new organization illustrates the role of education in the survival of Acadian culture. It also illustrates the commitment necessary on the part of the parents. Once again the burden of survival calls upon individual energies. Children alone cannot be expected to want to speak French and learn about their heritage without the support of the whole family. The Federation of Acadian Parents has a representative or development officer in Argyle, Clare, Halifax, Inverness, Pomquet, Richmond and Sydney. Like most Acadian organizations, it is linked to regional and national francophone associations of a similar nature.

In 1982, Acadian women formed their own organization called the Association des Acadiennes de la Nouvelle-Ecosse—three years before women were officially declared equal in the Canadian Charter of Rights and Freedoms. This group is also linked up with other women's organizations. In addition to cultural and linguistic issues, Acadian women face the same problems and prejudices as other women in North-American society. The Association des Acadiennes which serves as both a lobby and a service group has an advantage over other Acadians associations to the extent that it is able to focus on a number of social issues and to value the presence and contribution of different age groups. As Edith (Comeau) Tufts states in the conclusion of her book, *Acadienne de Clare*, the Acadian woman has made a discrete but enormous contribution to her society. "Her mission today goes far beyond her household...how can she not be concerned by laws that relate to housing, education, health and child protection?"[69] (TR) It is revealing to compare the women described in Léonie Comeau Poirier's autobiographical work to Janice, the central character in Germaine Comeau's award-winning novel *L'été aux puits secs* published in 1983. In the same way that Phil Comeau's films show the contradictions and complexities of modern life in the villages of St. Marys Bay, Germaine Comeau captures the feelings and choices of young Acadian women in the 1980s.[70]

The Acadians, and French Canadians generally, are closely linked to the culture of North America. But like other inhabitants of Nova Scotia, the Acadians have historical ties with their former homeland. Unlike the French Foreign Protestants who settled along the south shore of Nova Scotia in 1753, the Acadians have maintained—despite all odds and at great cost—their language and their culture. The Bouteliers, the Dauphinees, the Doreys, and other families who came from the Protestant principality of Montbéliard in northeastern France assimilated quickly and purposefully into the dominant English-language culture. Some of these families may be interested in their genealogical ties with France, but their own cultural future is not dependent in any way on connections with their country of origin. Since the Acadian culture has changed and is still changing, ties with France and other francophone countries are extremely important. These ties represent a source of support and constant renewal. The French language is not only the French spoken in Quebec and various Acadian regions of the Maritimes, it is also the French spoken in France, Belgium, Switzerland, Martinique, Gaudeloupe, Haiti and the countries of Africa.

After the consolidation of the Acadian provincial associations in the late sixties, the inter-provincial organization founded in the early 1880s, the Société nationale des Acadiens, began to focus on the renewal of relations with France. Since 1892, the Alliance Française had been making small annual donations in the form of money or books to various Acadian groups and institutions throughout the Maritimes.[71] In order to be closer to a large francophone population, the French Consulate was moved from Halifax to Moncton in the 1960s. After General de Gaulle's famous visit to the province of Quebec in 1967, the government of France began to take a much more active interest in the survival of the French language and culture in Canada. The following year, a delegation of four Acadians from New Brunswick, including the president of the Société nationale des Acadiens, went to France to explore the possibility of increased co-operation between France and the Acadians.[72] Since these initial contacts made in 1968, numerous programs have been established that have provided invaluable support to Acadians and their institutions in all three Maritime provinces. This cultural and scientific support takes the form of scholarships, exchanges, prizes, books, records and other learning resources. Over the past 20 years, the Société nationale des Acadiens has acted on behalf of the three provincial associations at the international level. In Nova Scotia, for instance, the Université Sainte-Anne, *Le Courrier*, Radio-Canada and the community radio station in Clare all benefit in a variety of ways from French government assistance.[73] Support from France and also from the government of Quebec has greatly strengthened the cultural framework of the Acadians, particularly in Nova Scotia where the francophone minority is small and broken up into several isolated communities.

The Nova Scotia government has recently recognized the value and importance of cultural and economic relations with France and other francophone countries. The Honourable Guy LeBlanc attended the 1987 Francophone Summit Conference in Quebec City. As Nova Scotia is not a bilingual province, he was invited to participate as a member of the delegation from New Brunswick. The first official government delegation from Nova Scotia visited France in October 1988. The members of the delegation were: Jean-Dennis Comeau, Advisor on Acadian

Affairs; Guy LeBlanc, MLA for Clare; Neil LeBlanc, MLA for Argyle; Robert Maillet, Regional Director for Small Business. The aim of this visit was to establish permanent contacts that would facilitate the development of commercial ties between small businesses in Nova Scotia and France.[74] Whether on a personal, commercial or political level, ties with France serve as a source of enrichment. The growth and future vitality of the Acadian minority in Nova Scotia depends heavily on co-operation and solidarity with other francophone communities—in Canada, the United States, the French West Indies, Europe and Africa.

The survival of the Acadians in Nova Scotia as a dynamic community that is allowed and encouraged to maintain its cultural and linguistic identity depends on support from other francophone societies, on the will of the Acadians themselves and above all on the committed tolerance of the English-speaking majority. Thousands of Nova Scotian Acadians since the beginning of the twentieth century have been obliged to assimilate into the culture of the majority. Assimilation in their case has invariably meant the loss of their ancestral language. Many Acadians today find themselves unable to speak French not because of choices they made, but because of the choices their parents or their grandparents were forced to make. Surely the majority of today does not have to perpetuate the intolerance of the past? Surely the majority of today can tolerate diversity?

NOTES

1. *Les héritiers de Lord Durham*, document prepared by the Fédération des Francophones hors Québec and made public in May 1977, page 19 of the section on Nova Scotia. According to Statistics Canada, in 1901 there were 45,161 individuals of French origin forming 9.8% of the total population.

2. Léonie Poirier, *My Acadian Heritage*, Lancelot Press, 1985, pp. 51-52.

3. Journals of the Legislative Council of Nova Scotia 1912, Appendix 5: Education, pp. 115-121.

4. Ibid., p. 121.

5. The play by Michel Tremblay *Les belles soeurs* (1968) is the best known work written in "joual", a Quebec dialect. The Acadian writer from New Brunswick, Antonine Maillet, published her play *La Sagouine* in 1971.

6. Félix E. Thibodeau, *Dans note temps avec Marc et Philippe*, L'Imprimerie Lescarbot Ltée, 1974, pp. 35-36.

7. Félix E. Thibodeau, *Dans note temps avec Mélonie et Philomène*, L'Imprimerie Lescarbot, 1978, pp. 64-65.

8. Laura Sadowsky, *The Chéticamp Waltham Connection: a Study of Acadian Ethnic Identity*, unpublished Master's thesis, Université Laval, 1987, pp. 151-153. See also: Anselme Chiasson and Annie-Rose Deveau, *L'Histoire des tapis "hookés" de Chéticamp et leurs artisans*, Les Editions Lescarbot, 1985, pp. 98-100.

9. Father Anselme Chiasson, *Chéticamp: History and Acadian Traditions*, translated by Jean Doris LeBlanc, Breakwater, 1986. See preface by Luc Lacourcière.

10. Barbara LeBlanc, *To Dance or not to Dance: The Case of Church and Group Social Control in Chéticamp*, unpublished Master's thesis, Université Laval, 1986, p. 140.

11. Father Chiasson's work in collaboration with Annie-Rose Deveau on hooked rugs was published in English in 1989 by Editions Lescarbot.

12. Father Anselme Chiasson, *Chéticamp: History and Acadian Traditions*, translated by Jean Doris LeBlanc, Breakwater, 1986, p. 9.

13. Léonie Poirier, *My Acadian Heritage*, Lancelot Press, 1985, pp. 16-17.

14. George Rawlyk and Ruth Hafter, *Acadian Education in Nova Scotia: an historical survey to 1965*, Ottawa: Information Canada (Studies of the Royal Commission on Bilingualism and Biculturalism, 11), 1970, pp.22-27.

15. Census of Canada, quoted in *Immigration and language imbalance* by Jacques Henripin, Manpower and Immigration, Ottawa 1974, p.20.

16. Journals of the House of Assembly 1938, Appendix 8: Education, p. 74.

17. Denise Samson, *Le Courrier*, May 30, 1990.

18. *La Loi sur les langues officielles au Canada*, special supplement published by the Fédération des Francophones hors Québec, March 1989. See also: *Les héritiers de Lord Durham*, op. cit., page 19 of the section on Nova Scotia. According to Statistics Canada, in 1971 there were 80,215 individuals of French origin forming 10.2% of the total population.

19. See for example: Robert Maheu, *Les Francophones du Canada: 1941-1991*, Editions Parti Pris, 1970; for assimilation rates in any of the provinces see *Les Héritiers du Lord Durham*, op. cit.

20. *Language and Society: The Official Languages Act Ten Years Later*, Autumn 1979, Commissioner of Official Languages; p. 9, p. 13.

21. *Le Courrier*, October 29, 1986; May 4, 1989.

22. Council of Maritime Premiers, Annual Report, 1986-1987, p. 6.

23. See: *The State of Minority-Language Education in the Provinces and Territories of Canada*, A Report by the Council of Ministers of Education, January 1983, p. 189. 1988-1989 statistics provided by the Department of Education, Research Section.

24. Brochure published by the Fédération acadienne de la Nouvelle-Ecosse on the occasion of its tenth anniversary: "1968-1978, 10e Anniversaire." The original name, Fédération francophone de la Nouvelle-Ecosse, was changed in 1972. As of July 1990, the membership of the FANE was 2,007 individual members in the seven regions which include Halifax and Sydney (*Le Courrier*, July 11, 1990).

25. *Le Courrier*, Dec. 21, 1988.

26. For a summary of all fifteen conventions held between 1881 and 1972, see special issue of *La Petite Souvenance*, "Un peuple à unir," La Société historique acadienne de l'Ile-du-Prince-Edouard, 1984.

27. For a complete list of all the branches throughout the Maritimes, see: Antoine J. Léger, *Les Grandes Lignes de l'Histoire de la Société l'Assomption*, Québec, Imprimerie Franciscaine Missionnaire, 1933, pp. 253-260. Regarding the development of the insurance company, see: J.-W.

Lapierre and Muriel Roy, *Les Acadiens*, Presses universitaires de France, 1983, pp. 51-53.

28. Georges Arsenault, *The Island Acadians*, op. cit., p. 160, p. 167; see also: *Les Héritiers de Lord Durham*, op. cit., section devoted to P.E.I.

29. *L'Evangéline* May 26, 1900.

30. J. Alphonse Deveau, *Les personnes éminentes*, Les Editions Lescarbot, 1988, pp. 35-38.

31. Ibid., pp. 51-55. See also: *The Legislative Assembly of Nova Scotia 1758-1983*, a biographical directory, edited and revised by Shirley Elliot, Province of Nova Scotia, 1984.

32. Father Anselme Chiasson, *Chéticamp: History and Acadian Traditions*, op. cit., p. 155.

33. J. Alphonse Deveau, *La Ville Française*, op. cit., p. 180.

34. Census of Canada, quoted in *Immigration and language imbalance* by Jacques Henripin, Manpower and Immigration, Ottawa 1974, p.20.

35. The teachers formed a representative committee called the Comité de programmation des écoles acadiennes.

36. *Les Héritiers du Lord Durham*, op. cit., section on Nova Scotia, p. 73.

37. Ibid., pp. 73.

38. Dr. Graham, interviewed by S. Ross in 1989, died in 1991. He is interviewed in Herménégilde Chiasson's film *Robichaud*, National Film Board, 1989.

39. *Les Héritiers du Lord Durham*, op. cit., p. 73.

40. *The State of Minority-Language Education in the Provinces and Territories of Canada*, op. cit., p.1. Quebec was the only province that did not subscribe to the statement although "the Quebec Minister of Education indicated that his province felt [it] represented a step in the right direction". The anglophone minority in Quebec has always been well served in educational matters.

41. Réal Samson, Andrew S. Hughes, *Les Acadiens et leur représentation à travers les manuels scolaires de la Nouvelle-Ecosse*, Atlantic Institute of Education, 1982, p. 9, p. 33, p.54 (a bilingual publication sponsored by Secretary of State and the Canadian Council of Christians and Jews).

42. Province of Nova Scotia, Department of Education, Sept. 14, 1983. The press release was in French and was entitled "Declaration de la politique concernant les écoles acadiennes". The text of Bill 65, entitled "An Act to Amend Chapter 81 of the Revised Statutes, 1967, the Education Act", appears in Chapter 20, Acts of 1981.

43. Tape recording of interviews with students and Mr. Boudreau provided by Réjean Aucoin to S. Ross in May 1985.

44. Quoted by Richard Julien in his article entitled "Chéticamp: An Acadian Community in Conflict" in *Historical Studies in Education*, Vol. 2. No. 2, 1990, p. 273.

45. For a detailed analysis of Acadian literacy levels, see the bilingual publication: Carmelle d'Entremont, *The First Step*, N.S. Department of Advanced Education and Job Training, 1990. The Collège de l'Acadie, not yet in operation, is designed to serve as a community college and will presumably combat illiteracy. Provincial funds have been set aside for this community college "without walls" that will provide long distance education via satellite. For a brief description, see the editorial by Richard Landry in *Le Courrier*, August 31, 1988. See also: *Le Courrier*, Dec. 20, 1991.

46. Jean-Louis Robichaud, *Du rêve à la réalité: l'implantation et le développement de l'école acadienne*, Meteghan: Conseil Scolaire—Clare Argyle School Board, p. 20.

47. Betty Dugas-LeBlanc, *Adolescence acadienne*, study sponsored by the Conseil jeunesse provincial de la Nouvelle-Ecosse and la FANE and authorized by Health and Welfare Canada, 1987, p. 21 (The author uses the term Richmond rather than Isle Madame). Some of the information in the report was published in *Le Courrier*, Jan. 27, 1988.

48. Jocelyne Marchand, "Campaigning for a Creeping Cancer: Cape Breton Acadians Battle Assimilation", *New Maritimes*, Jan.-Feb., 1990, pp. 8-12.

49. *Le Courrier*, April 5, 1989.

50. Statistics provided by the Department of Education, Research Section.

51. For further information see summary of Charles Castonguay's demographical research in *Le Courrier*, June 21, 1989. There are 10 times more young people capable of speaking French than there are young francophones in Saskatchewan, in Alberta and in Newfoundland and 20 times more in British Columbia.

52. Denise Samson, *Le Courrier*, May 30, 1990.

53. See: *The Legislative Assembly of Nova Scotia 1758-1983*, a biographical directory, edited and revised by Shirley Elliot, Province of Nova Scotia, 1984.

54. For federal Members of Parliament see: *Canadian Parliamentary Guide Parlementaire Canadien 1989*, Normandin, Toronto, pp. 387-389, pp.399-400, pp. 485-486.

55. Edith (Comeau) Tufts, *Acadienne de Clare*, no publisher indicated, 1977, p.47.

56. Information received from the Nova Scotia Provincial Library (Public Libraries Section), Department of Education; see also *Le Courrier*, Jan. 6, 1988.

57. *Association for Canadian Studies Newsletter*, Spring 1989, pp. 20-22.

58. Father Anselme Chiasson, op. cit., the author states that Charles W. Aucoin bought a radio that required earphones in 1925, p.225; see also:

Léon Thériault, *La question du pouvoir en Acadie*, Editions d'Acadie, Moncton, 1982, p. 229.

59. *Le Courrier*, April 26, 1989, editorial p. 4; *Les héritiers de Lord Durham*, pp. 32-43; Gilbert Maistre, *Revue de l'Université de Moncton*, Jan. 1971, p. 25.

60. *Report of the Task Force on Broadcasting Policy*, Minister of Supply and Services Canada, Ottawa, 1986, p. 208.

61. Ibid., pp. 529-530.

62. *Le tapis de Grand-Pré* is based on the children's book of the same name written by Réjean Aucoin and Jean-Claude Tremblay. English translation by Sally Ross and Barbara LeBlanc: *The Magic Rug of Grand-Pré*, Nimbus Publishing.

63. *Le Courrier*, Nov. 29, 1991.

64. Barbara LeBlanc, op. cit. (note 10), pp. 134-138. Barbara LeBlanc and Laura Sadowsky shared their research, the first two chapters of their theses are the same.

65. *Le Courrier*, editorial, May 24, 1989.

66. *Le Courrier*, Jan. 16, 1991.

67. In his recent study, Roger Bernard states that in 1986, 39.6% of Acadian husbands in Nova Scotia married a non-Acadian woman and 40.5% of Acadian wives married a non-Acadian. Roger Bernard, *Le choc des nombres: dossier statistique sur la francophonie canadienne 1951-1986*, Vision d'avenir, Fédération des jeunes canadiens français Inc., 1991, vol 2., pp. 215-228. In her article in *The Acadians of the Maritimes* (pp. 181-183), Muriel Roy states that according to 1971 statistics 1 out of 3 Acadians in Nova Scotia marry a non-Acadian, 1 out of 4 in Prince Edward Island, and 1 out of 10 in New Brunswick.

68. *Le Courrier*, May 17, 1989; *Le Courrier*, July 5, 1989, p. 19.

69. Details on the history and activities of the women's association: *Le Courrier*, June 21, 1989; *Le Courrier*, April 11, 1990; *Le Courrier*, June 27, 1990. Edith (Comeau) Tufts, op. cit., p. 88.

70. Germaine Comeau, *L'été aux puits secs*, Editions d'Acadie, Moncton, 1983 (awarded the Prix France-Acadie in 1983).

71. For relations with France, see: Léon Thériault, *La question du pouvoir en Acadie*, Editions d'Acadie, 1982, pp. 215-221.

72. The four delegates were: Léon Richard, S.N.A.; Adélard Savoie, President of the Université de Moncton; Gilbert Finn, President, Compagnie mutuelle l'Assomption; Euclide Daigle, Vice-president, Association Acadienne d'Education (listed in Léon Thériault, op. cit., p.218).

73. For details of this support, see: Le Courrier, Dec. 10, 1986, p.3; Le Courrier, Oct. 5, 1988, p. 12; for an example of the contributions of Quebec, see *Le Courrier*, August 1, 1990.

74. *Le Courrier*, Oct. 5, 1988, p. 12.

BIBLIOGRAPHY

The following is a selective bibliography of major works which the authors consulted. For more detailed information, see the Notes at the end of each chapter. The modern editions of seventeenth century texts contain the original French text and the English translation.

General

Aucoin, Father Charles, et al. *Les Régions acadiennes de la Nouvelle-Ecosse: histoire et anecdotes.* Church Point, Nova Scotia: Centre acadien, Université Sainte-Anne, 1982. Les actes du premier colloque des sociétés d'histoire acadiennes de la Nouvelle-Ecosse. This small publication contains five articles on five Acadian regions in Nova Scotia by Father Charles Aucoin, J. Alphonse Deveau, Gabriel LeBlanc, Réal Daigle, and Father Clarence d'Entremont.

Bernard, Roger, *Le choc des nombres: dossier statistique sur la francophonie canadienne 1951-1986.* Vision d'avenir, Fédération des jeunes Canadiens français Inc., 1991, 2 volumes. This study constitutes the most recent statistical analysis of various linguistic and life style trends of young French Canadians.

Clark, Andrew Hill, *Acadia: The Geography of Early Nova Scotia to 1760.* Madison, Wis.: University of Wisconsin Press, 1968. This is still a classic and provides a wealth of information on the pre-Deportation period.

Daigle, Jean, ed. *The Acadians of the Maritimes: Thematic Studies.* Moncton: Centre d'études acadiennes, 1982. This book is comprised of 15 in-depth articles and provides the best overall view of Acadian history and culture. The original French version was published in 1980 and is currently being revised and updated.

Dawson, Joan, *The Mapmaker's Eye: Nova Scotia Through Early Maps.* Halifax: Nimbus Publishing Ltd. and the Nova Scotia Museum, 1988. Most of the maps in this work pre-date the Deportation and give a visual perspective of early settlements in Nova Scotia.

Dupont, Jean-Claude, *Histoire populaire de l'Acadie.* Montreal: Editions Leméac, 1978. The work provides an illustrated description of various aspects of Acadian material culture throughout the Maritimes.

Fédération des Francophones hors Québec, *Les héritiers de Lord Durham* vol. 2. Prepared by the separate provincial organizations of the Fédération des Francophones hors Québec, 1977.

Lapierre, Jean-William and Muriel Roy, *Les Acadiens.* Paris: Presses universitaires de France, 1983. This work, published in the well-known "Que sais-je" series, provides a useful view of Acadian history from 1604 to the 1980s.

Maillet, Marguerite, *Histoire de la littérature acadienne: de rêve en rêve.* Moncton: Les Editions d'Acadie, 1983. This work contains useful biographical information on many writers and poets and gives an overview of Acadian literature which stems mainly from New Brunswick.

Massignon, Geneviève, *Les parlers français d'Acadie. Enquête linguistique.* Paris: Klincksieck, 1962, 2 volumes. A major linguistic study carried out in the field. It provides a global view of the richness and variety of the vocabulary used in all the Acadian regions in the Maritimes. Although Massignon's hypotheses pertaining to the geographic origin of the French families who settled in Acadie have been disputed in recent years, her monumental study contains a wealth of information.

Reid, John G., *Six Crucial Decades: Times of Change in the History of the Maritimes.* Halifax: Nimbus Publishing Limited, 1987. This book offers a unique perspective of the history of the Maritimes and provides a very clear and succinct analysis of the early settlement period and of the Deportation.

Université Sainte-Anne, *La vie acadienne en Nouvelle-Ecosse: être acadien aujourd'hui.* Church Point, Nova Scotia: Centre provincial de ressources pédagogiques, Université Sainte-Anne, 1985. This is a small book designed for secondary schools. It contains useful information on four Acadian regions in Nova Scotia.

Relations with the Micmac

Gould, G.P. and A.J. Semple, *Our Land: The Maritimes, the Basis of the Indian Claim in the Maritime Provinces of Canada.* St. Anne's Point Press, 1980.

Jaenen, Cornelius J., *Friend and Foe: Aspects of French Amerindian Cultural Contacts in the Sixteenth and Seventeenth Centuries.* Toronto: McClelland and Stewart, 1976.

Upton, L.F.S., *Micmacs and Colonists: Indian-White Relations in the Maritime Provinces, 1713-1867.* Vancouver, B.C.: University of British Columbia Press, 1979.

Early Explorers

Biggar, H.P., ed., *The Voyages of Jacques Cartier.* Ottawa: Publications of the Public Archives of Canada, 1924.

Biggar, H.P., ed., *The Works of Samuel de Champlain.* 6 vols. Toronto: Champlain Society, 1922-36.

d'Entremont, Père Clarence, ed., *Nicolas Denys: sa vie et son oeuvre.* Yarmouth, Nova Scotia: L'Imprimerie Lescarbot Ltée, 1982. This work contains a facsimile of Denys' original French text and an abundant series of notes.

Ganong, William F., ed., *Description and Natural History of the Coasts of North America (Acadia)* by Nicolas Denys. Toronto: Champlain Society, 1908.

Grant, W.L., ed., *The History of New France* by Marc Lescarbot. 3 vols. Toronto: Champlain Society, 1907-14.

Thwaites, R.G., ed., *The Jesuit Relations and Allied Documents.* 73

vols. Cleveland, Ohio: Burrows Brothers, 1896-1901. The first four volumes relate to French colonization.

Webster, John Clarence, ed. *Relation of the Voyage to Port Royal in Acadia or New France* by Sieur de Dièreville. Toronto: Champlain Society, 1933.

Charles de La Tour

MacDonald, M.A., *Fortune and La Tour: the Civil War in Acadia* Toronto: Methuen, 1983.

Louisbourg

McLennan, J.S., *Louisbourg: From its Foundation to its Fall 1713-1758.* London: Macmillan & Co. Ltd., 1918. 4th edition. Halifax, Nova Scotia: The Book Room Limited, 1979.

The French Regime

Pothier, Bernard, *Course à l'Accadie: Journal de campagne de François Du Pont Duvivier en 1744.* Moncton: Les Editions d'Acadie, Moncton, 1982. The author has also researched the emigration of Acadians to Ile Royale between 1713 and 1734.

The Deportation

Condow, James E., *The Deportation of the Acadians.* Environment Canada—Parks, 1986. This is an excellent bilingual booklet available at minimal cost. The English text was written by James E. Condow and the French text by Marie-Claire Pitre.

Griffiths, Naomi, *The Acadian Deportation: Deliberate Perfidy or Cruel Necessity.* Toronto: Copp Clark, 1969.

Griffiths, Naomi, *The Acadians: Creation of a People.* Toronto: McGraw-Hill Ryerson, 1973.

LeBlanc, Robert G., "The Acadian Migrations." *Canadian Geographical Journal,* July 1970, vol. 81, No. 1. Robert LeBlanc is the first scholar to provide clear graphic representations of the Acadian migrations. His work inspired the poster *L'odyssée d'un peuple* or *The Odyssey of a People* produced by the Canadian Parks Service in 1990.

Martin, Ernest, *Les exilés acadiens en France au XVIIIe siècle et leur établissement en Poitou*. Paris: Hachette, 1936.

Robichaux, Albert J., *The Acadian Exiles in Saint-Malo: 1758-1785*. Eunice, Lousiana: Hebert Publications, 1981.

The Fishery

Chaussade, Jean, *La pêche et les pêcheurs des Provinces Maritimes du Canada*. Montreal: Les Presses de l'Université de Montréal, 1983. This is an excellent overview of the fishery and is especially useful with regard to Acadian regions.

Innis, Harold A., *The Cod Fisheries: The History of an International Economy*. Toronto: Ryerson Press, 1940.

The Catholic Church in Eastern Nova Scotia

Johnston, A.A., *A History of the Catholic Church in Eastern Nova Scotia*, Volume I: 1611-1827; Volume II: 1827-1880. Antigonish, Nova Scotia: St. Francis Xavier University Press, 1960. Both volumes of this monumental study contain innumerable details on all the Acadian communities of Antigonish County and Cape Breton.

Prince Edward Island Acadians

Arsenault, Georges, *The Island Acadians, 1720-1980*. Charlottetown: Ragweed Press, 1989. Translated by Sally Ross. The original French version was published in 1987 by Les Editions d'Acadie (Moncton).

The Acadians of the Magdalen Islands

Chiasson, Father Anselme, *Les îles de la Madeleine: vie matérielle et sociale*. Montreal: Les Editions Leméac, 1981.

The Acadians of Saint-Pierre and Miquelon

Poirier, Michel, *Les Acadiens aux îles Saint-Pierre et Miquelon 1758-1928*. Moncton: Les Editions d'Acadie, 1984.

Political Representation in Nova Scotia

Elliott, Shirley B., ed., *The Legislative Assembly of Nova Scotia 1758-*

1983. Department of Government Services, Province of Nova Scotia, 1984. This is a very useful biographical directory.

Education

Council of Ministers of Education, *The State of Minority-Language Education in the Provinces and Territories of Canada.* A Report by the Council of Ministers of Education, Canada, 1983. Bilingual publication.

d'Entremont, Carmelle, *The First Step.* Nova Scotia Department of Advanced Education and Job Training, 1990. A bilingual publication that provides a detailed analysis of Acadian literacy levels.

Martel, Angéline, *Official Language Minority Education Rights in Canada: From Instruction to Management.* Office of the Commissioner of Official Languages, January 1991. Bilingual publication.

Arichat

Touesnard, Paul A., "The Growth and Decline of Arichat: 1765-1880." Unpublished Master's thesis, Dalhousie University, 1984.

Argyle

Boucher, Neil, *The Development of an Acadian Village: Surette's Island 1859-1970.* Yarmouth, Nova Scotia: Les Editions Lescarbot, 1980.

Campbell, Joan Bourque, *L'Histoire de la paroisse de Sainte-Anne-du-Ruisseau.* Yarmouth, Nova Scotia: Les Editions Lescarbot, 1985.

d'Entremont, Father Clarence-J., *Histoire de l'An Mil au Traité de Paris (1763)* 5 vols. Eunice Louisiana: Hebert Publications, 1981.

d'Eon, Désiré, *Histoires de chez-nous.* Yarmouth, Nova Scotia: L'Imprimerie Lescarbot Ltée, 1977.

Clare

Comeau, Germaine, *L'été aux puits secs.* Moncton: Les Editions d'Acadie, 1983. A novel.

Dagnaud, Father P.M., *Les Français du Sud-Ouest de la Nouvelle-Ecosse.* Besançon, France: Librairie Centrale, 1905.

Deveau, J. Alphonse, *La Ville Française*. Quebec: Les Editions Ferland, 1968.

Deveau, J. Alphonse, *Les personnes éminentes*. Yarmouth, Nova Scotia: Editions Lescarbot, 1988.

Deveau, J. Alphonse, ed., *The Diary of a Frenchman*. Halifax: Nimbus Publishing Ltd., 1990. As François Bourneuf lived in Argyle before moving to Clare, his diary which covers a very brief period of his life refers to both regions.

Doucet, Alain, *Littérature orale de la Baie-Sainte Marie*. Yarmouth, Nova Scotia: Sentinel Printing, 1965 and 1977.

LeBlanc, René and Micheline Laliberté, *Sainte-Anne: collège et université 1890-1990*. Church Point, Nova Scotia: Université Sainte-Anne, 1990.

Poirier, Léonie Comeau, *My Acadian Heritage*. Hantsport: Lancelot Press, 1985 and 1989.

Thibodeau, Félix E., *Dans note temps avec Marc et Philippe*. Yarmouth, Nova Scotia: L'Imprimerie Lescarbot Ltée, 1974.

Thibodeau, Félix E., *Dans note temps avec Mélonie et Philomène* Yarmouth, Nova Scotia: L'Imprimerie Lescarbot Ltée, 1978.

Thibodeau, Félix E., *Le parler de la Baie Sainte-Marie*. Yarmouth, Nova Scotia: Les Editions Lescarbot, 1988.

Tremblay, Marc-Adélard et Marc Laplante, *Famille et parenté en Acadie*. Ottawa: Publications d'Ethnologie, Musées nationaux du Canada, 1971.

Tufts, Edith (Comeau), *Acadienne de Clare*. Edith Tufts, 1977.

Chéticamp

Aucoin, Réjean, *Cap-Rouge: sur les traces des habitants*. Chéticamp, Nova Scotia: Les Amis du Plein Air.

Aucoin, Réjean and Jean-Claude Tremblay, *Le tapis de Grand-Pré*. Church Point, Nova Scotia: Centre provincial de ressources pédagogiques, 1986. Translated into English by Sally Ross and

Barbara LeBlanc: *The Magic Rug of Grand-Pré.* Halifax, Nova Scotia: Nimbus Publishing Ltd., 1989. A children's story.

Chiasson, Father Anselme, *Chéticamp: History and Acadian Traditions.* St. John's, Newfoundland: Breakwater Books Ltd., 1986, translated from the third French edition by Jean Doris Le Blanc.

Chiasson, Father Anselme and Father Daniel Boudreau, *Chansons d'Acadie.* Moncton: Ed. des Aboiteaux, 1942, 1944, 1946, 1972, 1979.

Chiasson, Father Anselme and Annie-Rose Deveau, *History of Chéticamp Hooked Rugs and Their Artisans.* Translated by Marcel LeBlanc. Yarmouth, Nova Scotia: Lescarbot Publications, 1988. The original French version, *L'histoire des tapis "hookés" de Chéticamp et de leurs artisans,* was published in 1985 by Les Editions Lescarbot.

LeBlanc, Barbara, "To Dance or not to Dance: The Case of Church and Group Social Control in Chéticamp." Unpublished Master's thesis, Université Laval, 1986.

Sadowsky, Laura, "The Chéticamp Waltham Connection: A Study of Acadian Ethnic Identity." Unpublished Master's thesis, Université Laval, 1987.

Chezzetcook

Labelle, Ronald, *La vie acadienne à Chezzetcook.* Special edition of *La Société historique acadienne, les Cahiers,* vol. 22, Nos. 2-3, 1991.

River Bourgeois

Boudreau, Ephrem, *Rivière-Bourgeois: paroisse acadienne du comté de Richmond.* Yarmouth, Nova Scotia: Les Editions Lescarbot, Yarmouth, 1984. The author has also written on Father Hubert Girroir and the Diocese of Arichat (see Notes, Chapter 4).

Boudreau, Ephrem, *Glossaire du vieux parler acadien: mots et expressions recueillis à Rivière-Bourgeois.* Montreal: Ed. du Fleuve, Collection Acadie, 1988.

INDEX